THE WARS OF FRENCH DECOLONIZATION

MODERN WARS IN PERSPECTIVE

General Editors: *B.W. Collins and H.M. Scott*

ALREADY PUBLISHED

Mexico and the Spanish Conquest
Ross Hassig

The Wars of French Decolonization
Anthony Clayton

THE WARS OF FRENCH DECOLONIZATION

ANTHONY CLAYTON

LONGMAN
London and New York

Longman Group UK Limited,
Longman House, Burnt Mill,
Harlow, Essex CM20 2JE, England
and Associated Companies throughout the world.

*Published in the United States of America
by Longman Publishing, New York*

First published 1994

ISBN 0 582 098 025 CSD
ISBN 0 582 098 017 PPR

British Library Cataloguing-in-Publication Data

A catalogue record for this book is
available from the British Library

Library of Congress Cataloging-in-Publication Data

Clayton, Anthony, 1928–
    The wars of French decolonization / Anthony Clayton.
        p. cm. — (Modern wars in perspective)
    Includes bibliographical references and index.
    ISBN 0–582–09802–5. — ISBN 0–582–09801–7 (pbk.)
    1. Decolonization—France—History—20th century. 2. France—
History, Military—20th century. 3. France—Colonies—
History—20th century. I. Title. II. Series.
JV1818.C62 1994   93-29506
325′.344′0904—dc20   CIP

Set by 14 in 10/12 Sabon
Produced by Longman Singapore Publishers (Pte) Ltd.
Printed in Singapore

CONTENTS

LIST OF MAPS

ACKNOWLEDGEMENTS

I like to tell my French friends that in the classroom of my preparatory school in Devonshire, in the Second World War long ago, hung two photographs. 'Ah, Churchill and Roosevelt of course', they usually say. While I am happy to be able to reply 'No, King George VI and Charles de Gaulle', this general French reaction, a grouping of *les anglo-saxons* probably opposed to French interests, is instructive. I hope this work may be seen instead as an example of goodwill that exists towards France and some understanding, on this side of the Channel, of her past difficulties. So it is to my French friends that I would want first to acknowledge my gratitude when writing both this book, and others that I have written on French military affairs. Their interest, and the common view we share on the need for close Franco-British understanding, have been my greatest help and inspiration.

I am also, again as with previous works, especially indebted to Ralph Goldsmith who has introduced me to so much French military history and records.

It is a pleasure to acknowledge the help of Andrew Orgill, the Librarian of the Royal Military Academy Sandhurst and all his staff, and of Longman Higher Education, to whom I am particularly grateful in allowing me to use some of the material on Morocco prepared for a chapter in Robert Holland's *Emergencies and Disorders in European Empires after 1945*. It has also been very helpful to discuss aspects of the French decolonization campaigns with colleagues in our Sandhurst War Studies Department, notably, Dr John Pimlott, Dr Francis Toase, Dr Ian Beckett, Dr H.P. Willmott, Dr P. Harris, and Mr N. de Lee.

I am very grateful also to the Editor of *The Times Literary Supplement* for arranging for me to quote from a review of C.R. Ageron's *Modern Algeria*, written by Elie Kedourie and published in the *TLS* of 10 July 1992.

Lieutenant-Colonel Jean Raffoux very kindly provided me with much useful material for the biographical notes.

For over twenty-five years Monica Alexander has miraculously converted my unsightly handwritten manuscripts into neat typewritten pages, and I am once again immensely appreciative of her work and patience.

Also exceptionally patient have been my wife Judith and our children Robert and Penelope. Absent-minded authors are not always the easiest of people with whom to live.

All translations are by the author.

1 INTRODUCTION: THE HISTORICAL PERSPECTIVE

Nothing in her history, recent experience, institutions or politics prepared France for any voluntary withdrawal from empire after the end of the Second World War. A study in perspective of France's wars of decolonization must, therefore, briefly return to the roots of the history of France herself, as deep in these roots lay major causes of the refusal of the general public and political figures alike, for so long, to acknowledge the anti-colonialism of the post-1945 world. This refusal led to large-scale and bloody conflict, far more costly in men and money than any decolonization campaign waged by Britain.

A brief comparison is useful. The British national tradition, as it evolved from the post-Roman Empire Anglo-Saxon era, had developed a loose, at times collegiate and generally anti-centralist style with as its main features Common Law, in which law grows out of custom, the break with Rome, the progressive erosion of royal central power – and a volunteer Army. In imperial affairs this style began to be reflected in the 1839 Durham Report envisaging self-governing Dominions with their own legislatures, and the 1931 Statute of Westminster confirming their full independence. The path for nationalist leaders in India and the larger colonies was, therefore, clearly marked out.[1] If they could convince Britain at some London conference of their responsibility, they too could claim dominion status through their developing legislatures. British political leaders, particularly in the Labour Party which was returned to power in 1945, knew Indian nationalist leaders personally and were prepared to trust, and be trusted by, them. There were also lobbies openly critical of empire, and a much wider proportion of the population who could see no further useful purpose in bearing its burdens. Political leaders, too,

1 For further comparisons of decolonization, see Dennis Austin 'The Transfer of Power, Why and How', in W. H. Morris-Jones and Georges Fischer, *Decolonization and After, the British and French Experience* (London, Frank Cass, 1980), chapter i; and Henri Grimal (trans. S. de Vos), *Decolonization* (London, Routledge & Kegan Paul, 1978), parts 1 and 2.

1

were very much aware of wider international criticism from the two superpowers, the Soviet Union and the United States, both anti-colonial though for different reasons, and also at the newly formed United Nations. Even if the end of the process, still less its gathering speed, was not foreseen in 1945, there was a general willingness to talk to nationalist leaders, whose co-operation was also seen as essential for economic development. Major military campaigns, for example to maintain a sovereignty over India, were not considered seriously. In any case the military force was not available; it was hoped to end wartime conscription quickly. The campaigns that were fought, Palestine, Malaya, Kenya, Cyprus, Borneo and Aden, were or became attempts to ensure that the independent successor regimes were acceptable to British political and commercial interests, generally successfully so in all except the first and last cases. Further, although regional strategic considerations played some part in policies towards particular colonies, the move towards and grant of independence to any imperial possession was never seen to present any direct strategic military threat to the metropole itself. Empire was far off and the worst possible damage to the metropole would be indirect and economic. Finally, for the imperial-minded sections of the populace, the rhetoric of 'Empire to Commonwealth' served in the 1940s and early 1950s to assuage pique and resentment over loss of prestige and formal flag sovereignty. Only the 1956 Suez crisis was to reveal the Emperor stripped of his clothing, a severe shock for many, and the first real intrusion of the consequences of imperial withdrawal into domestic politics. But by then decolonization was irreversible and consensus for it was not impaired.

The French national tradition and perceptions were very different. France's approach to constitution-making and law was that of the Roman Empire, *jus gentium*, the law for all peoples, based on a set of principles given out from the hub of the empire and applicable to all within it. This unitary concept of authority was complemented by Roman Catholicism which inherited from the Roman Empire the philosophy of doctrine prescribed by a superior authority, also for all to follow. The French Revolution changed particulars but not the general centralist approach. Jacobins and Bonapartists alike saw the French nation as one endowed with particular truths and wisdom, and also one entrusted with a mission to pass on these truths and wisdom to others, even if necessary by force. Behind all the differing policies pursued by France in different parts of her Empire lay, firmly rooted, this common mentality; France and French possessions must form an indivisible whole, and related to this, thinking on problems in absolute, rather than compromise, terms. Secession to the French mind was not an emancipation, it was a heresy.

French perceptions of the nation's history served to reinforce this attitude. Resentment over the loss of French Canada and French India in the eighteenth century set off a paranoiac attitude towards Britain, and later also the United States. It became the more important to acquire, and make French, areas of Africa and Asia. This perception was reinforced by the disaster of 1870; colonies were now held to be sources of military manpower as well as sources of international prestige and economic strength (the latter a mistaken view). Although the Revolution profoundly divided the nation, the need for empire and belief in a French *mission civilisatrice* spanned the divide. The French saw no paradox, apart from the question of the role of missionaries, in the working together of Republican and radical colonial soldiers and administrators alongside those of more conservative and Catholic, even royalist, views.

The legacy of the Second World War served only to strengthen these national perceptions. The bitterness of 1940 led, predictably, to a post-war wish to put the clock back to the pre-1939 era, and a belief in respect of empire that victor nations had every right to retain them. In 1940–42 the Vichy regime had drawn acceptance and a measure of legitimacy from the on-going French military and imperial control of West, and above all, North Africa, and both then and later French recovery was launched from the Empire.[2] The provisional government for the liberation had been formed in Algiers. Maghreb and colonial troops had formed the core of French military renaissance in large numbers, to be noted later. The French public went on to draw the comforting but false conclusion that this liberation was proof of their territories' loyalty to France. A weighty new factor to emerge was French fear of the Anglo-American partnership. It was argued that if France was to remain a world power she had to retain the Empire in order to resist subordination to *les anglo-saxons*, whatever the rest of the world might think. This view was for long held by the political Right and, in the early post-war months, on the political Left where Communists supported initial post-war French imperial re-assertion. Such sentiments were fuelled by deep suspicion over American

2 ' "Without her Empire, France would today be nothing more than a liberated country. Thanks to her Empire France is a victorious country" ', observed Gaston Monnerville, a political figure who became President of the Council of the Republic. Raoul Girardet, *L'Idée coloniale en France 1871–1962* (Paris, Table Ronde, 1972), p.196. The comment well illustrates the common attitude.

3

political activity in North Africa encouraging nationalists, and paranoia over the British presence in Syria and Lebanon.

These views were, of course, also ones that found generous support in the Army, whose structure needs explanation. France's organization of her imperial forces reflected the integrative nature of the French Empire just as Britain's organization reflected the devolved. The end of the British-officered Indian Army with its own general staff, Staff College, and career structure might bring the British Army nostalgia over the loss of agreeable postings (for officers but not for soldiers), and the loss of a number of battalions, but it brought no crisis of identity or confidence. The French case was, again, very different.

The French Army, although one institution, fell into three main components. The metropolitan Army was composed of conscripts whose service liability was limited to the homeland, and after 1945 Germany, unless they agreed to serve elsewhere. The *Armée d'Afrique* existed to garrison French North Africa and provide strategic reserves, some stationed in France, for the defence of the metropole. Its regiments were a mix, some like the *Zouaves* and *Chasseurs d'Afrique* largely white, some, notably the *Spahis* and *Tirailleurs*, indigenous with large French cadres, together with the Foreign Legion (*Légion Etrangère*). In addition there were the *Troupes de Marine*, from 1900 to 1958 styled *La Coloniale*, who existed to garrison colonies other than North Africa. Some of its regiments were white, others were indigenous, notably the *Tirailleurs Sénégalais*, despite the name recruited in all of French Sub-Saharan Africa. The *Armée d'Afrique* and *Coloniale* could be used anywhere. The officers of both were also often closely associated with colonial administration. The cadres, officers and NCOs of the *Armée d'Afrique* were metropolitan personnel, spending tours, sometimes whole careers, in North Africa while those of *Coloniale* served their entire careers in colonial soldiering.

Algerian *Tirailleurs* first figured in Europe in the 1870 campaign. A progressive 'drug effect' upon the French Army then followed, enhanced by the generally excellent combat performance of the *Armée d'Afrique* and *Coloniale* units. In the First World War 172,000 Algerians, of whom 158,000 were in combat units, served in the French Army, together with 54,000 Moroccans, 37,000 Tunisians, 160,000 Black Africans and 45,000 Malgaches. Most served in France, though many of the Black Africans were in second-line units.

The inter-war years saw massive use of Maghreb troops for imperial purposes and policing; the Algerian *Tirailleurs* became the work-horse of the Empire. In the 1930s' metropolitan birth-rate trough, numbers of Maghreb units were used for garrisoning France. Overall, prior to the 1939 mobilization 38.6 per cent of serving French Army infantry were Maghreb; of these Algeria provided 28 per cent. Twelve *Armée d'Afrique* divisions and eight *Coloniale* divisions participated in the May–June 1940 campaign; in these formations taken overall, a large majority of the soldiers were indigenous. The collapse of France heightened the drug addiction for Gaullists and Vichy alike. The 100,000-strong metropolitan army permitted by the Germans was totally unreal, but the North African *Armée d'Afrique* carefully tended by Generals Weygand and Juin was substantial. It was to form the bulk of the French Army's contributions to the Tunisian and Italian campaigns and provide the best of the formations of General de Lattre de Tassigny's 1st French Army that fought on the eastern flank of the Allied armies in the North-west Europe campaign.

Coloniale too found itself well placed at the end of the war. *Coloniale* officers were often more adventurous – and further removed from the decayed atmosphere of the metropole; the Communist spectre that appeared to haunt others in 1940 was less real to them. Almost all the first Gaullist units were *Coloniale*, from Equatorial Africa. At the end of the war 25 out of 100 serving (and politically acceptable) French generals were *Coloniale*, steeped in colonial ethos and tradition.[3]

In 1944–45 unit after unit of North or Black African troops crossed or recrossed France. Sometimes the movements had been especially arranged to impress the French populace that they were being liberated by themselves and not entirely by *les anglo-saxons*; sometimes also they were deliberately deployed in a role that British or US troops could not discharge, the curbing of left-wing insurrection. The pre-1939 years had also revealed the need to have troops of *'obéissance totale'* – more certainly reliable than conscripts – for internal security.[4] Paris in the 1930s was shielded by two of the best *Coloniale* infantry regiments (long-service white regulars) and the best *Zouave* (white *Armée d'Afrique*) regiment. Elsewhere other colonial units had served in this role – *Tirailleurs Sénégalais*, for example, intervening in a Marseille dock strike in 1939. Eight years later *Sénégalais* were again keeping order in Nice. And in September 1944 two regiments of horsed *Spahis* had been deployed in the Toulouse

---

3 Colonel P. Carles, *Des Millions de soldats inconnus* (Paris, Lavauzelle, 1982), p.157.

4 'The discipline and bravery of African troops represented at this time a force for order, still impenetrable to fashionable political ideas, that is to say one above all military, and of unquestioning obedience', translated from General R. Huré, *L'Armée d'Afrique, 1830–1962* (Paris, Lavauzelle, 1977), p.324.

area to restore order in places where Communists and anarchists, many Spanish, had established 'no-go' areas and rule based on terror. Both for great power status and in emergency domestic order, then, an on-going supply of soldiers from the Empire seemed indispensable and any loss unthinkable.

For the Army itself, there was no breathing space for any proper post-war consolidation, despite the desperate need for one. The need was particularly noticeable in the absence of any thought-out internal security doctrine or training. The French pattern of thinking in absolutes led too easily to overreaction, in contrast to the wiser British minimum force approach. The Second World War had opened with the trauma of defeat and division. One consequence of the defeat, to be played out again in the 1950s, was de Gaulle's belief that defence of national honour could in certain circumstances justify military disobedience to lawful constitutional commands, an extension of the beliefs – and practices – of generals serving in Africa from the 1890s onwards who frequently ignored or disobeyed instructions from Paris. The later renaissance had involved a welding together of de Gaulle's Free Frenchmen, the Vichy *Armée d'Afrique* that had joined the Allies in November 1942, and the French Forces of the Interior Resistance Groups inspanned into the Army in the winter of 1944–45. This difficult process was far from complete when the Indochina war began.[5] In addition there were acute shortages of money and equipment.

The immediate post-war months in France were ones of austerity even more depressing than that in Britain. The traditional pull factors of colonial soldiering made a renewed appeal – better pay, promotion and medals, an agreeable life style, particularly attractive after the 1947 pay reduction, and the lure of the frontiers of Empire and of the exotic; the French Army had long possessed a colonial, largely Maghreb institutional sub-culture of words, attitudes and concepts such as *baraka*, or personal luck. To these were added two new pull-factors, an escape into the purity of the *bled* for those who came to fear the incoming metropolitan consumer society, and lastly an escape to simple old-fashioned soldiering, for those who did not enjoy or could not master new technology. These attitudes were personified by Alphonse Juin, the outstanding French Commander in the 1944 Italian campaign, a soldier born and brought up in Algeria and with long North African service from 1910 onwards. Juin was Chief of the

5 'Broken by disaster, cohesion had not been truly restored by victory,' commented General Zeller in François Porteu de la Morandière, *Soldats du Djebel* (Paris, Société de Production Littéraire, nd), pp.88–9.

Defence Staff from 1945 to 1947, Resident-General in Morocco from 1947 to 1951 and Inspector-General of French forces from 1951. From 1952 onwards he enjoyed a unique status as France's only living Marshal, giving him considerable influence in political conditions already unstable.[6]

Finally in respect of the French Army, many, notably Juin, held the view that nationalism in North Africa would and did equate with Soviet Communism, posing a direct strategic threat to France herself.[7] Some were to go further and argue that if Indochina fell, then in turn would follow Asia, the Middle East and North Africa, with finally a challenge to southern Europe. This pattern of thinking obscured the reality; France's metropolitan defence burden was increasingly shouldered by America, Britain and later West Germany under Western European Union and North Atlantic Treaty Organization arrangements. If France had had a potential enemy on her northern frontier in the years 1947 to 1962, she could never have spared the soldiers or resources for the imperial periphery.

These great-power status and military linkages with empire were more significant than economic resources. France enjoyed a well-balanced economy, whose basic strength was to be proved by a remarkable post-war recovery despite severe war damage, political mismanagement and two vastly expensive military campaigns. In commercial terms, certain French companies prospered from manufacturing for or trading with overseas possessions, but the national economy was in no way dependent on them, and their lobby power, while vocal, was not decisive. The French commercial companies in Indochina had begun to prepare for change from the 1930s onwards, but those in Algeria, the other possession of substantial commercial profit, saw no such need.[8] Only in the late 1950s did a factor of national resource importance to metropolitan France appear, oil in Saharan Algeria. Preservation of French interests in this was to prove very significant in the ending of the Algerian war.

Of much greater street-level political significance were the human economic links, French residents in the overseas territories. The *colon*

---

6 For a biography of Juin, see Anthony Clayton, *Three Marshals of France* (London, Brasseys, 1992), chapters i, ii, iv, viii.

7 Bernard Pujo, *Juin, Maréchal de France* (Paris, Albin Michel, 1988), pp. 259, 333, 339–40.

8 The case of Indochina is examined in Jacques Marseille, *Empire coloniale et capitalisme française, histoire d'une divorce* (Paris, Albin Michel, 1984). A summary appears in his 'The Phases of French Colonial Imperialism', *Journal of Imperial and Commonwealth History*, VIII, 1985, 3: 127–41.

population in Algeria was approximately 975,000, in Tunisia 150,000 (mostly Italian in origin) and in Morocco 300,000. The vast majority were small farmers or working class, in Algeria protected artificially in a variety of ways against local competition in the markets. But some were large industrial proprietors or estate owners, the latter anxious to preserve a squirearchical life no longer available at home.[9] Indochina possessed a more truly ethnic French resident population of over 30,000; these had suffered severely in the war and looked to France for protection. Later, in strident terms and linked with factions within the Army, the *colons* of North Africa, particularly Algeria, were to do the same.

The political situation in the 1940s and 1950s reflected these and other specifically French factors. The Revolution had left a legacy of political and social division; the pursuit of national *gloire* (exaggerated self-respect) alone could re-cement these divisions. Empire in the past had provided both opportunities for showy – if at times also nervy – assertions of power in the name of *gloire*, and also the safety valve already noted through which those who were frustrated at home could recreate the society of their choice abroad. In turn such escape had contributed to domestic stability, the re-cementing.[10] No one sought change. In purely political terms the legacy of the Revolution seemed to necessitate – as the only means of securing legitimacy amid such sharp divisions and preventing rule by one man or one party – a national Assembly whose Lower House possessed very great powers, but which left the actual government with inadequate authority.

France's wars of decolonization took place within three political frames which do not precisely coincide with constitutional developments. The first was the brief period of de Gaulle's authority, from the Liberation to January 1946. The second was that in which power lay in the Lower House of the Legislature, the *Chambre*, resulting in the 22 governments between January 1946 and 1958. For its five-year span the *Chambre* was responsible to no one. The third saw the return of power to the executive, the second period of de Gaulle's authority

9 For an agreeable example see Jacques Weygand, *Goumier de l'Atlas* (Paris, Flammarion, 1954), p.30. Weygand wrote of one officer, 'The Foreign Legion had taught him to build, he has now become a gentleman-farmer in south Morocco' (the words 'gentleman-farmer' appear in the original French).

10 In a perceptive article, 'The Ends of Empire, Some Reflections on the Metropole', *The Round Table*, 317, (1991):86, Robert Holland observes that had the German nation possessed wider colonial responsibilities many frustrated men would not have turned on domestic out-groups.

beginning in May 1958, and the subsequent establishment of the Fifth Republic.

Only in the third of these frames and after much previous bloodshed could a French government start to break out from all the past conditioning and constraints. In the first frame de Gaulle faced a massive internal Communist challenge difficult to control, no national consensus on constitution-making, Anglo-American marginalization, and in respect of Indochina a lack of up-to-date expert advice. His own legitimacy and authority were far from secure and his views on empire as yet little developed. But with de Gaulle's departure from office in January 1946 policy became infinitely more incoherent.

The era that followed, only from October 1946 correctly described as the Fourth Republic, was bedevilled both by the constitution and the form of political life.

In the Fourth Republic's Constitution, the preference of the Left-wing parties for a *régime d'Assemblée* had only been slightly modified after the *non* vote at the 1945 constitutional referendum, and a Second Chamber with very little power was now provided. But the fundamental weakness remained. If the electoral mathematics failed to provide a majority for an important policy, a government was voted out, or more usually, resigned in advance leaving a vacuum that could take weeks to fill. Another major weakness was the voting system involving preferences and ensuring that voters voted for parties rather than men – individuals counted less, parties and party programmes counted for more.[11] In view of the divisions in French society coalitions then became inevitable and well-thought-out policy unlikely. In operation, where consistency in policy actually occurred it was often for the wrong reason and to prove unfortunate, as for example where particular ministries became fiefs of one or other political party. The Catholic Right-of-Centre *Mouvement Républicain Populaire* (MRP), especially its colonially minded faction headed by Bidault, who enjoyed especial prestige on account of his wartime resistance record, established almost complete holds on the Foreign, the Overseas Territories and later the Indochina Ministries. French policies in Morocco and Tunisia, and in Indochina respectively became stagnant, with any form of nationalism stigmatized as Communist-inspired.

11 In 1950–51 the Electoral Law was even revised so as to provide, for the 1951 election, a system whereby party lists of candidates could form alliances with other lists. An alliance winning an absolute majority of votes took all the places in a constituency, sharing out the seats proportionally. The measure was designed to weaken the Communists, and also the Gaullists.

In politics, there was on the one hand the extreme Left, the Communists, perceived increasingly, especially from 1947 on, as being under the orders of a foreign power, the USSR, and wishing to establish an East European type dictatorship, and on the other hand de Gaulle, ceaselessly advocating a stronger executive within a legislature properly and freely elected, but portrayed as seeking a personal dictatorship, a portrayal enhanced by his own contemptuous style. The presence and alien policies of the Communists denied the working class a fully effective political voice after 1947; the Communists championing the cause of Ho Chi Minh made it more difficult for other parties to contemplate negotiation with the Viet Minh. The Socialists were driven into coalitions with imperially minded parties further to the Right if they were ever to share any fruits of office, alliance with the Communists being impossible. In these coalitions the Socialists were ill at ease, at times divided, over economic policies, church–state relations and on occasions (but with little effect) colonial issues. The ill-ease led them to be the chief destroyer of governments, so as to be seen to be delivering goods in the next one.

At first, in the euphoria of the Liberation, the de Gaulle and Gouin interim administrations and the first three of the Fourth Republic governments, those of Bidault, Blum and (initially) Ramadier attempted Tripartism, a coalition of Communists, the Socialists and Centre parties, and the Right, the newly formed MRP. Tripartism collapsed in 1947 under a variety of pressures, most notably the international Cold War and French policies in Indochina. The Communists left the government and in political exile de Gaulle launched a new movement, the *Rassemblement du Peuple Français* (RPF), which initially attracted much support; since the MRP was in rivalry for votes with these Right-wing groups it could not afford to be seen to be soft on colonial issues. Politics was then reduced to interplay between factions composing the 'Third Force', some Radicals, residual MRP, other small non-Gaullist Right-wing groups and intermittently the Socialists and a few Gaullists. The 1951 election, as a result of changes in the electoral law, produced a further swing to the Right particularly after the disintegration of the RPF in 1952–53 when its members joined other Right-wing groups. Governments lived even more dangerously – and not for long – faced with major challenges; from the Right, after 1955 from the new populists of Poujade, from the Left, and from the lesser day-to-day challenges of commanding different majorities for different policies after wrangling, trade-offs and deals – in the words of one politician 'as many majorities as there are problems'. Political attrition and sheer physical fatigue became significant factors.

In military terms this political instability meant that the major decolonization wars were undertaken with no clear policy other than a vague formula – after the restoration of law and order by the Army political problems could be discussed. This formula was one on which agreement in a coalition could be reached but it offered the insurgents no promise of any political advance, particularly in view of France's declared aim of permitting no secession or exit from the French Union. Overall the decolonization dilemma was summarized in a nutshell by one commentator: 'To accord freedom to the overseas populations the only parliamentary majority was one which included the Communists; to defend the freedom which Communism would destroy, the only majority was one which included those who would refuse to grant freedom in Africa and Asia'.[12]

The political processes, from 1946 to 1958, were also unfortunately operated by figures mostly of modest, often second-rate abilities. Only a few, notably Pierre Mendès-France in 1954, could rise above the dilemmas and constraints to wrestle with the underlying problems. The political machine may have been faulty, but as will be seen, so too were the men. The Algerian crisis of April–May 1958 marked the end of the road, and another example of the predilection of the French people, in a moment of national emergency, to turn to a Caesar.

The third frame then, that of de Gaulle's return to power, is simple to outline in an introduction though the detail to follow in a later chapter is more complex. France now had a government with authority and beholden to no one. A policy to meet the need could evolve, and the government was strong enough to survive all challenge, even of violence from its own generals and demonstrations in the streets.

Lastly, there is the character of the French nation itself, particularly in Paris and large cities, excitable, anti-authority, with a tendency to rush to the barricades. Any process of decolonization was, in sum, bound to be chaotic for a country in which government and people were generally at odds with one another. France's greatest leader of the period, Charles de Gaulle, described his nation as 'the most fickle and unmanageable people on earth'.

---

12 Alfred Grosser, *La Quatrième République et sa politique extérieure* (Paris, Armand Colin, 1967), p.398, quoted in Frank Giles, *The Locust Years, the Story of the French Fourth Republic 1946–1958* (London, Secker & Warburg, 1991), p.369.

2 THE FRENCH UNION AND EMERGING NATIONALISM

The French Empire was second in size only to that of Britain and in 1945 was still at its greatest extent. By the end of 1962 all the major territories had attained independence, leaving France only a few very minor possessions, islands or small enclaves. This decolonization process was to involve France in two prolonged and large-scale campaigns in Indochina and Algeria, three medium-scale sequences of military operations, Madagascar, Tunisia and Morocco, and two brief but violent repressions, one temporarily successful in Algeria and one a failure in Syria. These latter both occurred in 1945 and may be seen as curtain-raisers to the campaigns that followed.

THE FRENCH UNION OF 1946

Centralist and Roman in style, the French saw their Empire as one that would in the 'formal' Black African colonies and in Algeria eventually assimilate indigenous peoples; this would at some remote date in the future be implemented by legislation removing any form of discrimination and entering the territory into the public collectivity of the French Republic, one and indivisible. In the words of Delavignette, a doyen of French colonial administrators:

> France faithful to a long tradition, regards her overseas territories
> as an integral part of the national community; she will not,
> nevertheless, reject the adjustments and adaptations which human
> and physical conditions overseas demand; but she believes that a
> wide measure of self-government for local groups will solve the
> special problems arising in Africa. Paris is not governed in the same
> way as Lyon, nor Lyon in the same way as Marseille, but the laws
> of the Republic are everywhere enforced.

At individual level, Delavignette saw peoples 'adopting a French nature'.[1] 'Freedom' therefore meant the attainment, either individually or collectively, of French citizenship expressed in terms no more diverse than the differences between an Alsatian and a Basque or Breton. The

protectorates of Tunisia and Morocco, some of the different components of French Indochina, and the League of Nations mandates of
Syria and Lebanon, it was appreciated, might have to evolve differently.
These were envisaged as dependent client states with a greater internal
religious and political autonomy, but with imperial defence, foreign
affairs and major economic policy – and commercial privileges –
retained by Paris.

This vision, seen in Paris as 'progressive federalism', was far from
coherent. Assimilation had actually been applied, after a fashion, in
the cases of the pre-Revolution Caribbean colonies and four communes
in Senegal. French citizenship had been granted to all. But full assimilation elsewhere, it was realized, would logically lead to France and
her legislature being swamped by overseas representatives, 'France the
colony of her colonies'. So an interim and indefinite stage of association
was thought appropriate for the Black African territories. Algeria,
although she possessed a Governor-General, was seen as part of metropolitan France, her *colons*, settlers, already qualifying for citizenship
and her indigenous inhabitants free to do so if they met rigorous
qualifications, in effect abandoning Islam.

In addition, in respect of Africa, there lay a deeply held French
belief in an essential unity of the two shores of the Mediterranean.
To many Frenchmen, the Mediterranean was but a river, and France
had a legitimate if squirearchical interest in any market gardens on
the opposite bank. As late as the mid-1950s, at the time of the outbreak
of the Algerian war, Mitterrand, then Minister of the Interior, could
say, 'From Flanders to the Congo there is one law, one single nation,
one Parliament. This is the Constitution and it is our will.'[2]

Even the Communists were not necessarily nationalist. At first
they had responded to the Communist International's call for colonial
freedom, but they moved progressively to demands for Communist
policies within the framework of the imperial union rather than the
ending of that union. In Algeria, for example, where the Communist
Party was in any case largely European, rhetoric centred on a non-racial
egalitarian Communist society replacing that of colonial capitalism.

Almost all of the French Empire had been acquired by conquest,
in the case of North Africa and Indochina often very bloody. Thereafter

1 *(opposite)* 'If I understand them aright, the Africans of today do not deny their
nature as Africans by adopting that of Frenchmen, neither will they consent to be
deprived of either one or the other.' Robert Delavignette, *Freedom and Authority in
French West Africa* (London, Frank Cass, 1967), pp.1–2, 150.
2 Frank Giles, *The Locust Years, the Story of the Fourth French Republic, 1946–1958*
(London, Secker & Warburg, 1991), pp.37–8.

the quality of French rule, at its best in Morocco, varied greatly elsewhere. In Algeria and in many of the Black African territories there had been abuses of economic exploitation, oppressive commutation of tax payment into labour, military conscription and local administrative misuse of power and corruption. In the years of the Second World War the need for reform in the 'formal' colonies was seen – but as an end in itself, not a preparation for political progress. To further this, and also both to further his own status and to attempt to modify American anti-colonial attitudes, de Gaulle had convened a colonial conference at Brazzaville, in French Congo, in January 1944. The conference was attended by French administrators from all over French North and Black Africa; no Africans were present (the 1960s representation of de Gaulle at Brazzaville as an African liberator is a product of African political mythology). While the conference made a number of extensive and constructive recommendations to end administrative abuses it offered no prospect of any advance to self-government or independence. Pleven, the Gaullist provisional government commissioner for the colonies, declared that France 'refuses all idea of autonomy, all possibility of an evolution outside the French bloc of empire; the eventual, even distant establishment of self-government is rejected'.[3] Nationalist politicians throughout the Empire took note.

The Fourth Republic's constitutional arrangements for the Empire reflected the Brazzaville theme. The preamble to the 1946 Constitution of the French Union – the new name for the Empire – firmly reiterated indissoluble unity. The Union was to be one of nations and peoples pooling their resources for development, but in political terms the ultimate goal was limited, in different styles for different territories, to a local autonomy. The Union was to comprise France, the overseas departments (the pre-Revolution colonies), the overseas territories (the post-Revolution colonies) and associated states and territories, a concept devised purely for Indochina. The word 'colony' was discarded. In most, but not all, matters the overseas departments were treated as part of metropolitan France.

The overseas territories were to elect a small number of members to the Paris parliament and the Assembly of the Union, and they also retained a local assembly. The associated states were to elect representatives to the Assembly of the Union and were to be represented in the Supreme Council of the Union. French control was assured by the fact that the President of France was President of the Union, and

3 William B. Cohen, *Rulers of Empire, the French Colonial Service in Africa* (Stanford, CA, Hoover Institution, 1971), p.167. Cohen's quotation is a translation from the officially published proceedings of the conference.

by a weighty French representation in both the Supreme Council and the Assembly of the Union. Algeria was viewed as part of France; Tunisia and Morocco, both technically being protectorates, were excluded from the Union. The exclusion was deliberate, it being thought that Arab nationalism would best be contained for a while within the protectorate structure with eventually a goal of 'co-sovereignty'. The local assemblies were simply to represent a controlled measure of administrative, and not political, devolution; real politics were to be in Paris. It was implicit that any increase in numbers of deputies elected in the overseas territories would depend on the speed of assimilation, a subject left vague. The President of the Republic, although President of the Union, was elected by the French parliament only, in which there was no representation from the associated states or the protectorates. One of the architects of this Union was Moutet, a Socialist minister for Overseas France, another the Right-wing Prime Minister, Bidault. Communist approval was obtained in a trade-off over the status of the metropolitan Civil Service. In essence, then, virtually nothing, except the labels and words, had changed. In teaching disastrous for the future, French school textbooks continued to emphasize to young children the importance of the overseas territories to France's status as a great power: 'European France is a medium-sized power, with overseas France she is a great power, the French Union.'[4]

Events within the Union were, however, moving in totally the opposite direction. Pre-war manifestations of nationalism had provided an early warning, generally ignored. The experience, common to all, of the Second World War was that of the collapse of France in 1940. Although the French in a variety of ways managed to limit the damage in their Empire, particularly in Africa, the loss of prestige was, nevertheless, grave. Thereafter, the experience of each territory varied, depending on proximity to Axis power.

INDOCHINA

The impact was greatest upon the territory collectively known as Indochina. The name itself is significant, the meeting place of the

---

4 Giles, *Locust Years*, p.37, quoting and translating from a specific school-book text cited in Raoul Girardet, *L'Idée coloniale en France* (Paris, Table Ronde, 1972), p. 288. In a survey of 4,193 people conducted in 1949, in 200 local government areas 81 per cent of people questioned answered 'yes' to the question 'Is it in France's interest to possess colonies?' Only 2 per cent offered an unqualified 'no'. Of a 25–34-year-old age group, 89 per cent answered 'yes' to a similar question: Jacques Thobie and others, *Histoire de la France coloniale*, II (Paris, Armand Colin, 1990), pp.414–15.

two big Asian cultures, mountains protecting the Chinese against the Indian. One and a half times the size of France, Indochina was a loose colonial amalgam of three very different lands, reflecting the meeting of the two cultures.

The largest of these lands, the present-day Vietnam, is a kidney-shaped composition of three distinct regions: Tonkin in the north, Annam in the centre-south, and the southern Mekong Delta region, called Cochinchina in the French colonial period. North-west Tonkin and some of the Annam central spine is mountainous and malaria-ridden. Much of the rest of Vietnam is watery land with rich soil devoted to rice cultivation. In the northern Red River Delta this cultivation had to be regulated by a system of dams and irrigation canals; it is in this area that the population is concentrated.

The pre-colonial history of Vietnam is complex. The Chinese dominated north Vietnam for over nine centuries, until A.D. 939. They continued to claim a titular suzerainty over Tonkin until the arrival of the French in the late nineteenth century. Even after the French conquest, Chinese influence remained in the political and social systems, Confucianism, Mahayana Buddhism and ideograms. Northerners migrated southwards along the coast, destroying the Champa kingdom in Annam and eventually penetrating into the Mekong Delta. Friction, however, remained between north and south, with civil wars in the sixteenth and eighteenth centuries. The north always saw itself as predominant, intellectually and culturally. The economies of north and south were, however, more equally linked as the north needed the south's rice, and later the south benefited from mineral development in the north, so justifying a political unity. The Vietnamese people, some 24 million in 1945, generally resemble the southern Chinese in appearance. But enclaves of earlier communities survived all over Vietnam, Thais and others in the north, Mois in the centre and south, Khmers in the Mekong Delta.

South and east of Vietnam lies Cambodia with her more homogenous population of Khmers, some of whom are descended from forebears ejected from Annam and the Mekong Delta. Distrust remained. The Khmers have darker brown skins, a different language and a different Hindu and Theravada Buddhist tradition. Cambodia is also a land of rice paddy, with highland plateaux to the east and mountains to the west. Between Vietnam and Thailand, landlocked and for the most part set on the mountain spine of Indochina, is Laos, whose hill peoples have a similar origin to that of the Khmers.

Common to all is the suitability of the terrain, whether paddy, rain forest, woodland or mountain, for guerrilla warfare, though flooding in the May-to-September wet season could slow down operations. Also to prove of military significance was the presence of many northern Vietnamese at work on plantations in the south, as well as in Cambodia. At the level of ideas it is worth suggesting that although the mandarin system had become discredited in Vietnam by the 1920s, certain concepts of Confucianism served to prepare ground for the events of the 1940s and 1950s. The Chinese usage of contradictory thinking could well be followed by dialectical materialism, the linkage of knowledge with power assisted a new ideology, justifying each other and concentrating the attention of men, particularly leaders, on their role and responsibilities within society rather than in any after-life. This in practice had created a social order of largely autonomous village communes, governed by councils of elders, all, in the mandarin age, under the central direction of a bureaucracy of holders of a true wisdom.[5]

French interest in the area opened with missionary activity in the eighteenth century. Colonial occupation began in the era of Napoleon III, with the taking of Tourane (Da Nang) in 1858, and Saigon together with much of Cochinchina by 1862. Cambodia followed next, a protectorate being established in 1863, but a first French attempt to occupy Tonkin failed. The final phase of French occupation included events that had similarities with those to follow over half a century later. China tried to oppose French penetration; Chinese irregular forces fighting under black flags defeated one French force but were in turn defeated in 1884. Negotiations between China and France then began to define the border; these – as was to be the case in 1946 – were interrupted and prejudiced by the actions of local commanders, both French and Vietnamese. In one of these, an attack on the border town of Lang Son, the French suffered heavy casualties and in Paris the government of Ferry had to resign. But by June 1885 the Chinese were obliged to accept a treaty recognizing French sovereignty over Tonkin, and the formal Union of Indochina was established in 1887. The French then proceeded to fashion and develop their colonial structures for the area. Under a French Governor-General at Hanoi, French-approved kings reigned in Cambodia and part of Laos. A French-approved emperor reigned over Annam and part of Tonkin. The remainder of Tonkin, though acknowledged as part of the Emperor of Annam's domain, was again directly administered by the French, as was also the 'incorporated colony' of Cochinchina in the south. The style of French administration was very close in all the

5 These points are made in Jacques Dalloz (trans. Josephine Bacon), *The War in Indo-China, 1945–54* (Dublin, Gill & Macmillan, 1990), p.5.

regions. French rule could claim, justly, to be bringing a large number of material benefits to the country, but the tax burden, both direct and indirect, was exceedingly heavy: wages were often miserable and labour forced to work far from home. Also, to prove significant later, some 10 per cent of the population of Indochina had become Catholic.

Laos and Cambodia were, in general, receptive to French protection, seeing it as security against Vietnam. It was in Vietnam that first resistance and later nationalism emerged. The French had to depose three emperors in the years 1885 to 1917. The new movements that appeared after the end of the First World War were initially a nationalist resentment against the French ruling and Chinese middle classes, and then Communist and religious groups.

The nationalist movement led to the formation in 1927 of the Viet Nam Quoc Dan Dang (VNQDD), largely Tonkinese and middle-class, inspired by the Chinese Kuomintang. The VNQDD was involved in the mutiny of locally recruited French Army Annamese *Tirailleurs* at Yen Bay early in 1930, an uprising very drastically suppressed and followed by the arrest and executions of VNQDD leaders.

The Communists were led by Nguyen Ai Quoc (Nguyen the Patriot), later better known as Ho Chi Minh (He who Enlightens). Nguyen, born in 1896 and the son of a middle-class Annamese, had travelled to Europe and become converted to Communism in the years before, during and immediately after the First World War. In Canton in the 1920s he formed a proto-nationalist movement and developed contacts with Borodin, the chief Soviet agent in China; he twice visited Moscow. In 1930 he formally founded the Indochina Communist Party, which from the start linked the overthrow of the French with agrarian anti-landowner revolution. Following the decapitation of the VNQDD and the failure of an attempt in 1938 by Bao Dai, the Emperor of Annam, to persuade the French to loosen their tight administrative control, the Communists gradually assumed leadership in anti-colonial sentiment. Ho was himself under sentence of death for complicity in unrest in Annam in the mid-1930s; other Communist leaders were executed. For a while Ho lived in Hong Kong, until under French pressure the British obliged him to leave. He then studied in Moscow from 1933 to 1936 and from 1936 to 1941 in China. These years developed Ho's remarkable personal mix of prudence, organizing ability, social charm and doctrinal beliefs. He was, however, even then criticized by some for being excessively nationalist and insufficiently Communist.

Two religious groups that were founded in the late 1920s were also to attract a large measure of nationalist support, particularly in the more liberal atmosphere of Cochinchina, in the 1930s. These were the Cao Dai and the Hoa Hao. The Cao Dai worshipped a supreme being who instructed his followers through the spirits of the dead; it included elements from several religions, spiritualism, freemasonry and Confucianism all with a Catholic church style hierarchy. The Cao Dai controlled an area north-west of Saigon. The Hoa Hao were a revived form of Buddhism; they controlled a rather smaller area west of Saigon. No adequate system of representation in any of the regions existed; assemblies and councils were consultative only and nominated by the administration. The last months of peace saw some Trotskyist splintering in the Communist Party and further decline of the VNQDD; on the outbreak of war the Communist Party, like that in France, was banned.

The 1940 collapse of France was more keenly felt in Indochina than anywhere else in the Empire. Vietnamese who had suffered under racial humiliation either in street relationships or in the abuse of their women, or who perceived themselves as exploited economically for little return, now saw the colonial power humbled. In addition there was the enormous local strength of Japan, while distance, and the British, until December 1941 anxious not to provoke Japan, prevented any reinforcement from the metropole. Under initial Japanese pressure, the French Governor-General, the very liberal minded General Catroux, stopped the supply of fuel to the Chinese fighting Japan. For this he was replaced by Vichy, he himself joining de Gaulle. His successor, Admiral Decoux, had only a small garrison, not well-equipped, at his disposal. He was obliged to make successive concessions to the Japanese in an effort to preserve an increasingly flimsy French sovereignty. In the late summer of 1940 Decoux was forced to concede air-base facilities in the north to the Japanese; later the presence of troops in the north and further bases in the south were conceded as well. An over-enthusiastic Japanese general launched a frontier attack on the French at Lang Son, killing over 800 French soldiers, before the concessions came into force. Encouraged by Japan, Thailand advanced border claims in Laos and Cambodia. Despite a sparkling naval success, French ground forces were inadequate to contain the Thais and territory was ceded in 1941. Over the next three years Decoux struggled to keep the Tricolour flying and to popularize French rule by developing social services and paying greater respect to local rulers and institutions.[6]

6 Dalloz, *ibid.*, p.36, also notes that the rhetoric of the Decoux era was one of 'national revolution' and regeneration exalting authority, responsibility and hierarchy, all presided over by Pétain as a remote, aged, all-seeing, almost Confucian figure. Dalloz suggests this pattern of loyalty was one easily transferable to new structures such as those of Ho and the Viet Minh.

By late 1944, however, the de Gaulle government had established itself in Paris and it rashly appointed a general to plan and direct future operations against the Japanese in Indochina, parachuting in specialist personnel. The Japanese learned of these plans. After their naval defeats, Indochina was an essential communication link to their forces in Malaya. In March 1945 they reacted brutally, arresting Decoux, executing publicly French military and political officers, and massacring garrisons – only one small gallant column escaping into China. There neither the Chinese nor the Americans, the latter obsessed by anti-colonial prejudices, were prepared to assist the survivors.

French authority was broken and, encouraged by the Japanese, Bao Dai proclaimed independence for Vietnam, appointing a government of non-Communist nationalists. In Laos and Cambodia similar proclamations followed. The realities of power in Vietnam were, however, different. In 1941, under a measure of Chinese Nationalist patronage, a coalition of Vietnamese nationalist groups was set up in South China. This coalition was known as the Vietnam Doc Lap Dong Minh – Viet Minh for short – the League for the Independence of Vietnam. Within this Viet Minh the Communists under Ho Chi Minh, now using this name, Vo Nguyen Giap and Pham Van Dong quickly acquired control. Ho himself was not initially trusted by the Chinese. Although relations improved for a while in 1942–43, by 1944 the Chinese had again become disenchanted with the Viet Minh, with important subsequent results. But neither they nor, as the war situation worsened for them, the Japanese were in any position to stop Ho and the Viet Minh from establishing a 'liberated zone' in the Thai Nguyen hills, north of Hanoi. Whether the Viet Minh actually operated effectively against the Japanese, as they claimed they were doing, is uncertain; more important was the Viet Minh's acquisition of US goodwill and some equipment and weaponry through intelligence-gathering and aircrew rescue. Further, in the north the Viet Minh had formed a cell structure, or more correctly two parallel cell structures, one by district and one by occupation. These, rather than Bao Dai's regime, controlled people's daily lives and began to enforce agrarian reform. The Viet Minh's position in Annam and Cochinchina was less strong, the Japanese having favoured other nationalists and the Cao Dai and Hoa Hao; the Viet Minh did, however, have followers, particularly among the northern labourers at work in the south.

The Allies' plans for Indochina had been heavily influenced by President Roosevelt's general dislike of the colonial system and his particular dislike of de Gaulle. Although the death of Roosevelt decreased some of the strength of these prejudices, his successor, Truman, giving priority to cordial relations with France, the Allies agreed at the Potsdam Conference of July 1945 that the immediate post-war administration of Indochina should fall to the Chinese north of the 16th Parallel, and to the British Admiral Mountbatten's South East Asia Command south of the Parallel. None of this could in any way be acceptable to de Gaulle who, from 1943, had been planning for a French re-assertion. The imprudent appointment of the general, already noted, had been an early move. Next, in March 1945, followed a statement of policy by the de Gaulle government, that Indochina was to have autonomy and a special position within the French Community; a policy in line with Brazzaville and far short of independence. A French Governor was to preside over a government of French and local ministers, the government was to be assisted by, but not be answerable to, a local assembly, and defence, internal security and all foreign affairs were to be retained by the French. Events on the ground, however, then gathered momentum. Bao Dai's government, discredited by acute food shortages, resigned on 8 August. Conscious that the Japanese were in confusion following the dropping of the atom bombs on Japan, Ho and the Viet Minh launched an uprising in Tonkin, taking Hanoi and forcing Bao Dai into voluntary abdication. In late August two French officials were parachuted into Indochina, one, Cédile, in the south and the other, Messmer, a future Prime Minister, in the north to assert a return of French authority and to present the new French policy. In the south the local Viet Minh ignored Cédile, in the north Messmer was arrested by them, only escaping with difficulty. Other contacts between the Viet Minh and the French fared little better. Finally, on 2 September Ho Chi Minh proclaimed the independence of Vietnam under the Viet Minh; the declaration was both one of independence from the Japanese and from the incoming Chinese, and covered all three component region *kys*, Annam, Tonkin and Cochinchina. France, Ho claimed, had been ejected in March. Although, to create a façade of nationalist unity, Bao Dai (under the title of Citizen Vinh Thuy) had an honorific post as councillor to the government, the Viet Minh were already at work consolidating power and, with increasing deliberate use of terror, eliminating moderate or pro-French opponents. Any French return would be on a stage set for conflict.

NORTH AFRICA

Tunisia

In contrast to the Viet Minh, the nationalist movements in the North African territories did not openly challenge the French during the war. The evident hope of all was that Allied, particularly American, pressure would force the French to grant post-war independence. In all three territories the loss of French prestige was highlighted by the physical arrival of the Allies and by the propaganda from Vichy, de Gaulle, the Italians and Germans before 1942, and the Communists, the British and, perhaps most important of all, the Americans thereafter. News of one influential independent Moslem Arab state, Saudi Arabia, of independence movements in other Arab and Asian territories, of the ideals of the Atlantic Charter, the Arab League and the United Nations was all circulating freely in the cities and in *colon* estates labour lines, ending the somewhat isolated state created by pre-war French rule. This rule had, however, provided emerging nationalist leaders with the sophistication and the skills necessary for both organization and domestic and international appeal. Islam, asserting that non-Moslems must never rule the faithful, added fuel. The detailed circumstances, however, differed in each territory.

Only Tunisia had suffered Axis occupation, and that brief, from November 1942 to April 1943. The territory had been occupied by a French Army in 1881 and had accepted protectorate status under the Treaty of Bardo. But Tunisia did not lose its sense of identity, which was in some respects safeguarded by the French system of indirect rule with the preservation of the beylicate. Tunisian nationalism in the form of the *Destour* Party emerged in the 1920s, reaction against European (largely Italian) land seizure being a major cause. This early movement was very conservative, led by the traditional families and unclear in its ambition. Tensions in Tunisia worsened in the 1930s as a result of the Depression and population growth. In 1934 the *Néo-Destour* (new customs) openly modernizing, nationalist party was formed, its most active and effective leader being the Sorbonne-educated lawyer Habib Bourguiba. Although the *Néo-Destour* preached both nationalism and social reform, Bourguiba remained an admirer of France and a believer in close relations with her. Nevertheless, the party was banned from 1934 to 1936, nationalist expression passing to an indigenous trade-union movement. Unrest, with small demonstrations, occurred in 1934, with a series of larger demonstrations in 1936 and further street-rioting in Tunis in 1938 following the arrest of two *Néo-Destour* leaders. In these riots 122 people were killed.

Bourguiba had been imprisoned from 1934 to 1936; after the 1938 riots he was returned to prison and his party was again banned. The Germans released Bourguiba, whom the Italians hoped to use. But Bourguiba refused Italian blandishments, though other *Néo-Destour* leaders co-operated with the Axis. Bourguiba returned to Tunisia in 1943 and although he promised support for the French for the duration of the war he was obliged, in fear of arrest, to flee secretly to Cairo in early 1945.[7]

In June 1943 as a gesture primarily intended to emphasize French return to authority, the acting Resident-General, General Juin, deposed the young Bey, Moncef, on a flimsy charge of supporting the Axis, though the more likely reason was some support he had given to the *Destour*. Juin, no friend of Maghreb nationalism, was himself embarrassed by this move, *'un acte impolitique'* dictated, he said, by the French *'pseudo-gouvernement'* in Algiers on a ruler who had remained always loyal.[8] After this deposition the French strengthened their hold on the territory by transferring some of the Bey's power back to French officials. Resentment could only grow, and the subsequent death of both Moncef and his successor served to strengthen Bourguiba, who also enjoyed American support, as the nationalist leader.

Morocco

Morocco appeared on the surface to be reasonably tranquil in 1945. The main reason for this was the quality of the French protectorate administration, which combined efficiency, a measure of economic development, and a very real respect for the dignity of the Moroccan Sultan, people and institutions. The French had begun to occupy Morocco in 1908, but had made only limited progress until the arrival on the scene in 1912 of General Lyautey who, with the exception of a few months in 1916–17, was to remain Resident-General in Morocco until 1925. The considerable military campaigns necessary to occupy the mountainous regions of Morocco had had to cease in the 1914–18 years, but were resumed from 1920 onwards. The years 1924–25 saw the massive uprising in the Taza mountains of North Morocco led by

7 In May 1943 Bourguiba was writing, 'Work together with France, anything outside the French frame is unhealthy': Habib Bourguiba, *La Tunisie et la France*, quoted in Wilfred Knapp, *Tunisia* (London, Thames & Hudson, 1970), p.131. His departure for Cairo was assisted by the American consul in Tunis, Doolittle. A useful account of Bourguiba's opposition to French rule appears in Norma Salem, *Habib Bourguiba, Islam and the Creation of Tunisia* (London, Croom Helm, 1984).

8 Marshal Juin, *Mémoires*, I, quoted in Bernard Pujo, *Juin, Maréchal de France* (Paris, Albin Michel, 1988), p.149.

Abd el Krim, initially against the Spanish but then also against France. This uprising was suppressed only with great difficulty in a campaign involving half a million troops, mostly French but also some Spanish. Campaigning to secure the final pacification of the Middle and High Atlas lasted from 1931 to 1934. The end result was that the authority of the central government of Morocco for the first time extended beyond the coastal plains into the mountain regions, a massive benefit.

There were, however, two specific difficulties, containing the germs of troubles to come. First, Lyautey, although perhaps Europe's greatest colonial proconsul, had had to make local arrangements with the *grands caids*, the great Berber chieftains of the Atlas, during the First World War when his military capabilities had been reduced to virtually nothing. Lyautey himself had a very clear vision for Morocco, of a progressive evolution of the whole people under benign French tutelage, to form an eventual equal partnership; he was opposed to any large-scale French settlement. His successors failed him, allowing substantial French *colon* settlement and developing Lyautey's wartime policy of expediency into a specific *politique des races*, in which France was seen to have a duty to 'protect' the mountain Berber peoples (who contributed massively to the *Armée d'Afrique*) against the designs of the coastal Arabs. A French-drafted decree of May 1930 reduced the role of the Sultan of Morocco, an Arab, in the Berber regions. This policy ignored the Moslem religious linkage of the Arab and the very varied Berber groups; religion and emerging nationalism, factors that united the two communities, were before long to become more significant than the ethnic divisions. Proto-nationalists chose to represent the Berber policy as an attempt by France to wean the Berbers from Islam. Suspicion began to replace trust, and the incalculable benefit of the ending of inter-tribal killings and banditry was no longer appreciated by the new generation. A few pre-war warnings of trouble to come had been evident in rioting in several Moroccan cities in 1937.

The second difficulty was one of competing focuses for nationalism. One was the young Sultan, Mohammed V, who at the age of sixteen had succeeded to the throne in 1927 and had been carefully tutored by the French. His dynasty, the Alouite, had ruled coastal Morocco since the seventeenth century, the dynasty claimed descent from the Prophet Mohammed which gave it the designation of 'Shereefian', and combined spiritual with temporal authority. Mohammed V had no particular animosity against the French, and had remained steadfastly loyal to them in the difficult war years. As he matured, however, Mohammed V's ambition for his country became one of following the path of Iraq and Saudi Arabia to a negotiated independence. He was also acutely aware that he could not afford to be seen as less nationalist than local political figures. The French, particularly strict Catholics such as Bidault, underrated the Sultan's political skills and regarded him as devious, venal and profligate – not altogether without reason. But in January 1943 the Sultan had made a great impression on President Roosevelt, who openly questioned the legitimacy and future of French rule with him, promising American support in ending it.[9]

The leading figures of the *Istiqlal* Independence Party were potential rivals to the Sultan. This party was formed in January 1944 from nationalist groupings, mainly bourgeois, that had started to express themselves in the late 1920s. On their formation they had addressed a manifesto to the Sultan and the French Resident-General demanding the ending of the 1912 Fez protectorate treaty and early complete independence. The French reacted by brushing aside the demands and arresting two leaders, Lyazidi and Balafry, on charges of collaboration with the Axis. Demonstrations in Moroccan cities followed. In attempting to control one of these, in Fez, Black African *Tirailleurs Sénégalais*, particularly resented in Morocco on racial grounds, opened fire killing more than 30. Numerous arrests followed. The event began to move Berbers closer to the nationalist cause and led the Sultan to be more outspoken, with consequences to follow from 1947.[10]

Algeria

If French rule was at its lightest in Morocco, it was at its most oppressive in Algeria, this rule to be the cause of the first 'curtain-raiser' uprising and repression. The French began to occupy Algeria in 1830 in an attempt, to prove vain, to save the restored but unpopular Bourbon dynasty. In a subsequent series of violent nineteenth-century campaigns France conquered the remainder of Algeria. One of the most important of these campaigns, from 1835 to 1847, was fought against a powerful indigenous chieftain, Abd el Kader, eventually defeated by Marshal Bugeaud. Conquest was followed by colonization, a large proportion of the settlers in fact being Italian or Spanish. All, together with the Jews, were given French citizenship in 1889. Land was seized, often ruthlessly, and a brief attempt by Napoleon III to protect the indigenous population came to nothing. *Colon* settlement increased greatly at the end of the nineteenth century though large

9 Elliot Roosevelt, *As He Saw It* (New York, Duell, Sloan & Pearce, 1946), pp.111–16.
10 Georges Spillman, *Du Protectorat à l'Indépendance* (Paris, Plon, 1967), p.122, for example notes the Sultan's demand for the removal of the Resident-General in 1945.

estate owners soon bought out many of the small farmers. A very large proportion of the new arrivals were townsmen, shopkeepers, artisans and craftsmen, who squeezed their Moslem rivals out. These latter were either reduced to poorly paid plantation or menial urban labour, or pushed into harsher and less profitable agricultural land. Immediately prior to the First World War conscription was imposed. Continuous large military manpower demands, with heavy casualties in both World Wars, contributed further to the immiserization.

In day-to-day life the *colons* consistently spoke of and to the Moslem population in disparaging terms, the *sale race* – dirty people. The French legal system disadvantaged Moslems; taxation bore more heavily upon them while education and medical services remained poor. Humiliation fuelled fear and hatred.[11]

Primary resistance, except in the Saharan south, had largely collapsed by 1858, though small-scale actions continued until 1860. There were, however, major revolts in settled Algeria in 1864 and 1870–71, an uprising in protest against conscription at Batna in 1916, and strikes and some urban rioting in 1936 and 1937.

Politically, the tradition of resistance was maintained after 1916 first by proto-nationalist religious groups and then by overt nationalists. As in Morocco, what had in the past divided the majority peoples of Algeria, the Berber Kabyles, from the coastal and plains Arabs assumed even less importance in the context of the factors uniting them; Islam and resentment over lost land and foreign domination in particular. From the 1930s Moslem teachers in Koranic schools, the most notable being the very influential Ben Badis, began the work of reviving Arab culture and religion. More sophisticated protest, when it came, took two forms. The first was a moderate demand for wider opportunities for Algerians voiced by Ferhat Abbas, the pharmacist son of a peasant farmer. Ferhat's aims, at least until 1936, were those of equality in taxation, education, the land and representation; assimilation should be the means to achieve this. Ferhat's followers were mainly from the small middle class, and he himself did not envisage any form of Algerian nation until the blocking by the *colons* of very modest reforms enfranchising the Moslem elite, some 20,000, proposed by the Blum Popular Front government in 1936, one of the very few Third Republic governments with a sense of accountability for overseas affairs. Even then and until 1941, Ferhat continued to speak of regional autonomy only.

11 For a detailed analysis of pre-1939 Algeria see Charles-Robert Ageron (trans. Michael Brett) *Modern Algeria*, (London, Hurst, 1991), chapters i and ii.

The second was a clear-cut nationalist call expressed by Messali Hadj, a man of limited formal education but considerable oratorical skill who for a brief period in the late 1920s flirted with Communism within the *Etoile Nord-Africaine*, a political organization based on Algerian workers in Paris. His aims moved towards a more nationalist and populist socialism when he returned to Algeria in the 1930s, but still with open talk of 'revolution'. In 1937 Messali formed the *Parti du Peuple Algérien* (PPA), but he was arrested later in the year. Both Ferhat and Messali had French wives, in the former case after divorce from a Moslem.

The political structures denied the Moslems any effective expression. At the top was the French Governor-General, in normal times appointed by the Ministry of the Interior in Paris, assisted by an executive Superior Council. For political purposes settled Algeria was constituted as three *départements*, Oran, Algiers and Constantine; Saharan Algeria was administered separately. Each *département* sent Senators and Deputies to the Paris legislature; there was also a local Consultative Assembly with virtually no powers. Originally the members of these bodies were elected only by French citizens; that is, *colons*. In 1919 a double electoral college system in which the French College dominated was instituted, the French College and a new Moslem College each electing half the members to the territory's Consultative Assembly. Voting rights in the Moslem College were limited to ex-soldiers, civil servants and property owners, though a few thousand even more carefully approved Moslems were permitted to vote in the French College. But procedural arrangements, such as the requirement for a two-thirds majority in the Assembly for discussion of a subject by the Superior Council, ensured that the voice of the *colons* dominated.

There was token representation of Moslems in the territory's Superior Council, and on the one council where Moslem sentiment could make some, albeit limited, impact, the *Délégations Financières*, which considered the budget. But in day-to-day matters the French administration's considerable direct law-making powers were generally under strong *colon* influence. In local councils where *colons* formed the majority, they had wide powers, including local taxation over Moslems. Where the *colons* were in a minority, French officials governed through *caids* appointed by themselves, a system that soon became filled with yes-men and corruption. Indigenous Moslems could only attain French citizenship by, in effect, renouncing Islam; by 1936 only 2,500 had bothered to do so. Unwisely, also, the administration in Algeria had given virtually no opportunities for local indigenous to serve within its ranks.

The few attempts by metropolitan governments to reform Algeria were thwarted by *colon* pressure, a clear example being the failure of Blum's reforms of 1936. The thwarting was both unfortunate in itself, and also in the lesson in respect of their own power drawn by the *colons*, who believed that their status should be one of protected privilege. It was a lesson watched further by the growing number, nearly 100,000, of Algerians working, slum-dwelling and learning politics in metropolitan France; it was these who had formed the proto-nationalist *Etoile* in 1926.

The war years were a grim experience for Algeria. They opened with extensive drafting; the fall of France denied Algerians the opportunity to go to France to work and stopped the flow of remittances from those already there at work. The years 1940–42 saw poor harvests, a typhus epidemic and all the difficulties of war – shortages of food, of clothing and of transport, and black markets. These deprivations fell chiefly on the Moslem population, who contrasted the widening gap between themselves and the full barns and cattle sheds of the *colon* farmers. At the same time the Moslem population's birth rate had begun to rise sharply. By 1936 the census figures were as follows:

	French	Moslems
Algiers Region	310,908	1,853,154
Oran Region	314,115	1,183,549
Constantine Region	188,354	2,494,653

The increase was particularly evident both in the growing density of the indigenous population in the country areas adjoining *colon* farms and in the towns and cities.

In February 1943 Ferhat Abbas, becoming a stage more radical, published his *Manifeste du Peuple Algérien*, demanding Algerian participation in the territory's government, and radical social and economic reform. In May he produced a supplement going further, demanding an Algerian state. But neither document called for violent revolution. Messali Hadj was arrested for complicity in an Army mutiny in 1941, a status converted to house arrest in 1944. The PPA had been formally banned in 1939, but Messali's message was projected and publicized by the PPA working underground, and a new grouping linking the PPA with the followers of Ferhat Abbas, *Les Amis du Manifeste et de la Liberté* (AML) was formed in Sétif in March 1944. Also involved were Moslem Scouts, Sports Clubs and certain Moslem *ulemas*. The

Scouts, for example, had taken the slogan of the Reformist *Ulema* leader, Ben Badis, 'Islam is my religion, Arabic my language, Algeria my fatherland', as their motto. Propaganda was printed by clandestine presses and sung in nationalist songs. Moslem *medersas* became dispensaries of political agitation.

As already noted, the arrival of Anglo-American forces in Algeria and the known war aims and policies of the Allies heavily strengthened nationalist sentiment. There was evidence of friendship between German and Italian prisoners and indigenous Algerians. As late as early January 1945, the *Deuxième Bureau* noted the satisfaction of many Algerians at the initial German successes in the Ardennes. A film concerning a pilgrimage to Mecca portraying King Ibn Saud drew tumultuous applause. In the French First Army fighting on the eastern flank of the Allied armies ejecting the Germans from France, General de Lattre de Tassigny noted with alarm that North African *Tirailleurs* were saying that they were being used, and killed, in the liberation of France while the French themselves contributed little.[12] To the horror of French officers, the green and white flag of Abd el Kader was found in the lines of one Algerian unit. Among the slogans seen and heard in this period in Algeria were '*Vive Messali*', '*A bas le colonialisme*', '*Pour la Charte de l'Atlantique*', and, most sinister, '*Tuez ces sales Français*'. It appeared to many Algerians that the foundations of French rule in Algeria were being shaken by external factors and that change could at last come about.

The de Gaulle provisional government of 1945, whose head had no love for the Algerian *colons* as they almost to a man had supported Vichy, had tried to initiate a measure of reform. The Brazzaville-type reforms of late 1943 and early 1944, the best that General Catroux, the Governor-General appointed by de Gaulle in 1943, could achieve in face of intense *colon* and conservative military opposition, gave political rights to further restricted categories of Moslems. In theory, all military and civilian posts were to be opened to Moslems. Moslem representation in local government bodies was increased from one-third to two-fifths; in the two electoral colleges, the franchise was extended to all Moslems over twenty-one for the Moslem College and in respect of the French College of some 450,000 voters an increased input of 50 to 60,000 Moslems was permitted, only one-half of these bothering to register. The measures appeased few and enraged many; frustration and resentment soured the atmosphere further. By April 1945, when

12 Maréchal Jean de Lattre, *Reconquérir, Ecrits, 1944–45* (Paris, Plon, 1985), pp.74–5, 131–2.

the nationalist propaganda offensive was in full spate, its declared aims had extended to include independence and eviction of the French, and its methods included boycotts and personal intimidation against Europeans and Algerians thought to be sympathetic to France. Minor officials, headmen and *caids* were threatened, and Moslems who drank alcohol were beaten up.

The Constantine *département* became the focus. The *colon* population was not only smaller than in the other *départements*, but also more scattered. Food shortages had been particularly severe, with bread rationed and fruit unobtainable. The Constantine area, too, had had a long tradition of leading opposition to French rule. The French military authorities were expecting trouble, the civilian administration was complacent. Both, however, were caught off balance by the scale and ferocity of the uprising. The garrison of Algeria totalled 115,000 but only 10,000 were in operational units; the remainder were in second-line units poorly trained, with inadequate cadres and equipment. The military commander in Algeria, General Martin, had, however, made careful contingency plans for rapid reinforcement.

Violence erupted in the small, shabby town of Sétif on 8 May, VE Day.[13] A procession several thousand strong, carrying placards demanding equality and the release of Messali, passed out of the control of the local gendarmes; Europeans in the streets were attacked and killed. The killings then spread to *colons* in isolated farms, forest stations or small gendarmerie posts, and lasted for several days. Certain specific features in the killings are noteworthy, as they were to recur on a larger scale in the next decade. Men roamed the streets with their index fingers pointing skyward – a sign of religious war; women ululated in support. Abd el Kader's flag was again to be seen. The actual killings were often of extreme ferocity, frequently disembowelling. Victims were targeted, killers using photographs. Killers generally came from sites other than those they attacked. Their victims were also selected symbolically, a magistrate and a priest were killed horrifically, the local *colon* Communist leader had his arms amputated and *colon* women were raped. Property destroyed included court houses, farms, barns and churches, all again of symbolic significance. The killers were urban or farm employees, they enjoyed the complicity of many local headmen and *caids* and the support of the mass of the

13 The uprising is summarized in my article 'The Sétif Uprising of May 1945: Cruelty and Terror in an Anti-Colonial Uprising', *Small Wars and Counter-Insurgency Campaigns*, IV, 1992. The summary is based on a volume of documents, *La Guerre d'Algérie par les documents, vol. I L'Avertissement*, published by the Service Historique de l'Armée de Terre, Vincennes, 1990.

local population. European deaths totalled 102, with many more injured.

The French reacted very firmly. In accordance with General Martin's plans and to the surprise of the insurgents, troop and gendarme reinforcements were flown in, and then moved around the affected area in half-track vehicles. Aircraft provided support. Cordon and search operations followed, and a cruiser shelled a coastal approach road used by insurgent groups. These operations lasted for two weeks, though smaller-scale pursuits into the hill ranges continued until the end of the month. In these 3,696 Algerians were arrested.

The local Constantine military commander, General Duval, repeatedly ordered that there should be no unnecessary bloodshed. These orders with one exception seem generally to have been observed, though passions were on occasions inflamed by the spectacle of mutilated corpses, and the *Tirailleurs Sénégalais* and *Légion* reinforcements were not trained in 'minimum force' counter-insurgency. The cruiser's shelling was limited to 23 6-inch rounds and a similar number from her smaller guns. The Army's artillery fired 658 rounds of which 440 were fused for intimidation. The aircraft were initially used for bombing and machine-gun fire, but as soon as possible were re-ordered to fly intimidation missions. Duval's reputation as the 'Butcher of Sétif' was somewhat exaggerated.

The exception was a massacre in the town of Guelma where the local sub-prefect, against standing instructions, authorized the formation of a local *colon* vigilante group.[14] These, probably fuelled on Algerian wine, went on a bloody reprisal rampage in which inhabitants of certain small settlements were subjected to general massacre, the bodies being disposed of in lime-kilns.

Insurgent and indigenous casualty totals remain a matter of controversy, nationalists grossly inflating the totals. The government of Algeria, after careful enquiry, assessed a figure of 1,340 killed. A figure of just under 3,000 appears more likely – 1,500 killed by civilians, 755 by the Army, 173 by the gendarmeries, some 200 by air attacks, with a lower total from naval gunfire. In addition, in the Constantine Region 157 men were condemned to death in military courts, to whom jurisdiction in these cases had been transferred. Of these, only 33 were actually executed. But inflation of totals had begun early. On 23 May 1945 the BBC, quoting Radio Madrid, offered 3,000 Europeans and

14 Guelma had had a particular history of killings of Europeans in small local uprisings. J. C. Jauffret speculates on a consequential siege paranoia: *L'Avertissement*, pp.249–50.

10,000 indigenous; the latter figure was supported by an article written by a sergeant in an American military newspaper. The PPA then moved to 35,000, projected to 45,000 by the FLN (*Front de Libération Nationale*) in 1954, and advanced to 80,000 in present-day Algerian writing. The figures, even their pre-1954 exaggerations, contributed to the overall sense of fear and destabilization.

The issue is complicated by the fact that reports of two enquiries into the events were aborted. The report of one was never published even if it was written. The second was under compilation by an enquiry commission of three. When the commission was about to go to Guelma its work was halted. No explanation was given at the time. A French historian, Jauffret, has recently speculated that behind this decision was a need to 'cover up' the Guelma events. Politics may have dictated the preservation of the reputation of the local sub-prefect who had been a declared Gaullist in a solidly Vichyist Algeria.[15]

The insurgents appear to have hoped that their uprising would spark off a general revolt in Algeria but no firm plans for this were made. After the outbreak of the uprising the underground PPA did attempt to mastermind an uprising timed for the end of the month, but it had been caught unprepared and the project was called off. There were, however, protest marches and riots in support of the Sétif insurgents in several Algerian cities; these led the French to claim later that a general insurrection had been planned in advance. The end of the uprising was marked by several mass formal acts of capitulation. The most important of these took place near Bougie, where *caids* and headmen, standing in front of their several thousand strong communities, mostly Babor and Oued Marsa, surrendered to General Martin who emphasized the occasion with bands, fly-pasts and gunfire salutes. In March 1946 an amnesty was proclaimed, most of the detainees being released. Among them was Ferhat Abbas, who had been arrested at the outbreak, and two of the future 'historic nine' founders of the 1954 National Liberation Army, Mohammed Khider and Larbi ben Mhidi.

The uprising alarmed the French Army, Duval warning that its suppression had only bought peace for ten years.[16] But the Army was not able to influence overall policy. The *colons* buried their heads further in the sands, on the one hand extolling benefits which they believed French rule had brought to all, on the other affirming that

15 *L'Avertissement*, pp.249–50. The commission, headed by a *gendarmerie* general, Tubert, assessed a death total of 15,000, but Tubert appears to have had his own reasons for inflating the figure.

16 François Porteu de la Morandière, *Soldats du Djebel* (Paris, Société de Production Littéraire, n.d.), p. 19.

all that was needed was a show of force to maintain that rule. These views simply produced sullen hostility from the mass of the population. Recriminations between the followers of Ferhat and Messali were bitter. For the Moslems as a whole, Sétif began the teaching of parallel lessons, violence appeared necessary to effect change; political moderation and the middle-class nationalism of Ferhat Abbas was unlikely ever to do so.[17]

SYRIA AND LEBANON

The second of the two curtain-raisers was the conflict, as sharp and as brief as Sétif, in Syria in late May 1945. The origins of this campaign lay in the great power arrangements made for the Middle East at the end of the First World War.

As a fruit of victory France received Syria and Lebanon, as League of Nations Class A mandated territories, after much complex military and diplomatic activity. Originally the area (together with Palestine and Jordan) had been one Ottoman Empire province with special local arrangements for the Maronite Christian area around Mount Lebanon. It had suited the French, however, to divide. They created a 'Greater Lebanon' from the Maronite Christian area with which France had had long-established cultural contacts, and areas to the immediate north and south which were Moslem. Syrian and Lebanese objections were overruled, Lebanon as structured by France (and until the 1960s) retained a Christian majority; the French believed that this arrangement would provide a check against any Moslem Arab nationalism that might emerge in Syria. The terms of Class A mandates provided for transition to full independence before too long. France, however, saw these two territories as one of the few tangible rewards for her suffering in the war, a foothold appropriate for a great power in the Middle East, and a counter to a total British monopoly in the region. She added these perceptions to those already held in respect of the essential unity of the French Empire, with the further fear that if Syria and Lebanon became totally independent, a dangerous precedent might be set for French North Africa.

With the exception of a brief period 1923–24 in which General Weygand had been High Commissioner, French rule under the Mandate

17 The poet Yacine wrote of Sétif: 'My sense of humanity was affronted for the first time by the most atrocious sights . . . The shock that I felt at the pitiless butchery that caused the deaths of thousands of Moslems I have never forgotten. From that moment my nationalism took definite form.' David Prochaska, *Making Algeria French, Colonialism in Bône 1870–1920* (Cambridge, Cambridge University Press, 1990), p. 238.

had been insensitive. As another stage in her divide-and-rule policy, varying administrative structures of autonomous zones and other divisions were created in Syria; central control rested in the hands of a large French bureaucracy not always well trained, in tune with the region, or free from corruption. In 1925 the Druze people, whose particular and very different version of Islam the French had hoped to use as one of the checks against the Sunni Islam of the increasingly nationalist Damascus elite, broke into revolt. The revolt lasted two years and was only put down with difficulty and severity; it left a legacy of bitterness that spread beyond the Druze community. In turn, the French suspected British connivance.

In the 1930s external and internal events both served to heighten nationalism. Externally, Britain gave flag independence to Egypt and Iraq, both becoming League of Nations members. The increasing number of Jews arriving in Palestine served also to arouse Arab feelings. Internally the French built an impressive modern commercial and French administrative infrastructure, but they seriously under-estimated the growing nationalism and made little effort to train local political or local administrative cadres. With one exception French governments continued to refuse to accept any concept of a Syrian unity. In 1938 one small area was ceded to Turkey. Worst of all, in 1936 the Popular Front government of Blum had negotiated and signed treaties giving a unitary Syria and Lebanon almost complete internal self-government after a three-year probationary period. The mandate was to be replaced by a treaty which would preserve French diplomatic, economic and military interests in a manner similar to the British position in Iraq. The Blum government then fell, and the more conservative Senate rejected the treaty, which in consequence was never ratified.

In Lebanon, Moslem leaders sought a return to Syria. In Syria herself a National Bloc alliance of political leaders had emerged in the late 1920s but the failure of the treaty negotiations led to its splintering. On the outbreak of war Puaux, the French High Commissioner, suspended the constitutions of both Syria and Lebanon, imposing direct French administration. The 1940 collapse of France, the adherence of the territories to Vichy, Vichy's tacit support for German help to the Iraqi nationalist uprising in April 1941, and the resulting overthrow of the Vichy regime by British, imperial and Free French forces after a short and bloody campaign threw both territories, but particularly Syria, into turmoil. French prestige suffered irreparable damage, the French reaction was to recoup it at the expense of the British. Nominal authority was transferred to the Free French, the more enlightened General Catroux being appointed Delegate-General. Prior to the Allied occupation, the Free French had promised to end the Mandate, but, supported by de Gaulle, Catroux ignored this undertaking. Catroux's position was, however, not strong, real power lay in the presence of British troops and the supreme authority of their Commander-in-Chief. Pre-war anglophobe suspicions flared into deep mutual distrust, evident in successive arguments and incidents. In respect of Britain and in sum, local British officials certainly were hoping for the ejection of the French, some actively working with local or other Middle Eastern nationalists for this.[18] The Foreign Office was more cautious, talking ambiguously of sympathy for Syrian long-term aims for independence and claiming a British role in any negotiations for this, while at the same time respecting French wishes to conduct the negotiations. Particularly controversial was the head of the British liaison mission and later Minister to the Levant States, Major-General Spears, a former francophile whose ardour had been damped by the events of 1940 and the rebarbative style of de Gaulle. Spears was a protégé of the Prime Minister, Churchill, who would support him against the Foreign Office.

Syrian and Lebanese nationalists argued that the Mandate had come to an end; the Free French countered by insisting that there must be a 1936-style treaty negotiation. Following the murder of a moderate nationalist during the period of Vichy control, and the flight of other nationalists to Iraq, the more militant Shukri al Quwatly had moved to the leadership of the National Bloc. Quwatly wanted full independence, not a 1936-style internal self-government, and he believed playing Britain and France off against each other might achieve this.

Catroux constituted Syrian and Lebanese governments, headed by moderate nationalist figures acceptable to the French, in the autumn of 1941; he did not, however, restore the suspended constitutions. Amid much Anglo-French diplomatic confusion he and de Gaulle further proclaimed both territories 'independent', with France retaining direct control over the armed forces and police, and indirect control over the administration, economy and communications. Final details were to await negotiation after the war. These arrangements failed to satisfy the militant nationalists.

The next four years saw a succession of incidents in a complex

18 The whole complex sequence is set out in Ariel Roshwald, *Estranged Bedfellows, Britain and France in the Middle East during the Second World War* (New York and Oxford, Oxford University Press, 1990). Also useful is S.H. Longrigg, *Syria and Lebanon under French Mandate* (London, Oxford University Press, 1958); and Henri Lerner, *Catroux* (Paris, Albin Michel, 1990).

power struggle between the local governments, Catroux, his less liberal subordinate Helleu, de Gaulle, Spears and London. Spears, expanding his mission to the size of a rival administration, wanted free elections. Catroux initially saw this as open to too much British influence, but came to believe elections were necessary for the reputation of France. De Gaulle took a harder line, forbidding the elections and demanding the dismissal of Spears, but he was himself constrained by his other colonial need of the time, to be allowed to assert himself in Madagascar. Axis military successes, and then the Allied preoccupations following the North African landings, imposed delays. But in late 1942 Catroux at last succeeded in extracting permission from the newly formed National Committee in Algiers in which de Gaulle was not in control, to restore the pre-war constitutions, and hold elections. Three months later, in February 1943 Catroux restored the 1939 constitutions and set up new interim administrations headed by moderate nationalists of his choice – Quwatly and more militant nationalists declining. Catroux was then moved by de Gaulle to Algiers to assert the Gaullist interest, but also to continue to supervise policies in Syria and Lebanon. The long-deferred elections followed at a time of economic hardship and food shortages in July and August. The National Bloc gained a large majority in Syria, the militant Quwatly becoming President. In Lebanon the election took the form of a contest between French-backed and British-backed candidates, the French using dubious electoral methods. The British-supported candidates won and promptly sought to end the Mandate and declare themselves fully independent. On 11 November Helleu reacted by arresting most of the Lebanese cabinet, dissolving the assembly and appointing a new, subservient, leader.

Strikes and demonstrations followed. Under a British threat of martial law, Helleu was forced to release the arrested leaders whom Catroux from Algiers thought it wise to reinstate – to the fury of de Gaulle. But the lesson perceived by nationalists in both territories was that full independence must be secured before the British left, and any willingness to negotiate fully with the French would undermine their claim that the Mandate was finished. Overall, the legacy of the events was to contribute to the passions and violence of May 1945.

A lull followed; Catroux attempted belatedly and in vain to buy the time necessary for the recovery of goodwill, French prestige and strength before final negotiations. He transferred most internal affairs to the two governments but insisted on retaining control of local forces, denying the two governments their own armies. Friction with the British remained acute despite the recall of Spears in December 1944 in the interests of wider Franco-British relations. Foreign Office policy vacillated, but several indications suggested to the French that British officials and soldiers, at local level, still had designs for British hegemony in Syria. In April 1945, to strengthen his hand in the negotiations he planned, de Gaulle personally ordered the despatch of troops to Syria and Lebanon. The first battalion was justified to the British as a replacement, for the next two no camouflage was attempted. One of the units was a black *Tirailleurs Sénégalais* unit, which served to enrage Arab feeling. At the same time the French negotiation proposals were announced – France was to retain a pre-eminent position, with special diplomatic, economic, cultural and above all military base privileges. Both Syria and Lebanon promptly rejected the proposal and demanded withdrawal of the French forces. Street disturbances in Beirut, Damascus and other Syrian cities followed, developing into a full-scale armed revolt in Syria by 28 May with the French deploying tanks, armoured cars and troops. Open street fighting erupted in Homs and Damascus itself. On the thirtieth, and despite an order to desist from the Delegate-General, General Beynet, a ferocious artillery and mortar bombardment supported by air-to-ground strikes opened against certain areas of Damascus, under the direction of General Oliva-Roget whose mental state appears to have been disturbed. A large number of people, probably some 400, were killed or injured in the bombardment and the poorly controlled follow-up street operations by the Senegalese. Homs was also bombarded.

The British reacted by ordering a return to barracks of all the French units. US approval for this order followed very quickly, and the still considerable strength of the British in Syria ensured compliance. In fury de Gaulle lashed out against the British; he even said to the British ambassador in Paris that his one regret was that he had insufficient strength to go to war with Britain. Local French officials alleged British direction of the street rioting.

These events left the British masters of Syria and Lebanon, the French position destroyed. Under pressure from the British and the Americans the French came to abandon their hopes of a negotiated settlement in which the two territories might remain part of a French Union with garrison rights for French troops. Harassed by a sequence of partisan-style attacks on barracks and French property they conceded their last card, control of locally raised military forces, but to no avail. The last French troops left Syria in April 1946, the last Delegate-General departing, almost unnoticed, in July. For a while the French had entertained a vain hope that they might survive in Lebanon, but they were obliged to withdraw from there also by early 1947.

The withdrawal was eased by the desperate French need for American aid in post-war reconstruction, by the perception of many that France's other priority was the defence of Western Europe for which a friendship with Britain was essential, and by the departure from office of both Churchill and de Gaulle in July 1945 and January 1946 respectively. The British acted as brokers, arranging a formula of joint simultaneous withdrawal.[19]

So ended a brief decolonization conflict. If the main cause was the continuing French refusal to acknowledge a very clear, and not unreasonable, nationalism, an important contributory cause of the hard line of the French, the events of November 1943 and the bloodshed of May 1945, was French resentment of the British, a pre-war inferiority complex inflamed to passion by France's post-1940 status of sick relation in the eyes of Britain and America. Particularly affected was de Gaulle, who repeatedly refused to allow Catroux to make concessions that might have created some bridgehead between France and the nationalist leaders. To de Gaulle these nationalists were the tools of the British, a misconception that brought about the disastrous end that he was trying to avert. But British local officials and military commanders, Spears, and ultimately Churchill must also carry some responsibility.

Whether, if there had been no British presence, the outcome would have been any different is doubtful. As with her other, larger campaigns to follow, France gained virtually nothing through her military efforts. But one result common to both Sétif and Syria was scapegoating, a distrust of Britain and America not confined to the French military. The loss of Syria and Lebanon was perceived, in bitterness, as almost entirely the result of British machination. As at Sétif, no timely political lessons for elsewhere were drawn.

19   In the event, criticism at the United Nations led the British to advance their date of withdrawal. The small French garrison, in apprehension, followed suit.

3 INDOCHINA, 1945–50

The French see their war in Indochina, in purely military terms, falling into three phases: the 1945–46 attempt to reassert total control; the local colonial war period, 1947 to the end of 1950, in which France seriously underestimated the developing insurgency; and the last period of large-scale conflict including a new international dimension, ending with the catastrophe of Dien Bien Phu in 1954.

THE IDEOLOGICAL CONTEXT

A major characteristic of the war, however, was the ideological, planned strategy of the Viet Minh insurgents which suggests a slightly modified periodization. Some ideological introduction is therefore essential for any understanding of the campaign, which was not simply guerrilla warfare but revolutionary guerrilla warfare. The revolutionary theory had its origins in von Clausewitz, Marx, Engels and Lenin, was formalized by Mao Tse-tung and received practical additions from the Viet Minh's military leader, Giap. From Clausewitz, the early-nineteenth-century Prussian military philosopher who was no revolutionary but who had seen guerrilla warfare at first hand, came certain specifically military analyses: insurgency could redress the military balance in favour of the weaker force and, given favourable terrain, insurgency could make a hostile occupation difficult. Insurgency could oblige a superior enemy to disperse some of his forces so weakening any concentration to destroy an opposing force – Clausewitz always thought in terms of insurgents behind the enemy lines complementing a national army facing the enemy. Finally Clausewitz, from Spanish and German experience, saw insurgency as inspiring and harnessing patriotism within a principle of resistance everywhere but nowhere tangible – the insurgent should always strike and move on, avoiding a set-piece battle.

Clausewitz thought in terms of wars between nations. Marx and Engels were to reformulate these principles in terms of class conflict.

The main tenets of Marxism, the conflict inherent in any unequal dependency relationship between men engaged in exploiting the material world in either agricultural or, later, industrial, production, is well known; the conflict would end with the destruction, through its own internal oppressive contradictions, of capitalism and the subsequent triumph of socialism and later full communism. Followers of these tenets, seen as inevitable and imposing a sense of historic mission, should join in and hasten the revolutionary process. Faced with the practical problems of directing a revolution based on an urban seizure of power, Lenin had found the need to create a tightly disciplined party for social control, and also the need to proclaim a new revolutionary morality in which any measure that served the revolution was in order. In theoretical terms he added the tenet that imperialism was the final stage of capitalism.

Mao Tse-tung developed his analyses from his experiences in China's war against Japan. Revolution in China would require the means by which a poor peasantry could defeat a modern military force. The agrarian masses would need first to have explained to them not only the methods of insurgency but also the essential Clausewitzian linkage between the political and military objectives, the political commitment of the people being the more important as it engendered the will to win. Specifically, he saw a campaign of three merging phases. The first was the political mobilization of the masses in preparation for a long struggle; in this phase military activity would be confined to the securing of safe areas, usually remote, training and organization. In the safe areas the foundations of communist society would be laid, in particular in respect of land reform and adult education. In the second phase military activity would be extended, but its aims would remain limited to acquisition of some further territory, forcing the enemy to disperse, and to the undermining of the enemy's morale. All the political work would of course continue. The third phase would be one of open conflict, in which the insurgents' formal forces would attack from the safe areas they held while, behind their opponents' lines in an essential unity of front and rear, peasant insurgents would progressively swamp and overrun the enemy's fixed positions and lines of communication.

Mao's views and writings greatly influenced Ho Chi Minh and his military leader, Giap. The latter, however, influenced also by a Vietnamese writer, Truong Chinh, made several significant additions to the teachings of Mao. In all phases Giap advocated the use of terror which Mao had assessed as counter-productive. Giap argued that terror coerced the masses and raised the commitment and morale of the insurgents at the same time substantially reducing those of their opponents. Giap, further, saw this psychological victory as an essential condition for success on the field of battle, particularly if a favourable world opinion could also be assured. From the Viet Minh perspective, therefore, the first phase can be seen as starting rather earlier than 1945, with the political organization of the Viet Minh cell structures and the securing of the 'liberated zones' from 1941 onwards.

THE FRENCH RETURN

De Gaulle's provisional government had started specific military preparations for a French return to Indochina, earmarking *Coloniale* troops in the autumn of 1944. In June 1945 General Leclerc de Hauteclocque was selected by de Gaulle to command an expeditionary force; three divisions were envisaged, though only one was likely to be ready before 1946. De Hauteclocque as a captain had immediately rallied to de Gaulle in the summer of 1940, adopting the name Leclerc. He had had a brilliant wartime career, his division entering Paris and Strasbourg.[1] By upbringing a devout Catholic aristocrat, the war experience had taught Leclerc to think for himself in political matters. He was to approach the problems of Indochina with a remarkable clarity of vision, forming views at variance with the narrow-minded and withdrawn former monk, Admiral d'Argenlieu, whom de Gaulle later appointed as High Commissioner.

The situation facing Leclerc was unpromising, with the proclamation of Ho Chi Minh's provisional government in Tonkin and, as agreed at Potsdam, Chinese (Nationalist) military occupation. Ho Chi Minh was, however, prepared to tolerate the presence of a French administrator, Sainteny, in Tonkin as a lever to remove the Chinese, whose leaders were building up, generally by buying, a political following, while their soldiers were looting and pillaging in the style of conquerors rather than allies. In the south, vengeful insurgents and French civilians and garrison survivors were harassing and killing one another, the troops of defeated Japan offering no discouragement. To restore order, and also under the provisions of Potsdam, a British force arrived at Saigon on 12 September 1945. The role of this force, commanded by General Gracey and composed of Indian Army units, was in theory to be limited to the control and removal of the Japanese.

1 For an account of the career of Leclerc, who was created a Marshal of France posthumously, see Anthony Clayton, *Three Marshals of France* (London, Brasseys, 1992). Leclerc's aide-de-camp in Indochina attributed his liberal approach to a humanism produced by his firm religious beliefs.

In the event Gracey found himself obliged to proclaim martial law, after which he handed over administration to Cédile, the French official who had earlier been parachuted into the south.[2] Cédile, with the aid of British and Indian troops and some 200 French soldiers who came with Gracey, re-asserted order, concluding a truce with the insurgents. Two ugly incidents, however, fuelled racial passions. The first was a small-scale roughing up by French settlers of Annamese, which in riposte was followed by the 'Heyraud massacre', in which some 400 people, mostly French, were cruelly kidnapped or killed almost certainly by the Viet Minh.

Leclerc arrived in Saigon on 5 October but had only the remnants, much reduced, of the Vichy garrison regiment and the 200 newly arrived men to command for several weeks, until his expeditionary force began to arrive from France. With a remarkable mixture of political and military skill he, nevertheless, set about the re-assertion of French control in the south, initially with the use of Gracey's men and later with French units as they became available. First he directed the local French community of administrators and businessmen to revise their attitude towards the Vietnamese, a message received grudgingly; he then arranged for the disarming and progressive return home of the Japanese. The immediate Saigon area under control and, with more forces at his disposal, Leclerc next broke up the Viet Minh insurgent groups that surrounded the city and then despatched motor-borne or water-borne columns out into Cochinchina.[3] These columns moved quickly, often at night; areas penetrated would then be consolidated with infantry sweeps. In the cases of the more powerful rebel groups, artillery and aircraft were used in support. The French columns were, however, told wherever possible to use minimum force, avoid brutality or looting and make friends with the local peoples. After an area had been cleared, efforts were made to restore economic life.

Leclerc himself commanded with energy, personal direction and disregard of danger, with outspoken awards of blame or praise, and with efficient intelligence-gathering. Above all he injected a sense of morale, high standards of behaviour, team spirit and the teaching to the indigenous peoples that the aim of the campaign was as much political, a liberation from Japanese and Viet Minh terrorism together

2 Labour Party politicians argued that Gracey here exceeded Mountbatten's instructions on non-intervention. He was, however, faced with anarchy, and Mountbatten advised Cédile to negotiate with the Viet Minh; Bevin, the Labour Foreign Secretary, defended his actions.

3 Notable among the column leaders was Colonel, later General, Massu.

with economic recovery, as purely military.[4] However, although the rebel groups were generally only lightly armed and were also divided amongst themselves, including both Cao Dai and Hoa Hao, the difficulties to be experienced by the French in the future were already emerging: harassment of the French columns by snipers and in ambushes; sabotage of bridges and roads; and, most difficult of all, the identity of insurgents, apparently innocent paddy-field villagers by day but guerrillas after dark.

Leclerc complemented his successes in Cochinchina with resolute action in Cambodia. On a flying visit to Phnom Penh he personally arrested the anti-French Prime Minister, Son Ngo Thanh, so enabling the King, who wished to retain the French link, to appoint a more moderate successor. By the end of November French forces were entering Cambodia and southern Laos: in January 1946 French forces landed from the sea in south Annam. By the end of February economic life was restored south of the 16th Parallel.

This notably successful campaign had cost the French forces 630 killed and 1,000 wounded, but this cost and ever more evident difficulties heightened Leclerc's doubts over the longer-term future. He began openly to express the view that a full military reconquest of Indochina was not feasible and that the best military power could achieve would be the formal re-assertion of sovereignty to strengthen the French position in political negotiations.

Re-assertion of sovereignty, however, had to include the key areas held by the Viet Minh, north Annam and Tonkin, for which Leclerc prepared another move of notable diplomatic and military skill. His plans provided for French pressure, from Paris and within Indochina, on the Chinese to withdraw their 150,000 troops, negotiations with Ho Chi Minh using their common interest in removing the Chinese, and military preparations, in the event a build-up to 65,000, for re-occupation of the north. The departure of the Chinese, to begin on 1 March, was eventually conceded grudgingly by the various factions within the Chunking government.[5] Agreement was expedited by the manpower needs of the Nationalists in their fight with the Communists, and a promise by France to renounce her pre-1939 treaty concessions in China. Ho, alarmed by the Chinese who were now supporting a number of anti-Viet Minh VNQDD figures, and at this time having

---

4 Leclerc's operations in this respect followed the pattern set by Lyautey in Morocco earlier in the century; they also foreshadowed both the personal style and the strategy of General Templer in Malaya in the early 1950s.

5 Chinese military maps of the time showed Tonkin as part of China. After a number of incidents of violence in both Laos and Tonkin, the last Chinese departed in July.

no other friends abroad, was prepared to recognize Sainteny. Discreet, sometimes covert, negotiations opened in late 1945, Ho demanding a French acceptance of full independence and a progressive withdrawal of French troops. Striking his benign, scholarly 'Uncle Ho' image, he also mounted a political window-dressing operation by first dissolving the Communist Party (while preserving its structures), and then after concluding an agreement with the VNQDD nationalists, holding an 'election' on 6 January which was won by the supposedly broad-based Viet Minh 'front', though at Chinese insistence, Giap was appointed a minister.

Ho was at the time much criticized by some harder-line Communists as being more nationalist than Communist. He was at this point undoubtedly willing to accept a negotiated settlement, which he believed possible after the exit from office of de Gaulle in January 1946. On 6 March Ho signed a preliminary agreement with Sainteny in which Vietnam was recognized as a free state of the Indochinese federation within the French Union, with further negotiations on future status and diplomatic representation to follow. The Vietnam government agreed to accept the return of French troops to replace the Chinese, but the troops were to withdraw in phases, to be replaced by the successor government's army over a five-year period.[6] Ho also agreed to a referendum on the issue of any unity of the three *kys*, Tonkin, Annam and Cochinchina.

Leclerc had no illusions over Ho, believing that after the agreement Ho would continue to manoeuvre to remove all French political influence, but he also believed that Vietnam would stand in need of French help, economic and other, and on that need a fresh partnership could be built in accord with the new conditions of post-war Asia.[7] At the time of this agreement d'Argenlieu was in Paris; but he was to return very critical, the attitude also of the old colonial bureaucracy.

The agreement, however, provided Leclerc with the assurance he needed that the Viet Minh would not oppose his arrival at Hanoi, an assurance essential for the safety of some 22,000 harassed and victimized French residents in Tonkin.[8] His ships arrived in the Haiphong

6 Giap saw the 6 March agreement as a tactic, comparing it with Lenin's 1918 Brest-Litovsk Treaty with the Germans.

7 On 14 February 1946, for example, Leclerc sent a telegram to Paris strongly advising the French government to promise and use the word 'independence'. His overall view is best summarized in a note that he wrote on 5 December 1946: 'In sum, since we do not have the means to break Vietnamese nationalism by force France should try by every possible means to align her interests with those of Vietnam.'

8 Leclerc had in reserve a full assault plan had there been Viet Minh opposition, but Ho's orders were obeyed.

River on 5 March, and after a 30-minute exchange of fire with the Chinese, who then capitulated, his troops landed and began moving into Hanoi and later all Tonkin. The atmosphere was generally friendly, the French Army vehicles carrying both the Tricolour and the Vietnam colours. Leclerc himself met Ho, who was greatly impressed by his straightforwardness, and they agreed on cease-fire arrangements. Leclerc supported Ho's request for early negotiations in Paris and went as far as he could in limiting French involvement in purely Vietnam internal affairs, though he did not accept Ho's claims in respect of Cochinchina.

Leclerc's remarkable success, at a cost of 37 killed, secured the return of the Tricolour in the north, but it met with hostility from d'Argenlieu and no support in Paris. D'Argenlieu first secured the stalling of negotiations in Paris and then, on his own initiative, and using non-Communists, began to create a separate client state in Cochinchina totally divorced from Hanoi.[9] This move precipitated bloody Viet Minh attacks under a local Cochinchina leader both fanatical and cruel, Nguyen Binh, who was at the time supported by the Cao Dai and also the Hoa Hao in their respective areas. Leclerc and Sainteny protested in vain that all this would be seen by Ho as a breach of faith and strengthen the Viet Minh hardliners. Leclerc, his warnings that France was heading for a guerrilla war that she could neither win nor afford ignored, and with even his military command authority by-passed, returned home in July.[10]

In sum, in these months a deal could have been struck, though without doubt before long Ho would have used independence within the French Union as a basis for a Communist dictatorship – but such a dictatorship might not have been Moscow- or Peking-driven.

THE OUTBREAK OF OPEN WARFARE

D'Argenlieu, however, was backed in his view that full French control could and should be restored by the Gouin and the subsequent Bidault governments in Paris; these both included the Socialist Moutet as Minister for the Overseas Territories. D'Argenlieu also arranged for a press campaign advocating firmness to be launched in France. Under Tripartism the Gouin and Bidault governments also included the

9 D'Argenlieu, on 1 July, proclaimed a respected doctor, Nguyen Van Thinh, as President of Cochinchina. On 10 November, Nguyen committed suicide, apparently in despair over the limited powers he was allowed.

10 D'Argenlieu arranged for Leclerc's recall. On one occasion he compared Leclerc's meetings with Ho and Giap with Munich in 1938.

Communists; those few interested in Indochina still envisaged a future French Union including a Communist France and a Communist Indochina, while others faced with d'Argenlieu's press campaign, supported a policy of re-assertion for fear of losing the patriotic vote.[11] Ignoring the terms of the 6 March agreement, d'Argenlieu offered only local talks at Dalat, an Annam hill station. At Dalat Giap dominated the other Vietnamese groups, re-asserted a claim to Cochinchina and demanded full independence; the only agreement reached was for a conference in Paris in the summer.

In May, however, because of their opposition to the proposal for a unicameral French legislature, the MRP ministers caused the fall of the Gouin government and the Paris conference had to be delayed until July, following an election in June for a constituent assembly. In this election the MRP gained at the expense of the Socialists, a gain that led to the formation of the Bidault government; Bidault himself was increasingly alarmed by Ho Chi Minh's communism.[12] In a mistrustful atmosphere the conference eventually concluded a *modus vivendi* agreement in September, the Viet Minh making several economic and cultural concessions but the French offering nothing implying independence. In the uneasy truce period that followed Giap, now supposedly out of office, used the time to further clandestine preparations for conflict, launching a number of terror attacks on the French.[13] His main targets, however, were the middle-class, non-Communist nationalists, in particular the VNQDD whose leadership was killed off and replaced by fellow travellers or deliberately betrayed to the French. Other opposition figures were arrested. The worst killings were in Cochinchina, where scores of traditional figures and nobles were assassinated.

As the terrorism spread the French forces, poorly trained and often poorly led, reacted to the clashes with excessive severity. The French further enraged the Viet Minh by seeking to protect Thai and Moi minorities in Viet Minh held areas. On the Viet Minh side, Ho

11 The USSR, whose line the French Communists followed, did not recognize Ho Chi Minh's government at this time. For the Kremlin, France was the bigger possible prize.

12 Bidault chose a *colon* banker rather than a cabinet minister to head the French team.

13 Giap later remarked that the truce saved the Viet Minh in the south. His preparations extended to the formation of organized regiments for frontal combat; by September 1946 he had stretched French consent to the formation of a few units to replace the Chinese to 35 infantry and three light artillery units all under training. The Viet Minh also printed their own money for use in the areas they controlled, and burgled banks for French-backed money for arms purchases.

reformed his government in November, openly bringing back Giap. The French claimed that one of the economic concessions given in Paris by Ho entitled them to customs revenue, hitherto collected by the Viet Minh and used for purchases of clandestine arms. Tensions mounted. On 11 November Ho Chi Minh made a personal appeal to Bidault to intervene, but his appeal was delayed, in dubious circumstances, at d'Argenlieu's headquarters. It only arrived in Paris on 26 November, too late to avert a bloody shooting incident at Haiphong on the twentieth. Other clashes followed elsewhere. General Valluy, Leclerc's successor and at the time Acting High Commissioner, demanded the withdrawal of Viet Minh forces from the area; the Vietnamese prevaricated. Two days later, with the approval of d'Argenlieu and Bidault, Valluy ordered retribution.[14] French ships and artillery bombarded Haiphong, causing a number of casualties.[15] Troops entered the city after five days of fighting.

At this crisis point, following the November French General Election in which the Communists made gains and the MRP this time suffered losses, there was an unfortunate interregnum in Paris. The veteran Socialist leader, Blum, eventually formed a new Socialist minority government but this was only a temporary measure pending the election of the Fourth Republic's first President in January 1947. Some in the Viet Minh leadership hoped Blum would be less confrontational, but another message from Ho was again mysteriously held up and Moutet, on a visit to Indochina, made no effort to meet or even contact Ho. Local negotiations broke down and both armies deployed for conflict. After nightfall on 19 December the Viet Minh launched a massacre of French troops and French civilians, 43 being killed. On the twenty-first Ho formally proclaimed war against the French; the second phase of the war had begun.

Blum himself favoured negotiation, even sending Leclerc to Indochina to report on the situation and asking him to return with full authority, an offer Leclerc, at de Gaulle's behest, declined.[16] Blum could do no more and was, in any case out of office after the election of Auriol as President. His successor was Ramadier, who, although like Moutet a Socialist, held the general national view on the status

14 Valluy issued the orders direct to the French colonel commanding in Haiphong, bypassing the French northern commander, Morlière, who had counselled caution.

15 The Viet Minh claimed more than 6,000 civilians were killed; the actual number – as at Sétif and Damascus – was likely to have been very much less, probably 300–500. Survivors' accounts were apt to be exaggerated.

16 De Gaulle, apparently, argued that weakness had led to the loss of Syria and Lebanon, and that d'Argenlieu, who had also been a war-time Gaullist, should not be removed. Moutet also felt that d'Argenlieu could not be replaced so quickly.

of France and the Union, a view reinforced by the grossly over-confident military command and the MRP Minister for War, Coste-Floret.[17]

The French opened the campaign by clearing the Viet Minh from the Hanoi area. They were also able to re-occupy almost all of Laos. But they were not sufficiently strong to prevent a Viet Minh withdrawal to pre-prepared and provisioned safe areas in the north; they were only able to relieve sieges of Nam Dinh and Hué with difficulty, and the situation in Cochinchina remained precarious. An uprising in Madagascar delayed the arrival of some badly needed reinforcements; when these arrived pacification of Cochinchina was seen as the first priority.[18] This took longer than expected, but when it was largely accomplished, two operations were launched in October – November 1947 designed to cut off the Viet Minh in the Thai Nguyen hills, using parachute troops for surprise, artillery, and aircraft, mostly Spitfires. Viet Minh casualties, some 10,000, and weapon losses were very heavy, including the death of the Finance Minister, but contrary to French assessment the losses were not fatal. Conclusive French pursuit offensive operations were not feasible as sizeable numbers of troops were required to secure vital areas under constant attack in the north, Annam and Cochinchina. But at this point the French were confident of victory and remained reluctant to train large numbers of Vietnamese: they even reduced the size of their own forces. From the Viet Bac, the remote north-western mountain area that they controlled, the Viet Minh would launch attacks or mount ambushes, and then slip away, avoiding a pitched battle in which French firepower would dominate. They also operated a scorched-earth destruction policy. The conflict was characterized by innumerable small local engagements all over Vietnam, some of them very bloody for both sides. Ho briefly tried to make a seemingly conciliatory concession by again briefly dropping Giap from his government; the French saw this as window-dressing, comparable to Communist tactics in Europe.

The emerging scale of the conflict and its severity was a major contributory cause of the political upheaval in Paris of spring 1947, the end of Tripartism. The Communists refused to support a vote of credits for the Indochina war. This, set in the wider context of the

17 An interesting description of the colonial attitudes of the Socialist Party at this time appears in Jacques Thobie and others, *Histoire de la France coloniale* (Paris, Armand Colin, 1990), vol. II, pp. 429–32. The authors comment on the paradox of emancipatory rhetoric and a mental inability to accept emancipation in practice. Moutet later defended his policies by saying that there was no alternative in a government in which Bidault was Foreign Secretary.

18 The pacification was complex, the religious sects – Cao Dai and Hoa Hao and others – at first trying to retain a foot in both the Viet Minh and French camps.

tense atmosphere of the Cold War and with a domestic wages dispute as a catalyst for crisis, rendered the position of the Communist ministers in Ramadier's government intolerable. On 5 May 1947 they were dismissed and the Communists now moved to opposition to the war and support for Ho Chi Minh.[19] The Communists' departure left the Socialists as the acceptable Left and the MRP in the centre, greatly strengthening their position when it came to political bargaining against the Socialists.

Ramadier had hoped for negotiations with new, non-Communist, Vietnam leaders, a French aspiration to last until 1954 in various forms. D'Argenlieu was replaced by a Radical politician, Bollaert, in April 1947.[20] Bollaert was given the task of talking with any Vietnamese willing to negotiate within the declared French framework and he made contact several times with Ho Chi Minh. The military were opposed to any such negotiations with the Viet Minh whom they saw, rashly, as almost finished. While Ramadier and Bollaert both constrained Valluy, limiting the size and scope of his operations by specific directives and denying reinforcements, Valluy in turn ensured that the armistice terms offered were impossible for Ho to accept. This oscillation was to undermine the French effort for two years.

In 1947 there were particular as well as general reasons for the attitude of Valluy and Coste-Floret, the War Minister. In the summer and autumn of 1947 France was in turmoil, with food shortages, inflation and major strikes which were reasons for genuine hardship, all exploited by the Communists to create a near-revolutionary situation. Gendarmes and police were out on the streets of Paris, civil war seemed near. The government, pressed additionally by the Gaullist RPF who made gains in local elections in October, had to show firmness in confronting Communism at home and therefore, by extension, abroad. The Socialists vacillated, and Ramadier, exhausted, resigned in November 1947. The next administration, that of Schuman (MRP), included Coste-Floret at the Ministry of Overseas Territories, the beginning of the long MRP hold on the Ministry responsible for Indochina. His first task was to reshape policy in the light of the failures of the autumn military operations and Bollaert's first initiatives.

19   The Communist leader, Thorez, over-estimated his strength; he believed the exclusion could only be temporary.

20   Ramadier first offered the post to Leclerc. De Gaulle again advised refusal, arguing that the politicians would not give Leclerc the resources necessary and would then blame him for failure.

THE BAO DAI POLICY

Coste-Floret's solution for Indochina was, on the one hand one of trying to build a non-Communist alternative to the Viet Minh, an alternative to which France might devolve a limited measure of internal self-government, with, on the other hand, the use of military power to force the surrender of the Viet Minh. But Coste-Floret's devolution never extended to true independence, international standing and a truly effective national Vietnamese Army. This in turn made the position of Coste-Floret's chosen agent, the former Emperor Bao Dai, impossible.[21] If he accepted less than the independence sought by the Viet Minh he was discredited in the eyes of his own people, but the French would not give him what he needed for credibility. He had little real following of his own. The Cao Dai and Hoa Hao broke formally with the Viet Minh in 1946 and 1947 as did a third smaller but better-organized sect, the Binh Xuyen. These all gave Bao Dai some tactical support in their respective fiefdoms. The Catholics also initially supported the Viet Minh; under papal pressure they moved to a more neutral position, attempting to keep both the Viet Minh and the French out of the two bishopric areas they controlled directly. In practice the Viet Minh continued to use the bishoprics as safe refuges, despite local militia garrisons supposedly supporting Bao Dai. Emperor Bao Dai was a man of considerable ability, but – with both dubious morals and a diffident streak in his character – was not temperamentally suited to play either the role for which he was cast or the one to which he personally aspired.[22] His personal weaknesses of character led French officials and politicians to believe, wrongly, that, given a façade of power, he could be easily manipulated. He had left Indochina in 1946 and, while living mostly in Hong Kong or France, sought from 1947 to 1949 to prise more generous concessions out of Paris, pointing out the true independence gained by India, Burma and, in 1949, Indonesia.

Talks and negotiations dragged on until 1949 amid the vacillations of the Schuman, Marie and Queuille governments, in all of which Coste-Floret remained the minister responsible. In March 1948 Bollaert secured Bao Dai's acquiescence to the formation of a provisional government, and in May 1948 this was duly formed, headed by General

21 The Bao Dai policy had in fact been advocated by Catroux in the years before the Second World War; as for Syria, he envisaged a political structure similar to that created by Britain in Iraq. D'Argenlieu had also favoured the policy.

22 One possible reason for this diffidence may have been that, according to some sources, Bao Dai was not born into the imperial dynasty but had been adopted. The point is obscure. He also enjoyed sport and gambling, to excess.

Nguyen Van Xuan. In June, at Along Bay, Bao Dai signed an agreement promising Vietnam's adherence to the French Union, and in March 1949 there followed the formal Elysée Agreement between Bao Dai and President Auriol. Under this agreement Bao Dai was recognized as the head of an 'independent' and unified Vietnam, 'independent' being qualified by recording that it would be restricted by membership of the French Union. A specially convened Cochinchina assembly then voted for the reintegration of Cochinchina into Vietnam (thus reversing previous French policy), and as a next step a 'State of Vietnam' was proclaimed on 2 July as a preliminary towards a move to full Associate State status, to be given to Laos and Cambodia as well as Vietnam.

These limited concessions made by France also reflected growing anxiety over the Communist successes in China. The details of the concessions were criticized as too great by the political and Catholic Right, notably Bidault; many Socialists would have preferred to negotiate with the Viet Minh or with Bao Dai's head of government, Vice President Xuan. Bollaert had resigned in late 1948 in irritation over Bao Dai's prevarications, but his successor, Pignon, continued to implement Coste-Floret's Bao Dai policy. In accordance with this policy French Union Associate status was given to Laos in July and to Cambodia in November, France of course retaining defence and foreign affairs, though Laos was permitted missions in Thailand and the United States. It was hoped that this would strengthen the credibility of the Associate State status given to Bao Dai's Vietnam in December; in this case a small Vietnam Army was to be allowed and foreign missions in China and Thailand permitted. But overall policy was to remain, very obviously, in French control and special legal privileges for French citizens were also secured. On his return Bao Dai was not allowed the use of the former imperial palace, which was retained for the French administration. Ratification and implementation were dilatory, providing further fuel for Viet Minh propaganda condemnations and distrust among Bao Dai's ministers, notably after the June–November 1950 Pau administrative conference. Although Bao Dai could claim that he had gained what had been denied to Ho Chi Minh in 1946, the months that followed showed only too clearly that none of his successive governments was capable either of arousing any genuine mass support for him or even of administering the subjects and departments devolved upon them by the French.

MILITARY OPERATIONS, 1948–49

In the field, French military operations in 1948 and early 1949 continued to be limited by lack of manpower and indecision in Paris. The Viet Minh in Tonkin and Cochinchina concentrated on political education, recruitment and training; limited guerrilla activity was, however, continued in most areas, on a rather larger scale in Cochinchina. Blaizot, the new Commander-in-Chief, wanted to lead a powerful force into the Viet Minh stronghold, the Tonkin mountains.[23] Both Bollaert and Pignon feared this would leave the economically important Cochinchina denuded of troops so that Viet Minh guerrillas could strike, expose French weakness and discredit Bao Dai's government.

Effort was then first concentrated on the Red River Delta with, later, Cochinchina. Both efforts met with some success, in Cochinchina General Boyer de Latour du Moulin methodically encircling the Viet Minh stronghold in the Plain of Reeds. But, overall, in the indecisions and half-measures of 1948 an opportunity was lost. The policy oscillations and inadequacy of numbers left the French with the on-going dilemma of whether to concentrate in one area at severe risk to others, or disperse in a strategy largely defensive and one seen as such. Command of the cities and roads was generally maintained, though ambushes became ever more dangerous. The French appeared to control the rice fields and jungle by day, but the Viet Minh ruled at night. The Viet Minh deliberately resorted to torture; the French reprisals often mirrored the terror.

In 1949 the military balance tilted further against the French with the final victory of the Communists in China; the Communist world as a whole was also strengthened by the first Soviet atomic weapons and the founding of the German Democratic Republic. The first problem was that of 40,000 defeated Nationalist troops, many with their families, arriving at the border willing to part with their weapons to anyone who would let them cross. These had to be disarmed and interned. Communist troops started to arrive on the Tonkin border in December, so providing a safe haven for the Viet Minh. The Viet Minh, with growing numbers of irregular insurgents were now able to field some 30 regular units in open attacks, initially on the smaller frontier posts, and with ambushes on the roads leading to the larger ones, notably the Route Coloniale 4 which linked Lang Son and Cao Bang.[24]

23 General Salan had briefly succeeded Valluy but had then been replaced as too outspoken in his demands for additional troops.

24 Some evidence suggests that the creation of the Viet Minh regular units was hastened deliberately to attract Chinese support for these operations.

Giap then launched a more central attack which, at some cost, succeeded in precariously linking his liberated Viet Bac frontier area with insurgent units in the Red River Delta.

The French Army suffered increasingly heavy casualties and loss of morale. Two small-scale successes could, however, be claimed by the French. In Cochinchina Nguyen Binh had been forced to open a formal offensive against the French in order to secure his rice supply. The very able local commander, General Chanson, who had succeeded Boyer, deployed mobile reserves with skill to defeat each successive attack over a four-month period. At the end of this period Nguyen Binh had lost several thousand men and been forced back into remote refuge areas. A terror assassination unit slipped into Saigon was also destroyed a little later. In Tonkin, the local French Commander, General Alessandri, re-occupied most of the Delta area in methodical operations lasting from October 1949 to April 1950, so depriving the Viet Minh of rice, recruits and money. In May, Alessandri scored a further apparent triumph by quickly recapturing the border fort of Dong Khe which had fallen to a sudden Viet Minh attack.

These successes were over-valued. To many Frenchmen, in France or in Indochina, it still seemed that victory was near. Cochinchina and the Delta appeared to be subdued, Bao Dai appeared to be credible, it appeared possible to hold or at least contain the northern border. Neither the efficacy of the Viet Minh political indoctrination and military training, nor the provision of Chinese equipment was as yet evident, and Chanson's food control strategy was preventing southern rice from reaching the Viet Minh forces in the north. Dong Khe's fall was attributed to a lack of steadiness among its Moroccan defenders; its speedy recapture was seen as proof that a French parachute battalion could defeat a Viet Minh brigade. And attention was, in any case, to be diverted to a scandal within the French political establishment known as 'the Generals' Affair'.

In April 1949 General Revers, Chief of the General Staff, was sent by Ramadier, at that time Defence Minister, with the approval of Coste-Floret, to Indochina to report on the situation. Revers, a general of left-of-centre views, produced a military report in which he sensibly advocated withdrawal from the isolated forts on the Chinese border; a second part of the report suggested that the Coste-Floret MRP policy was wrong, that independence should be real and that Bao Dai was ineffective. Revers's friends included another General, Mast, and unfortunately a shady wheeler-dealer, Peyré; Revers evidently hoped to arrange that Mast replaced Pignon, and that Mast would establish an effective Vietnam government, perhaps under Xuan.

Revers's report was leaked, in murky circumstances probably contrived by Peyré, but which led to MRP accusations of a Socialist conspiracy. The recriminations in the autumn of 1949 were behind closed doors, but in January 1950 press reports led to the appointment of a Commission of Enquiry. The Commission's work was leaked to the outside world by one of its members, a Communist. The Commission's conclusions, bitter recriminations and charges of political, financial and personal impropriety occupied newspaper headlines for most of 1950. The wider results were unfortunate: military contempt of politicians; public disenchantment with the Fourth Republic; the MRP, not all of whose members had hitherto believed in Coste-Floret, now rallying to him; the discrediting of the Socialists together with their doubts over the Bao Dai policy; and, in Indochina, the lowering of the stock of Bao Dai still further. Overall, attention was distracted from the growing menace on the Chinese border, where Giap was now alerted to the likelihood of a French withdrawal from the border posts.

The affair raged in a year of industrial unrest (troops having to be brought to France from Germany) and inflationary food prices. The Socialists brought down the Queuille government on 6 October; after a three-week interregnum Bidault formed the next administration in which Letourneau replaced Coste-Floret. Letourneau was to remain the Minister responsible for Indochina until May 1953.[25] The continuity did not, however, free him from the indecisions, contradictions, policy bargaining and political uncertainties that precluded clear thinking and realistic action. An early example, in the climate created by the Revers affair and his own lack of experience, was Letourneau's rash decision to set aside the Revers recommendations – and also the view of the even more experienced and able General Juin – and maintain the border garrisons.

THE DISASTERS OF 1950

As on earlier, less important, occasions, French troops were simply insufficient in number for a fast-changing situation. In much of Annam there were no French garrisons; in Cochinchina there were areas where all that the French could manage were infrequent searches. The Viet Minh here could organize with impunity. The Viet Minh were now receiving Chinese equipment – in particular, guns, mortars and

25 Letourneau served generally as Minister for Overseas France from October 1949 to June 1950, and specifically Minister responsible for Indochina from July 1950 to May 1953.

anti-aircraft weapons – across the border from early 1950. In January 1950, Peking officially recognized the Viet Minh – so obliging the Soviet Union also to do so. In July, China sent a strong training mission and opened training camps. By the end of 1950 the Viet Minh had five small divisions or equivalent formations in the field. In September, Giap, using more than 20 battalions of his best units together with artillery, began to launch heavy attacks on the posts on the border mountain ridge, again capturing Dong Khe. He then, piecemeal, destroyed the French column, three battalions strong, that had belatedly on 3 October been ordered by Carpentier, Blaizot's successor, to withdraw from Cao Bang.[26] Carpentier's inept and over-confident plan ignored specific intelligence advice, with the consequence that a four-battalion column, including an elite parachute unit sent to assist the withdrawal, was destroyed as well. The disaster, costing the French over 4,800 dead or missing with many more wounded, led the French to evacuate Lang Son, with its stores and weapons, without a fight, after which they were progressively squeezed out of almost all northern Tonkin. Personal conflicts between Carpentier and Alessandri in Tonkin, and between the two column commanders, played a large part in the disasters.

By the end of November Carpentier had prepared plans for a withdrawal from Hanoi, which Ho Chi Minh claimed he would occupy by Christmas. To add to French anxieties, Nguyen Binh had returned to the attack in Cochinchina. Chanson, however, remained able to limit his impact and eventually Nguyen Binh was killed by his own followers on his way to explain his failures to Ho.

In contrast to the optimism of the summer, the French situation at the end of 1950 could hardly have been less promising. In France, the war was now generally unpopular, many Socialists and the Radical leader, Mendès-France, now vociferously opposing it.[27] Even more serious, Indochina had become the subject of furious anti-war propaganda by the Communists and associated organizations on the themes of atrocities, 'the dirty war' and the 'emperor of the night clubs'. Militants organized strikes in arsenals and ports where personnel or

26 Carpentier had wanted to retain the forts to block communications between China and the Viet Minh, to support ethnic minorities loyal to the French, and to ensure that the beaten Chinese Nationalists were disarmed by the French. By July 1950, however, the forts were no longer in a position to perform any of these functions.

27 Polls taken reflect the change in public attitudes. In July 1947 37 per cent favoured on-going military operations, and 37 per cent favoured negotiations with the Viet Minh, generally supported by a further 5 per cent who wanted order first restored. By July 1949 only 19 per cent supported prosecution of the war and at least 49 per cent ending the conflict; of this 49 per cent, 11 per cent favoured total withdrawal: Jacques Thobie and others, *Histoire de la France coloniale*, vol. II (Paris, Armand Colin, 1990), p.378.

equipment were loaded, and the sabotage of stores. Gendarmes had to be used to protect the embarkation of troops; returning wounded could not be flown back to Paris for fear of demonstrations and the national blood donor organization could not be used for them. Citations for bravery could not be published. Conscript soldiers could only be sent to Indochina if they volunteered; very few did so. The campaign accordingly bore very heavily on the professional regulars of *Coloniale*, the *Légion Etrangère*, and North African *Tirailleurs*, used in increasing numbers from 1950 onwards.[28] The heavy casualty rate, 3,500, of whom 352 were officers, killed since September 1945, further lowered morale. But, as before, the more the Communists agitated, the less possible it was to negotiate with Ho Chi Minh, many arguing that if Vietnam was lost the rest of the French Empire would soon be lost as well. Coste-Floret raised a ghost from France's past by arguing that surrender after one defeat would be a repetition of 1940.

The total French forces had risen from the 60,000 of Leclerc to 100,000 under Valluy, and to 145,000 by 1950. Until that year a very large percentage of the ground troops were based in forts of concrete and bamboo. Soldiers spent their time either out on patrol, on guard or at rest. Increasingly, 'rest' was a misnomer, the rest period becoming one of nervous anticipation or plain terror if sudden gunfire was heard at night. Otherwise rest was a mix of poor, over-spiced meat and fish, good beer, brackish '*choum*', a local rice beer that quickly affected the brain, an unpleasant wine made from a concentrate, water made drinkable only with pastilles whose foul taste was removed by aniseed, cards, old magazines, the military brothels, and for a large number (of all races) a semi-permanent Indochinese wife or *congai* with, perhaps, children. Some *congais* were Viet Minh agents, others were rapacious, but many were devoted consorts, who were, with their children, later to be abandoned. The better forts secured a village community with schools and a market, but all posed problems of supply. Many were overrun in fanatic Viet Minh assaults, with horrible consequences for the garrisons. The elite pursuit group units of the latter part of the campaign were continuously on the move, when terrain permitted, by vehicle, boat, air move or parachute drop. Local leaves were spent in gaming, drink, the countless brothels of Saigon and, for a few, drug dens.[29] The French Navy played an active role,

28 Leclerc had refused to have black *Tirailleurs Sénégalais* in Indochina; his successors reversed this policy.

29 Pierre Carles, *Des Millions de Soldats Inconnus* (Paris-Limoges, Lavauzelle, 1982), p. xvii, offers a fascinating description of a soldier's life in Indochina, on which this brief outline is based.

with ship-to-shore bombardments in coastal areas, strikes from carrier-borne aircraft, and the transport of troops along waterways in a whole variety of small craft. Neither Blaizot nor Carpentier were effective commanders. A few staff officers were Communists, and until their removal they would covertly help the insurgents.

In contrast, the months of preparation by the Viet Minh had been well spent. The regulars, now over 20,000 men, were able to concentrate and outnumber the French at places of their choice. They were supported by regional units of largely part-time insurgents who co-ordinated the strikes of the regulars with the part-time, village-level guerrillas. The men were tough and needed only coolie porters for movement, usually by night. Constant political indoctrination by political commissars of almost monastic zeal operating the two parallel cell systems and teaching by parrot fashion repetition of political clichés was backed by public sessions of self-criticism. Drastic punishment, including public execution, was awarded to offenders. All this ensured conformity, discipline and vigilant security; human weaknesses such as gambling, flirting with girls, drinking or even complaining were forbidden. The indoctrination, stressing the themes of revolution and independence, ensured on-going fanaticism. The uniform dress and trappings reflected Chinese influence; the actual political message was more Soviet-inspired. The message was communicated by carefully orchestrated mass singing and slogan chanting by military and labour units. Porters, men and women in their hundreds, carrying loads on their backs or on bicycles kept the fighting units supplied. Traditional French area-by-area methods of pacification could no longer succeed in face of this continuous political corrosion. An area the French thought to be in their grasp would be quietly subverted by nocturnal visits from political officers and regional unit officers. Above all, this subversion ensured ever-growing popular support for the Viet Minh in the forms of food, intelligence, disinformation for the French, concealment and recruits.[30] Only a small minority of Vietnamese in the 'liberated areas' opposed the pro-Chinese wing of the party and its increasingly revolutionary policies; some of these defected to Bao Dai. The politicization was culminated by the formation of the all powerful Lao Dong (Workers) Party on 3 March 1951, in which all the cadre posts and most of the founder members had been members of the former Communist Party.

Even the most casual glance at any book containing photographs

30 In respect of intelligence, the Viet Minh also often received massive help from the intelligence organizations of Communist countries and left-wing Western journalists, authors and politicians.

of the Indochina war will show the gap in military sub-culture facing the French in this area of monsoon Asia. This gap particularly confused generals with extensive North African experience, such as Carpentier. Almost invariably the climate and terrain assisted the Viet Minh and, off the roads, hindered the French whose maps were generally out of date. In the southern swamps and paddy fields soldiers trudged through mud, often ambushed from banks; the capture of one palisaded village could occupy a battalion for twelve hours and roads had to be protected by watch towers 1 kilometre apart. The forest-covered mountain areas posed even more daunting problems. Aircraft strikes could not always be effective. The movement of French tracking units were observed, especially if artillery was deployed, while the French themselves never escaped from the virtual impossibility of telling which rice farmer or highlander was by day an innocent peasant but after dark a killer.

1 (*opposite*) Bao Dai headed his first government himself under the title of 'Head of State' while 'retaining' the title of Emperor. In early 1950 Bao Dai passed the premiership to Nguyen Phan Long, who incurred French displeasure for his approaches to the United States. In May 1950 he was succeeded by Tran Van Huu, a known francophile with a reputation for corruption. Huu's first ministry fell apart following quarrels among ministers from the religious sects. His second ministry, formed in February 1951, was one of technicians and independents. This lasted until June 1952, when Nguyen Van Tam, another known subservient francophile, was appointed. Tam proved increasingly unable to hold the different rival factions together, and in chaotic political conditions was replaced by Bao Dai's cousin, Prince Buu Loc, in December 1953. Buu Loc lasted until June 1954, when in the extreme post-Dien Bien Phu circumstances, Bao Dai appointed Ngo Dinh Diem.

4 INDOCHINA, 1951–55

The enforced withdrawal of the French from the north-east of the country and the ability of sizeable Viet Minh formations to operate from this consolidated 'liberated' area as a 'front', to co-ordinate with insurgents attacking in the 'rear', marked the opening of the final stage of the war. But despite the apparently desperate predicament of the French, two factors were briefly to work to French advantage.

THE CONFLICT INTERNATIONALIZED

The first was the opening of the Korean war in June 1950. This Asian war accelerated a change in American attitudes that had already begun; American aircraft and medical supplies now arrived in a steady flow. By October 1952 American aid covered over 75 per cent of the cost of the war. The American public and government now perceived the war not as a campaign of colonial repression but as part of a world-wide struggle against Communism, a perception that soon led to the 'domino theory' – if one state fell to Communism, others would follow. The French shrewdly despatched a regiment to the UN force in Korea specifically to strengthen this perception of a common struggle. It came also to be held strongly that a defeat of the French Army in Indochina would mean that American attempts to build a security system in Europe would fail; a strong and confident French Army was to be a cornerstone of this system. But to confirm this new perception it was necessary for the French to make some more realistic concessions to Bao Dai; in particular a real Vietnam Army. The war was to be both Americanized and Vietnamized. This was a policy that served also to recapture some critical French Socialists, especially when Bao Dai's ministers, partly to try to display an independence from the French, attempted to approach America directly for support. Such a move had earlier led the French arbitrarily to dismiss one Vietnam Prime Minister, Nguyen Phan Long.[1] American involvement, however, still further enraged the Communists, who represented it as American preparation for a strike against Communist China.

L'ANNÉE DE LATTRE

The second factor was that the frontier disasters had led the Pinay government, faced with criticism and recrimination, to despatch to Indochina a soldier of exceptional ability and resolution, General de Lattre de Tassigny, as both Commander-in-Chief and High Commissioner.[2] Of the other three very senior French generals who had gained their reputations in the Second World War, Leclerc de Hauteclocque had been killed in an aircraft accident in 1947, Juin's interests lay in North Africa, and Koenig refused the command as the government would not accept his stipulation that conscripts be sent to Indochina. There was an element of both drama and the gambler in the sixty-one-year-old de Lattre's acceptance of the responsibilities. He was also much affected by the death rate of young French officers and by the appeals of his only son, serving in Indochina. The 'Year of de Lattre' that followed was both a personal *tour de force* and a personal tragedy.

Although he had never before been to Indochina, de Lattre analyzed the territory's problem clearly and constructively; he was no old-fashioned imperialist. He also worked well with Letourneau, though he was sometimes in advance of political thinking in Paris. His first priority was military. Immediately on his – carefully stage-managed – arrival in December 1950 de Lattre addressed groups of demoralized officers and soldiers on the theme of firm command: 'From now on you will be commanded.' He next showed this resolute grasp by issuing orders that Tonkin was to be held and all plans for withdrawal to the south scrapped.[3]

On 13 January the Viet Minh opened a massive attack on Vinh Yen, only 32 kilometres from Hanoi. The attack was made by some 25 battalion-sized units, the attackers assaulted in successive waves, screaming and generally at night, some in suicidal attacks, some bound together by the ankles in groups so that the wounded (and the dead) would maintain the momentum. De Lattre personally directed the defence using flares dropped by aircraft to illuminate the scene, and

2 For an account of the remarkable career of de Lattre, see Anthony Clayton, *Three Marshals of France* (London, Brasseys, 1992). Like Leclerc, de Lattre was formally created a Marshal posthumously, though in de Lattre's case the process was initiated while he was still alive.

3 At almost the same time another equally resolute general, General Ridgway, was adopting the same measures in Korea.

napalm. French units were rushed up from Cochinchina by any and every means; after six days of fighting the Viet Minh attacks ceased, their casualties totalled at least 1,600 dead, over 400 captured and 3,000 wounded. The French victory gave their own forces both time and encouragement.

Next de Lattre ordered the urgent construction of a line of mutually-supporting concrete blockhouses, eventually to total 900, with many of the sites selected by de Lattre himself. These covered the Delta area and the approaches to Haiphong and Hanoi. The blockhouses served three purposes: for the better protection of the civilian population; as a barrier against Viet Minh mass attacks; and as sally ports for de Lattre's second main tactical concept, that of mobile combat groups. These comprised two or three battalions carried in armoured half-track vehicles, accompanied by armoured cars and light field-guns. The groups could quickly clear areas, relieve posts under siege, or seek out a Viet Minh stronghold. Working closely with these groups were increased number of parachute troops and air-to-ground strike aircraft. Control and command procedures were made much more efficient; intelligence was gathered from interception of Viet Minh signals.[4] The situation stabilized, at least temporarily; de Lattre paid a visit to Paris to secure further troop reinforcements, obtaining an extra dozen units, nine infantry and three artillery. This reinforcement was not all that he thought necessary but was all that the government of Queuille, who had succeeded Pleven, was prepared to provide, the cost of the war since 1945 being estimated at over £700 million (1951 values). Queuille assessed that the French contribution to the defence of Europe must be his priority, so adding to the lengthening tale of 'too little and too late' in respect of Indochina.

Giap, now commanding in total in Vietnam more than 170,000 men, a total considerably larger than that of the French forces, unwisely decided to attempt another formal mass attack, this time aimed at the Delta. Five small divisions opened this on 23 March with, in the French rear, intensification of guerrilla activity in the Delta itself. De Lattre had just returned from his visit to France and was unwell; he nevertheless, against his staff's advice, correctly saw through a Viet Minh deception plan. He recognized the real direction of Giap's main frontal thrust, a small town called Mao Khe, rushed up reinforcements, and inflicted a second heavy defeat on the Viet Minh. Night air reconnaissance, a new technique, contributed greatly to the French

4 Throughout these last years of the campaign the French were able regularly to decipher the Viet Minh logistics signals and from time to time the operational ones. The former provided invaluable material in respect of movements.

success; naval gunfire from a cruiser and two sloops on the Da Bach river were also important. De Lattre followed this victory with two sweeps into the Delta, the first a success, the second rather less successful.

Along with these achievements de Lattre was also making political progress. With some difficulty he pushed Bao Dai into appointing a Defence Minister efficient enough to help with his next major policy, the rapid creation and expansion of Bao Dai's Vietnam Army. An initial target of an army of 115,000 was set, but, despite all de Lattre's efforts, it was not reached until 1953. De Lattre himself feverishly supervised the opening of cadre schools. He also ordered each French unit in Vietnam to raise a second battalion from the local population. At a purely political level various major state departments and economic institutions were made over to the Vietnamese. They were also permitted diplomatic representation in London, and at the end of the year France sought UN membership for all the Associated States, a move vetoed by the Soviet Union. The number of French administrative officials was greatly reduced but attempts to persuade Bao Dai to hold anything more than local-level elections failed.

The military problem, however, remained. Giap, learning from his mistakes, moved to a closer co-ordination of front and rear for his next attack. This was again aimed at the Delta and was launched in the Ninh Binh area on 28 May, catching the French by surprise and cutting off lines of communication.[5] In this attack de Lattre's son was killed, a bitter blow to a man now falling seriously ill with cancer. De Lattre once more rushed in reinforcements by air and water, and again inflicted a bloody reverse on the Viet Minh frontal attack. He then mounted a six-battalion sweep operation to clear his rear areas during which he firmly occupied the two bishopric enclaves. But a typhoon hampered the operation, enabling a large proportion of the Viet Minh to escape. Another setback was the assassination of General Chanson by a Cao Dai dissident.

The sympathy aroused following the death of his son, and his own reputation, success and clear determination to give Vietnam a meaningful autonomy gained de Lattre more local support than any previous French official had aroused since Leclerc, Bao Dai even identifying himself openly with him. De Lattre himself saw the future in terms of increased American military support as essential to provide the fire power necessary for the front, with the use of local Vietnamese troops as the only effective counter to the insurgent behind the lines.

5 The French refer to this battle as the Battle of the River Day.

He continued to throw all his weight into the expansion of the Vietnam army, particularly its officer training, convincing many that France was offering a genuine independence while the Viet Minh only offered a Marxist dictatorship directed by China.[6]

Although now a very ill man, in September 1951 he also visited the United States to win support for France; he met President Truman and senior officials, his charismatic personality making a very effective impression.[7] He briefly returned to Indochina in October where, with General Salan, he directed the desperate defence of Nghia Lo against mass Viet Minh attacks aimed at turning his inland flank. He then mounted a last offensive that in a brilliantly planned manoeuvre, designed in part to impress America, he took the strategically important city of Hoa Binh. But no substantial concentration of Viet Minh appeared to do battle. His pain-wracked condition then obliged him to return to France, where he died in January 1952. In the Second World War de Lattre had shown himself capable of total changes of strategy and tactics when necessary. Had he fought in Indochina at the peak of his powers he might have countered the rear insurgent as well as the frontal attack and so secured a strong political and military negotiating position for France and Bao Dai; he had no illusions over the possibilities of any total victory. Neither Letourneau, who took over the post of High Commissioner to hold jointly with his ministry, nor Salan as Commander-in-Chief could hope to match his volcanic genius.

STEADY DETERIORATION, 1952–53

Letourneau's twin responsibilities were difficult to combine – he had in any case to be based in Paris; further, the considerable power that he now held diminished the prestige of Bao Dai. Salan was an able commander with an impressive career as a fighting soldier and experience of Indochina behind him. He had, however, a complex

6 Any documentary study of the Indochina war must include de Lattre's speech at the prize-giving of a leading Saigon *lycée* in July. One section ran:

Be true men. If you are a Communist, then join the Viet Minh. There there are men bravely fighting for a bad cause. But if you are patriots fight for your country, as this is your war. Build a national army to take over from the French Army. Young men of Vietnam, I feel for you as I feel for the young men of my own country.

7 De Lattre had earlier attended a conference at Singapore in May, at which he presented the French campaign in Indochina as the centre-piece of Western strategy to contain Communism. The British reaction had been cautious, the American more receptive. Both at Singapore and in the United States de Lattre deliberately chose to play the lead role, doubting the stability of the governments in Paris.

personality, with ambition and a taste for intrigue concealed behind an inscrutable manner. Known as '*le mandarin*' or '*le chinois*', he did not inspire trust; events later in Algeria were fully to confirm this reputation. He also distrusted both the reliability of the Vietnam Army which the Viet Minh were seeking to infiltrate, and its capabilities. De Lattre's programme of rapid expansion lost momentum; instead, more Vietnamese were recruited into French units.

In 1952 the French military situation slowly deteriorated again. In a series of costly attacks mounted over two months by three divisions, Giap wore down the French forces in the Hoa Binh area; at the same time he infiltrated two divisions into the Delta. Faced with the usual problem of inadequate numbers, Salan skilfully withdrew from Hoa Binh, and in March and April used the troops effectively to clear out and inflict heavy casualties on the Delta infiltration.

Checked at least in part in the Delta, Giap returned to the forests and mountains of the north, seeking to outflank the de Lattre line. Here his preferred style, infiltration, possessed a further advantage; even when the French could identify infiltration it was virtually impossible to deploy artillery. The area also offered two further benefits to Giap: the inability of the French to defend the Thai and Moi ethnic minorities in the area undermined their loyalty to the French; and Giap was also able to pose a threat to Laos. Violent fighting took place from September 1952 around Nghia Lo, which Giap attacked with three divisions.

Salan met the challenge with a new tactical concept, the 'hedgehog' air–land base, a large strongpoint defended by an outer perimeter of gun posts and forts with interlocking fields of fire, and an airstrip for secure supply. From these 'hedgehogs' sorties supported by both light aircraft and artillery could be mounted. At the first of these, Na San, in the Nghia Lo area, Salan repulsed a three-division Viet Minh attack, inflicting heavy casualties but again not winning any decisive success. Also largely unsuccessful was a two-pronged, 30,000-strong attack launched by Salan's mobile reserves against Viet Minh supply bases north of the Red River. Salan himself came to be criticized as faint-hearted.

The enlarged scale of the fighting and the increasingly defensive strategy forced on the French became even more clear in 1953. Although Bao Dai's government and Letourneau had agreed on a further expansion of the Vietnam Army, the Vietnam government insisted that they operated under their own command. This in practice limited their initial use, when they became available in any sizeable numbers, to the south. The main threat remained in the north. To counter a large-scale Viet Minh invasion of upper Laos in April 1953 Salan created two new 'hedgehogs' at Luang Prabang and in the Plain of Jarres. These – and sheer exhaustion – temporarily checked the Viet Minh. But at the same time Giap began to revive activity in the lower Mekong, south Annam and Cochinchina, so threatening to take Cambodia from the rear. In one particularly horrifying attack in July 1952 at Cap Saint-Jacques 25 French women and children were killed. In Cambodia the Viet Minh linked with the local Khmer Issarak movement headed by Son Ngoc Thanh, the Cambodian leader removed by Leclerc, in the jungle, threatening to take Cambodia from the rear. To retain credibility, the Head of State, King Sihanouk, began to press the French for complete independence.[8]

This military challenge coincided with a major political setback for French policies in Indochina. On 8 May 1953, without any prior warning to Letourneau in Saigon, the Mayer government in Paris abruptly devalued the Indochinese piastre. The piastre had been fixed at 17 francs in 1945, it had declined to some 7 francs by 1953. Speculators of all types – Viet Minh, French and Vietnamese – had been profiting in a scandalous situation that should have been ended earlier. But any ending by France would appear to invalidate the 'independence' of the Associated States, and as such had been resisted by Letourneau.

The devaluation decision, delivered so arbitrarily as it was, had precisely this effect, arousing the indignation of the governments of the three Associated States, with, in particular, a further weakening of the status of Bao Dai. In contrast, in areas held by insurgents the Viet Minh were gaining political credit from their 'Land for the Tillers' redistribution programme, a measure designed as a reward for the hardships being suffered by the peasant population, the support of the middle and landowning classes now no longer being needed.

In the summer Sihanouk forced France's hand by dramatically appearing in Bangkok and declaring to the world that he would not return to Cambodia unless France granted full, unrestricted independence. Concessions were promised in August, and in November President Auriol gave way announcing that the French Union would

8 The Cambodian story is complex and can only be summarized here. A Provisional Assembly elected in 1946 had proved to be very hostile to the French; its successor, elected in the next year, was even more so. The politics also reflected internal vendettas among royal princes and nobles. In September 1949, King Sihanouk dissolved the Assembly and ruled personally. Restlessness continued; a further election again returned the anti-French Democratic Party. Sihanouk once more appointed himself Head of Government in June 1952 and dissolved the Assembly, imprisoning his critics, in January 1953.

now permit full independence to member states – a clear acceptance of France's declining military prospects in Indochina and also of the end of the 1946 concept of the French Union. To make matters worse, revelations of corruption and an internal political crisis in Vietnam highlighted the lack of support for Bao Dai. Two national conferences, one in September and one in October 1953, served only to reveal the sectarian and other rivalries in the anti-Viet Minh camp; other than the rejection of Communism the only subject of agreement was opposition to Bao Dai and his corrupt government.

The piastre fiasco, and a subsequent commission of enquiry, also destroyed Letourneau. The Laniel government appointed a Gaullist, Jacquet, as Minister for Indochina, with a civil servant, Dejean, as 'Commissioner-General' in Saigon. The change of title, it was hoped, would indicate that Dejean's role would be increasingly ambassadorial.

These concessions also coincided with a change in the international climate. Stalin had died in March 1953; his immediate successor in the Kremlin, Malenkov, spoke of the need to reduce international tension, particularly in the Far East. The Korean war was ending. Both the Pinay (March to December 1952) and Mayer (January to May 1953) governments had without success attempted to make secret contacts with the Viet Minh. The Laniel government, which after a 36-day crisis largely caused by the European Defence Community issue, had succeeded that of Mayer in June 1953, began to hint openly that it might negotiate with the Viet Minh. Ho Chi Minh in a speech in December 1953 replied indicating willingness to talk, linking, in order to tap Left-wing opinion in France, American support for the war with American wishes to re-arm West Germany as all part of a world-wide American imperialism. However, in the Laniel government Bidault had returned to the Foreign Office. There, although he had now come to realize that complete victory was out of the question, he was able to obstruct and delay Laniel's proposal to send Savary, a Socialist Deputy, to the Viet Minh to discuss possible negotiations, arguing that the French negotiating position had first to be strengthened. By the time Bidault had agreed to this project the French military position had deteriorated rather than improved, as Bidault had hoped.

American aid, too, was fast proving a mixed blessing, the United States making it clear that she regarded the price of her aid as greater French involvement and commitment to the war, and a measure of American commentary upon policy and operations that was resented in Paris. Nationally, support for the war was declining fast, some Radicals, most Socialists, a few MRP and all the Communists calling for a negotiated solution. Among the few who wanted the war to continue were those who argued that so great a French military effort in Indochina was an excellent reason for opposing the European Defence Community project – the absence of French troops giving a re-armed Germany too great a preponderance.

While willing to open negotiations, Laniel agreed with Bidault that a precondition for these should be a significant French military success. Accordingly General Navarre, who in May had been selected by the Mayer government to replace Salan, was instructed to adopt an overall defensive strategy in the north for a year, during which time only minor tactical offensive operations should be conducted to mop up the Delta and retain combat efficiency. In this period preparations could be completed for a military blow late in 1954 or in 1955 which would bring the Viet Minh to the negotiating table in a suitably chastened frame of mind. The British government welcomed the initial defensive strategy; the Americans, however, wished to see an offensive that would inflict earlier and greater damage upon the Viet Minh. When the French asked for a further massive aid contribution on 1 September threatening disengagement if this was not forthcoming, the United States repeated the American desire for an early offensive and the requirement that US military officers supervise planning.

French and American delusions were strengthened by some evidence of vigour in the Vietnam government under its new premier, Nguyen Van Tam, and by the apparent success of Navarre's early operations.[9] These included an occupation of Lang Son by airborne troops in July, a large-scale sweep in the Hué area of Annam, and a difficult but successful withdrawal of the French garrison from Na San. In October occurred a further spectacular French success with the virtual destruction of a Viet Minh division preparing to infiltrate the Delta.

DIEN BIEN PHU AND GENEVA

Despite these successes Navarre had, however, to choose the area for the desired final strike at the Viet Minh in response to challenges presented by them rather than his own personal preference. He himself had been selected deliberately because he had no previous experience in Indochina, and this lack of experience was now to prove one reason for his undoing. He was led to assess that the most serious of the

9 Nguyen Van Tam's government was an ill-assorted mix of ministers, Catholics, Cao Dai, Hoa Hao and one VNQDD. It was supported by the Right-wing Dai Viet movement, which had grown powerful, largely through use of terror.

challenges facing him was a renewed Viet Minh threat to Laos, into which Giap, contained elsewhere, was attempting to infiltrate a division. Laos had been given formal full independence on 22 October 1953 but the Viet Minh support for the Pathet Lao insurgence movement had enabled the Pathet Lao to dominate one border area. It was thought by Letourneau and other political figures that, if French guarantees of a full independence to be protected by France were to be meaningful and serve as a pattern for Cambodia and Vietnam, the defence of Laos must take priority. Navarre's other main concern was a Viet Minh-held area on the Annam coast south of Da Nang; this he attacked without success in an offensive in January 1954.

In detail, Navarre further assessed the key area in the north to be around the small town and airstrip of Dien Bien Phu, from which he would be able to dominate the Laos border and all the communication routes with Laos, China and Tonkin. American advisers supported this assessment, some seeing it as a possible future base for operations against China. Navarre did not, however, at this early stage envisage the area as one for a decisive battle and the two defects of this chosen area, its 300-kilometre distance from Hanoi and the surrounding hills, were only appreciated too late. Navarre himself commanded from Saigon, remote, comfortable – and *louche* and out of touch. French intelligence assessed that the terrain and the one single, poor-quality road would prevent Giap from deploying more than 20,000 troops, and that his logistic support would permit of the arrival of only a small number of guns no larger than 75 mm, whose range would be insufficient for fire from the hills. The plan was freely discussed in the French press, so alerting Giap. He nevertheless had to surmount considerable criticism from Central Committee members when he proposed a lengthy period of preparation involving the construction of hundreds of kilometres of supply trails and communication trenches, and then committing the flower of the Viet Minh to a decisive pitched battle.

On 20 November 1953 Dien Bien Phu, which had been in Viet Minh hands for a year, was taken in an airborne assault. Its conversion to a giant hedgehog began at once, five strongpoints, all given girls' names covered the airstrip, two more covered the central position, and one was sited 8 kilometres to the south.[10] A twelve-battalion garrison was envisaged and the pick of the Army in Indochina ordered

10 During a visit to Paris in November 1991, Giap commented that the hardest decisions he had had to make in his career were to veto a proposed rush attack on Dien Bien Phu on Christmas Day 1953 which he knew would fail, and to plan for the set-piece battle later.

to provide it.[11] Politicians and other visitors were invited to admire the base's strength. But as the garrison moved in, so, quietly, began the Viet Minh investment, with combat forces totalling 60,000, far greater than the French expected, and artillery including 24 105-mm guns, together with 700 lorries and thousands of black-clothed men and women porters for supply. To prevent any stiffening of French strength in the area Giap ordered new guerrilla offensives in the Delta, the Annam highlands and towards both central Laos and Luang Prabang.[12]

While both sides were preparing for battle, developments were taking place on the international stage. Early in 1954, at the great powers' Berlin Conference, Molotov, the Soviet Foreign Minister, had proposed a further conference to include China, to consider wider international issues – in particular, Korea but also Indochina. The proposal was followed up and arrangements were made for a conference to assemble at Geneva on 26 April. The conference was to be chaired jointly by Britain and the Soviet Union; France, the United States, China, Bao Dai's Vietnam, the Viet Minh, Laos and Cambodia were all represented, as well as India, Canada and Australia.

Giap's investment of Dien Bien Phu, and the opening of the Viet Minh attacks on 13 March were timed with an eye on the Geneva Conference. Navarre was later to argue the Geneva Conference had unfairly raised the stakes. In the initial assault the Viet Minh, in wave attacks always providing a local numerical superiority, overran a *Légion* battalion holding *Béatrice*, one of the outer strongpoints covering the main airstrip. The next day, *Gabrielle*, the other northern strongpoint, fell, and on the fifteenth the airstrip came under Viet Minh artillery fire from well-dug-in hillside positions, the death knell for an air–land base. Supplies and reinforcement units could then only reach the French by parachute drop at great risk.

The only hope for the garrison now rested on American intervention. A plan was prepared for this jointly by General Ely and Admiral Radford, the French and American chiefs of staff; the plan was sup-

11 At the time of the fall of the fortress the garrison comprised three battalions of *Tirailleurs Algériens*, one of *Tirailleurs Marocains* together with a battalion-sized unit of Moroccan irregular *goumiers*, six *Légion Etrangère* battalions (of which two were parachuted), two *Coloniale* parachute battalions with one additional company, two locally recruited Vietnam infantry and one parachute battalion, a French metropolitan Army parachute battalion, a *groupe* of *Coloniale* artillery whose gunners included a large number of West Africans, and one squadron of tanks.

12 In late 1953 it was estimated that 5,000 out of the 7,000 Delta villages were in Viet Minh hands: Jacques Dalloz, *The War in Indochina 1945–54* (Dublin, Gill & Macmillan, 1990), p.160.

ported by Dulles, the US Secretary of State and Nixon, the Vice-President. The plan provided for raids by 60 American B29 long-range heavy bombers, escorted by carrier-borne fighters which would also contribute air-to-ground support.[13] A special war committee of the French Cabinet composed of the Prime Minister, Foreign Minister and the several defence and armed services ministers requested this operation. Dulles, however, became cautious, aware that such involvement would not be popular domestically, and on 5 April proposed a collective security pact for Vietnam of Britain, France, the United States, Australia and New Zealand. President Eisenhower, too, was cautious, being advised by General Ridgway, the former US Army commander in Korea, that close bombing might not prove effective but could instead lead to a large-scale Asian war.

As the condition of the defenders worsened following a Chinese re-supply of artillery shells, French pleas for help were renewed on 24 April. Dulles sought at least token British support, so that intervention could be presented as joint. The Foreign Secretary, Eden, sought the advice of the Prime Minister, Churchill, who, sharing the same doubts as Eisenhower, very firmly refused. Both Churchill and Eisenhower then agreed that no action should be taken before the Geneva Conference.

The doomed garrison fought on, slowly losing ground to successive Viet Minh attacks, with ever-mounting casualties incurred both on the ground and during the frantic efforts at air support and supply. On 7 May General Cogny, the French Commander in Tonkin, signalled to Colonel de Castries, the garrison commander, 'You are going to be overrun. No surrender, no White Flag'.[14] By the evening of the seventh the last strong point, *Isabelle*, had been overrun. The French lost their entire garrison, which with last-minute reinforcements had totalled over 15,000 men. The valour of the garrison, notably the *Légion* and the *Coloniale* units but also some of the North African *Tirailleurs*, was legendary by any standard, an epic later somewhat to reduce the bitterness of the defeat. Many of the legionnaires were Germans who felt that they had in any case little to live for. The Viet Minh too performed remarkable feats of bravery and only achieved victory at

13 No real significance need be attached to an offer, made by Dulles to Bidault, of two atomic bombs. Bidault knew they would not save the fortress; Dulles knew that President Eisenhower would be most unlikely to approve it. The offer was a gesture only.

14 With the appointment of Navarre, de Lattre's team of able commanders had been recalled. Command in Indochina now lacked experience, hence the absence of any general at Dien Bien Phu.

the cost of immense casualties, at least 20,000 overall, and exhaustion.[15] France had suffered the biggest colonial war disaster in her history. The event, as Giap had hoped, coincided with the formal opening session of the Geneva Conference, at which Bidault stonily blamed the Viet Minh for the war and accepted their presence at the conference only for the purpose of arranging a cease-fire, not for any further negotiation.

The immediate and most important consequence of Dien Bien Phu was the collapse of any further support for the war in France. Bidault and the Laniel government survived for a month, in order not to change the negotiating team at Geneva. Bidault still refused to negotiate with the Viet Minh though he sought a cease-fire with guarantees for a free Vietnam. With considerable skill he played on possibilities of American intervention, something which at this point the Soviet Union feared as being likely before long to involve China, and so, through the Sino-Soviet pact, the Soviet Union also. Bidault was also initially opposed to any partition of Vietnam. The Americans were prepared to threaten intervention, but were divided as to whether to carry it out. Their threat was made primarily to deter any Chinese military intervention; detailed contingency plans were prepared, and this planning activity made known. But the divisions between the hard-liners and those who believed France must try and negotiate a settlement, as the American public would not support intervention, led to an offer of American intervention on conditions that made such action unlikely.[16] This check slightly modified Bidault's attitude, and he began to make contact with the Viet Minh leaders and speak of partition; he also offered a French withdrawal from Laos and Cambodia if the Viet Minh would also withdraw.[17] Overall, French aims were now realistically assessed; military withdrawal was inevitable but the threat of America's replacing France could be used to secure a continuing French influence and presence.

15 The French lost approximately 3,000 killed and 10,000 taken prisoner; some 2,000, mostly locally recruited Thais, deserted. Viet Minh casualties have been estimated at 8,000 dead and 15,000 wounded.

16 These conditions were, in detail, a formal request by France that Thailand, the Philippines, New Zealand, Australia and Britain must support intervention and the United Nations endorse it; that the Associated States must have total independence; that American intervention would be naval and air only; that there would be a common command structure; and that there would be approval of the intervention and conditions by the French parliament.

17 The point is important. Although the breakthrough in the negotiations occurred after the fall of Laniel it was Bidault who first realized that, by making some concessions and talking to the Viet Minh, France could negotiate to secure some aims and avoid total humiliation.

On 12 June the Laniel government fell and was succeeded by the Mendès-France government.[18] Mendès-France, a Radical, was known for his sharp criticisms of conservative policies in Indochina and North Africa. In a curious mix of the use of France's still considerable residual strength in Indochina, of his known wish now to end the war, and of threat, Mendès-France turned to the Geneva Conference and demanded a treaty within four weeks. If no agreement were reached he said, he would authorize the despatch of conscripts to Indochina and then resign. The sincerity and realism of Mendès-France, and his willingness to negotiate with the Viet Minh, served to recoup some of the prestige lost to his country following military defeat. It also injected purpose into a conference in which debate had declined to the exchange of sterile diatribes.

The basis of this final stage of the negotiations then became a demarcation within Vietnam, a project which Eden had been pressing upon the largely uninterested Soviet Foreign Minister, Molotov, with some success, and which Molotov was able to persuade Pham Van Dong, the chief Viet Minh negotiator, to accept. The Viet Minh perceived that partition, providing a firm base for their long-term aims of a unified Communist Vietnam, would serve their interests better than any form of 'leopard spot' settlement. The French were prepared to sacrifice Hanoi and Haiphong for the same reason, consolidation being preferable to Viet Minh-controlled areas in the south. Debate then centred on the demarcation line, the French seeking the 18th Parallel, the Viet Minh the 13th. Unexpected help in securing this compromise solution came from China, which had suffered severely in the Korean war, needed Western trade and above all, general international recognition and admission to the United Nations. Peking appears also to have foreseen that the French would withdraw completely, leaving a vacuum in the south which the United States would seek to fill. The Chinese were therefore prepared to urge compromise on the Viet Minh leadership. So, despite American opposition led by Dulles, on one occasion extending to a threat to withdraw from Geneva, and with Eden and Chou En-lai acting as brokers, Mendès-France was steered to negotiations with Chou. Dulles modified the American stance to setting out acceptable conditions which, in turn, led on to agreement upon a demarcation line close to the 17th Parallel, with mutual withdrawals from Laos and Cambodia. China also continued with her more rational and traditional Chinese policies by

18 Mendès-France was supported by the votes of the Communists, which he disowned. The MRP distrusted him because he was known to oppose the European Defence Community project, a major issue in French politics at the time.

supporting the existence of the Laos and Cambodia monarchies. This package, together with the cease-fire agreements, was signed on 20 July, amid some reluctance in the hard-line wing of the Viet Minh, some of whom spoke of Chinese betrayal. If the deal was crude it nevertheless averted a dangerous confrontation, and represented a tribute to the patient diplomacy of Eden.

In detail, the agreements provided for a cease-fire throughout all three states of Indochina. In respect of Vietnam, each side agreed to withdraw behind the demarcation line within 300 days, in which time free population movement would be allowed. Almost a million people moved from the north to the south in this eight-month period. Neither zone was to join any military alliance or build military bases. Free elections for all Vietnam were to be held in July 1956; the French encouraged the mass migration southwards with an eye to a strong anti-Communist vote which optimists believed might reverse the result of the war. For Cambodia it was agreed that the Khmer Issarak be disbanded, that French and Viet Minh forces should withdraw and no further foreign forces should be permitted, and that elections be held in 1955. For Laos, which had in fact been secured by the French sacrifices at Dien Bien Phu, the French were allowed to retain bases at Vientiane and Seno together with a garrison of 3,500. Other non-Laos forces were to withdraw, but the Pathet Lao insurgents were to hold two north-eastern provinces until a political settlement was reached. An International Control Commission drawn from India, Canada and Poland was to supervise the agreements in all three states. The agreements were embodied in a 'final declaration' of the Conference, a document of unclear legal status.

The agreements were also not subscribed to by either the new government in the south of Vietnam, headed now by the formidable Ngo Dinh Diem, or the United States. Diem, a veteran nationalist, had refused to serve in Bao Dai's first ministry and had been outspokenly critical of him. Strongly francophobe, he had been appointed by a reluctant Bao Dai only under American pressure. Diem entered a reservation that he doubted whether free elections would be possible in the north; their delegation had opposed partition and sought to create a neutral zone in the Catholic area. The United States merely 'took note' of the agreements; a little later President Eisenhower stated that, while he hoped the conference and its agreements would bring peace, the United States was not a party to them. Two days later Dulles spoke of the need to prevent what was now referred to as North Vietnam from becoming a base for the expansion of Communism.

Military activity between the fall of Dien Bien Phu and the cease-fire had been limited. The French suffered two reverses, one in Laos and one more severe at An Khê in Annam, but gained one success in a final Delta sweep operation.

COSTS AND CONSEQUENCES

With the cease-fire, the eight years of war came to an end. The total of French and Associated State forces had continued to rise, by 1953–54 totalling approximately 375,000. A breakdown for the summer of 1953 well illustrates the composition:

Metropolitan Frenchmen and personnel from the pre-1789 colonies: ground forces	54,800
Metropolitan Frenchmen: naval and air forces	25,000 (approx.)
Légion Etrangère	19,000
North Africans	29,500
Black Africans	18,000
Indochinese	53,100
Vietnam Army	151,000
Cambodian forces	13,000
Laos forces	13,000

Casualties totalled 11,000 Frenchmen killed with a further 4,500 missing, 20,899 wounded and 5,000 prisoners; 7,500 Légion killed with 3,000 missing and 5,349 prisoners; 4,500 North and Black Africans killed, 2,500 missing and 6,000 prisoners, together with 24,347 Légion, North and Black Africans wounded. From the prisoner totals 2,350 Frenchmen, 2,867 Légion and 2,290 North or Black Africans were never repatriated, almost all having died in captivity. Also, in the years 1947 to 1954 more than 2,000 soldiers deserted.

Of the indigenous Vietnamese directly serving with the French forces 14,093 were killed, 12,830 were missing believed killed (though some may have deserted), 26,924 were injured and 14,060 taken prisoner; of these latter 13,200 were never repatriated.[19] In the Associated States forces 17,600 were killed or missing, 12,000 wounded and 9,404 taken prisoner, of whom 9,247 were not repatriated. Figures of village guard and other irregular local units do not exist, but their numbers killed, if known, would increase the overall total of approximately 77,000 known killed given here.

Viet Minh casualties are unknown but may have totalled at least 200,000 killed; some experts estimate a much higher figure. The high death rate among prisoners was caused because they were often made

19 A very large proportion, for one reason or another, apparently joined the North Vietnam forces.

to march long distances, even if wounded, in conditions of deprivation, thirst, starvation, dysentery, beriberi and malaria. In camps, prisoners, most of them diseased and debilitated, would be subjected to programmes of forced labour and political indoctrination, the issue of food to prisoners being based on Viet Minh perceptions of their conversion and progress.[20] A large number of Frenchmen succumbed. Of greater long-term significance was the number of North Africans, particularly Algerians, who became ready converts to the cause of anti-colonial conflict expressed in these conditions.[21] These were to return home with ideas on and experience in insurgency, to make an important contribution to the campaign to follow in Algeria. The Black Africans proved largely impervious to Viet Minh propaganda.

In France the mass of the public felt relief that the war was at last over. But it was also felt that the United States had promised help, and then, when it was desperately needed, failed to provide it. In French North Africa, as will be seen in the chapters that follow, Dien Bien Phu acted as a catalyst for change in French policies first in Tunisia and then in Morocco.

Within the French Army itself the defeat had major consequences. Many officers shared the belief of a betrayal by the Americans. There was a widely held view that the major reason for the defeat was vacillating political leadership, in particular the politicians' refusal to allow conscripts to be sent to Indochina, seen not only in terms of the provision of inadequate forces but also in terms of a failure to bring the perceived realities of the conflict home to an indifferent general public, in particular, in respect of Dien Bien Phu.[22] Navarre argued that he had been given no clear instructions concerning the defence of Laos, and as the reinforcements he needed for this were not forthcoming he had had no option but to revert to the 'hedgehog' strategy. He also lacked what in numbers could have been a battle-winning weapon, helicopters, as these were not yet sufficiently developed. French intelligence, too, throughout the campaign was unimaginative, generally well informed on the Viet Minh regular units but failing to understand, penetrate or produce counter-gangs from

20 Red Cross visits to prison camps were not permitted until after the cease-fire.

21 It should, however, be remembered that many North Africans, particularly Moroccans, remained steadfastly loyal to their French officers, even if so doing they earned their captors' disfavour.

22 Surveys of public attitudes to press reporting of the Indochina war show clearly that the public generally submitted to the war but did not feel committed to it. In May 1953, only 30 per cent of the population bothered to read press reports about the war; by February 1954 the total had dropped to 23 per cent: Jacques Thobie and others, *Histoire de la France coloniale*, vol. II (Paris, Armand Colin, 1990), p.381.

the irregular Viet Minh. This intelligence – and security – weakness resulted in ever-increased ambushing of supply columns, and with the improved weaponry available to the Viet Minh, of armoured columns as well, bound as they were to the limited number of roads.

But the wide general conclusion drawn by many French officers was that in a conflict of this type, the efforts of the entire nation, and not simply cadres of regular officers and NCOs, must be committed; and that a new combat doctrine of a total war against revolutionary movements must be developed. The psychological warfare staffs were especially blamed for failure in this respect. Both these conclusions and the general feeling that 'it must not happen again' were to have disastrous consequences in France's next major colonial campaign, Algeria, before the lesson was finally learnt that social and nationalist challenges cannot be crushed by technical solutions.[23]

This chapter must, however, end with an outline of the consequences of the French defeat and the Geneva agreements in Indochina. On the wider international stage the triple Communist challenge, Malaya, Korea and Indochina, led to the South-East Asia Collective Defence Treaty signed in September 1954. The signatories, Britain, France, the United States, the Philippines, Australia, New Zealand, Thailand and Pakistan, agreed in the event of an attack upon any member, that each country would act in accordance with its constitutional procedures and also consult in the event of an attack on any other country in the area. The United States saw this as doubtfully adequate. President Kennedy's inaugural speech in January 1961 promising to meet any burden, pay any price, support any friend and oppose any foe in support of liberty, reflected the crusading zeal and self-confidence of America at the time.

Cambodia, lying to the south of the 17th Parallel, was able to preserve peace and a great measure of stability for fifteen years under Prince Sihanouk, who resigned his role as King but remained Head of Government. To meet the Geneva agreement conditions, he formed a national political movement that convincingly won a reasonably free election in September 1955. Cambodia then withdrew from the French Union and declared herself non-aligned. The tragic end to this period of stability in the 1970s was caused by Sihanouk's dictatorial personality on the one hand, and the Vietnam War and its overspill, on the other.

Laos, bordering North Vietnam and China, could only gain a

23 In particular, the French Army's grief over its abandonment of communities and minorities loyal to it was profoundly to influence commanders in Algeria in the early 1960s.

lesser measure of stability. The Viet Minh never withdrew from the north. Prince Souvanna Phouma, who wished to see his country neutral, continued to be faced with challenges from the political Left and the Right. By 1960 these challenges had taken the form of two rival armed camps receiving backing from the United States and the Soviet Union respectively. President Kennedy, with considerable skill, paved the way for a fourteen-power, second Geneva Conference specially convened for Laos; this secured stability until, like Cambodia, Laos became dragged into the vortex of the Vietnam war.

In Vietnam, the French withdrew from the North within a year. South of the demarcation line Viet Minh units were transferred back to the North, but much Viet Minh cell structure remained. A French military command under General Ely remained until July 1955, but power passed increasingly into a partnership of Ngo Dinh Diem and his US patrons, who planned South Vietnam as a second South Korea. Bao Dai from Cannes tried feebly and ineffectually to play off rival factions within the regime. The Americans steadily pushed the French aside, taking over from them the provision of military aid, and despatching first training teams and then Special Forces units. In 1955 Diem used some of the aid to destroy the religious sects, which the French had built up partly as a force against the Viet Minh, but also later as a counter to the Vietnam government. The Cao Dai and the Hoa Hao, each with their private armies, had become states within a state; only a little less powerful was the Binh Xuyen, which had established a grip on Saigon through control of the police. Suppression of this latter sect involved street battles in Saigon itself. Diem next moved against Bao Dai himself, a carefully managed referendum in October 1955 opting for a republic in which Diem proclaimed himself President. In March 1956, Diem allowed the election of a constituent assembly for South Vietnam, so signalling formal partition. This republic was able in a few respects to draw upon the historic divisions between North and South Vietnam, though Diem, a northern Catholic, could attract little personal following. The regime itself became a corrupt dictatorship of Diem, his family and entourage, to the mounting dismay of its American sponsors. In Hanoi, Ho Chi Minh, alarmed by the growth of American influence, tried to urge upon the French the need to remain to prevent South Vietnam becoming an American client state. No will for this remained in Paris though French diplomats on the spot, including again Sainteny, tried to work for accommodation between North and South. In North Vietnam propaganda teams of pretty girls in political song and dance troupes, together with huge posters of Ho, Mao and Lenin, fanfares, red banners, and slogans, all accompanied the Viet Minh entry to Hanoi. Politicization of young people began at once, though a token tolerance was extended to Christians. But the grim post-war conditions led to a peasant uprising against the Viet Minh in Ho Chi Minh's home province, Nghe An, in late 1956; the rising was brutally suppressed.

The elections required by the Geneva agreement were never held in either North or South Vietnam. The North, confident of an electoral campaign in which they would be able to win, if necessary by terror, repeatedly called for a poll. Diem flatly refused. None of the signatories of the Geneva agreements was willing or able to enforce elections. Least able of all was France, now heavily involved in Algeria and also in recriminations over the defeats in Indochina, these recriminations often being the vehicles for attacks on any who sought a negotiated solution in Algeria. From 1957 onwards the North then turned to military activity in the South, the new behind-the-frontier Viet Cong guerrillas launching a campaign of sabotage, assassination and terror. In October 1961 Diem accepted a recommendation by local American military officers and agreed to the arrival of US Army combat units, a move authorized by Washington a little later. By January 1962 there were 3,000 American servicemen in South Vietnam; by July 1962, 6,000; and by the end of the year, 11,000. The stage was prepared for the outbreak of the second Indochina war.

Suffering enormous costs in men and resources and with no tangible offset gains, France had been ejected from Indochina. Ho Chi Minh, also at prodigious cost, had won a long war. But, still inspired by an ideology that served to prevent the conflict from remaining local, Ho was now faced with the prospect of a second war, to prove infinitely more destructive and bloody than the first.

5 MADAGASCAR, 1947–49

While the Indochina war was gathering momentum, and before the violence of the 1950s in North Africa, France was faced with an uprising and a two-year military campaign in Madagascar in 1947–49. The uprising is important for several reasons: the structure of the insurrection, the severity of the repression, some effect of this repression on French domestic politics, and the effect of the uprising on the nature of subsequent Malagasy nationalism.[1]

FRENCH RULE IN MADAGASCAR

The French occupied Madagascar in a military campaign in 1895, though a further eight years of subsequent pacification operations were necessary.[2] The most powerful polity in the island at the time had been the Merina kingdom in central Madagascar. The Merina are a people of Malayo-Polynesian origin; the other 18 or so peoples of the island represent differing mixes of Bantu and Malayo-Polynesian ancestry, language and custom. The French first destroyed the Merina kingdom, then put down the *menelamba* (red shawls), a largely Merina popular revolt, and finally suppressed other primary resistance movements mounted by the non-Merina peoples. A limited number of French settlers and business people arrived in the first 40 years of the twentieth century, and the quality of the colonial administration fell somewhat after the departure of the modernizing and able General Gallieni in 1905. Gallieni had, however, taken some advantage of the resentment caused by Merina hegemony, and in some cases oppression

---

1 No work purely on the uprising exists in English. Jacques Tronchon, *L'Insurrection malgache de 1947* (Paris, François Maspero, 1974), is the most useful and reliable of studies in French.

2 The metropolitan army, jealous of the successes of the *Troupes de Marine* in West Africa, had tried to lead the occupation campaign. The results were disastrous, 4,613 soldiers dying from disease against a total of 25 killed in battle. The lesson drawn was that colonial campaigns needed specially trained soldiers, the major factor in the decision to restructure the *Troupes de Marine* as '*La Coloniale*', colonial infantry and artillery, in 1900.

of the non-Merina peoples, especially the northern Sakalava, by ensuring that each ethnic group was administered by its own chiefs. His successors developed this into specific divide-and-rule, an offset against one of the main French colonial achievements – the establishment of one administration for the whole island.

A number of pre-war and Second World War factors combined to prepare the ground for the one, major, post-1945 uprising in a French Sub-Saharan African colony. Some of these factors were common to all French colonies, some particular to Madagascar. Common to all was an economic structure that favoured the metropole, protecting its manufactured products by a high tariff and excluding foreign competition.[3] In the case of Madagascar, local arrangements also favoured an advantaged French settler community which exerted pressures on the colonial administration. An additional, much-resented, irritant was the racial attitudes of some of the Chinese, Creole and Indian executives of the big commercial companies.

Also common to all French African colonies was abuse by administrative officers, in particular the *indigénat* system of wide authoritarian powers of sentence for very minor offences held by officials, and the *prestation* system whereby payment of an often high rate of tax was commuted to days of compulsory labour. Madagascar suffered further from an additional system of conscription for the purposes of military labour instituted in the 1920s.

Malagasy peoples, particularly the Merina, had for historic reasons a generally higher level of political consciousness than the peoples of France's continental African possessions. This caused many to resent the imposition of the French language and the substitution of French national holidays, such as Bastille Day, for traditional Merina events such as the *Fandraona*, or Festival of the Bath purification ceremony that linked the Merina monarchy with local communities. Malagasy perceived themselves as second-class citizens in their own country. But perhaps most important of all in the formation of post-war attitudes was the fact that Madagascar, alone of France's Sub-Saharan possessions, saw the French defeated on the field of battle. The occupation of Madagascar by British and Commonwealth forces in 1942 had been resisted unsuccessfully; a myth of French military superiority was thereby very visibly destroyed. The better-educated Malagasy, also, quickly saw the British Commonwealth self-governing dominions as an ideal to follow.

3 Japan, for example, was in a position to offer numerous cheaper manufactured goods to Madagascar, but was prevented from doing so.

Protest against the French had begun as early as 1913 with the formation of a mainly Merina secret society, the *Vy, Vato, Sakelika* (VVS).[4] The French authorities closed the VVS down with numerous arrests in 1915–16. A new campaign appeared in the 1920s headed by a failed French settler, two French Communists, and a number of Malagasy including some Merina aristocrats, these latter beginning a partnership with the French Left to continue for over 30 years. Their criticism of French rule became strident, and the French turned again to repression with arrests and a severe press law. In the late 1930s, and as a consequence of the Paris Popular Front government, the press restrictions were eased and the system of conscripted military labour being used for public purposes ended. But by 1939 nationalist papers and tracts were again vocal, calling for independence.

In addition to the experience of local French military defeat, other events in the war years further fuelled militant nationalism. The pro-Vichy government imprisoned pro-Communist nationalists. Trade suffered as a consequence of isolation and there was a severe famine in 1943–44. Some of the Madagascan soldiers serving in France in 1940 later joined the Resistance, learning the skills of *maquisards*.[5] Locally grown foodstuffs, in particular rice, were ruthlessly requisitioned. After the installation of a Gaullist colonial government hopes were raised but the limitations of the Brazzaville reforms soon became evident. Although the unpopular wartime requisition and *indigénat* powers were abolished, independence was not to be considered. The post-war French Union constitution seemed to offer little for Madagascar, and, as in Algeria, there were separate French and Malagasy electoral colleges for the deputies to be sent to Paris.[6] The *colon* lobby, the *Ligue des Intérêts Franco-Malgaches*, had influential connections in Paris, and the military argued that Madagascar's strategic importance in the Indian Ocean called for a continuing French presence.

In February 1946 a new nationalist party, the *Mouvement Démocratique de la Rénovation Malgache* (MDRM) was formed from an earlier political faction, its declared aim being independence within a loose French Union. Initially the MDRM enjoyed a measure of approval from both Paris and the colonial government, which saw it as an *interlocuteur valable*. It was mainly Merina – aristocrat, bourgeois

4 Mervyn Brown, *Madagascar Rediscovered* (London, Damien Tunnacliffe, 1978), p.260, notes the meaning of *Vy, Vato* and *Sakelika* as iron, stone and network.

5 Generally, the French held a low opinion of Malagasy as infantry soldiers though some were used to man machine-gun posts in the Maginot Line in 1939–40. Malagasy were used more extensively in the *Coloniale* artillery and logistics units.

6 The population totals at this time were some 37,000 French *colons* and 4,150,000 Malagasy.

and peasant – but it did include both in its leadership and its 300,000-strong membership people of other ethnic groups. It was skilled in propaganda, presenting itself as a mass party. As its strength grew, however, the colonial administration began to view the MDRM as a major challenge rather than a partner. Two of the other smaller political parties in existence at the time were more exclusively Merina.[7] The impression of a Merina bid for hegemony created by this one large party together with the two smaller ones aroused fears among some of the coastal peoples and former slave classes. These fears were played upon, and perhaps even initiated by, the French as a new form of the *politique des races*. They resulted in the emergence of the *Parti des Déshérités de Madagascar* (PADESM), which rapidly grew in numbers, to the alarm of the MDRM which saw the activities of PADESM as encouragement for the French to delay political progress. The MDRM leadership, never very cohesive, became more divided, some counselling moderation and patience while others spoke of war. In some areas the MDRM became a cover for several secret underground revolutionary movements that had been formed in the war years, in particular the *Jeunesse Nationaliste Malgache* (JINA), and the Parti Nationaliste Malgache (PANAMA). The former drew its adherents from the south of the island, the latter from the north. These societies saw themselves as successors to the 1896 *menelamba* tradition of rural *jacquerie*.

The local provincial assembly elections, held in January 1947, took place in a very tense atmosphere with sporadic, isolated acts of violence.[8] The MDRM-controlled local press sought to use the tension and revolutionary feeling to its advantage and talked of revolt; the PADESM talked of civil war.

THE REBELLION OPENS

The uprising itself broke out on the night of 29 March. Apart from large numbers of ex-soldiers, the precise ethnic or social composition of the insurgent groups remains obscure. Certainly, what was intended to be a largely nationalist uprising was very soon reduced to a regional one, the east coast, its hinterland escarpment and the south-east. The extreme south and the west did not participate, and were generally opposed to the rebels. This eastern escarpment area, some 800

---

7 These were the largely Protestant *Parti Démocratique Malgache* (PDM) and the Catholic *Mouvement Social Malgache* (MSM).

8 The tension was heightened by the French deciding that the final stage of the elections should be single college, a move that ensured the defeat of the MDRM by an alliance of PADESM and *colons* in three of the assemblies.

kilometres in length and 160 kilometres in depth, was rocky, mountainous, and thickly forested. It was an area well suited for insurgency.

The opening attacks took place at Diego Suarez, where the local *Tirailleurs Malgaches* mutinied, at an army camp at Moramanga on the escarpment, and at several locations on the east coast. Generally the French were well prepared and informed. A planned attack on Fianarantsoa further south was forestalled by the French, and another planned attack, on the capital Tananarive, had to be cancelled by the insurgent leaders. At the Moramanga camp some 2,000 insurgents, mostly armed with matchets or spears with only a few possessing firearms, did achieve surprise. They attacked the camp's garrison of *Tirailleurs Sénégalais*, killing a number. The *Tirailleurs* retaliated with reprisals against the local civilians. Elsewhere Malagasy known to be pro-French, French settlers, officials, PADESM leaders, administrative offices, and other military posts were attacked, railway lines torn up, bridges destroyed and telephone wires cut. During the two years of the fighting 350 soldiers and 200 civilians, mostly French but including other Europeans and Asians, were to be killed by the insurgents.

By April the French had lost control of most of the south-east, and about a quarter of the island and Tananarive was cut off. In the area controlled by the insurgents a loose provisional government was created. This was headed by a Merina, Razafindrabe, of the lowest social caste who had served as a junior official, in the north, and a Betsileo teacher, Radaoroson, in the south. The population of this area totalled some 1,600,000 and was made up of more than 10 big ethnic groups, a sizeable percentage of the island's population. These very heterogeneous peoples were all directed to produce side arms, food and uniforms for the insurgents, gather intelligence and prepare shelters to conceal insurgents from aerial reconnaissance and bombing. The political aims of the insurgents centred on a return to a Madagascar community that they saw as having been destroyed by France, this return to be achieved not only by ejecting the French but also by dismantling the state structures located by them. The insurrection as a whole was a strange combination of articulate political and administrative directives from the provisional government on the one hand, and a mixture of wish and delusion in the reports of foreign, particularly American, military forces arriving in support sent to insurgent field commanders on the other hand, all together with specific instruction and apparent belief in talismanic medicines and oaths that were said to deflect bullets or stop a French opponent moving along a road or path.[9] The medicines had a drug effect which must have been known to, and misused deliberately by, at least some of the insurgent commanders to inspire their men. Sorcerers were present in many groups. The insurgents were severely handicapped by an acute shortage of firearms. It is doubtful if they ever possessed more than three machine-guns and 150 rifles of varying types – these were given to the ex-soldier members of the different groups; other insurgents were limited to spears. Insurgent tactics followed a pattern of an encirclement of a target area, the cutting of access and escape routes by felling trees, and finally a mass assault by waves of drug-crazed spearmen.

Initially these tactics proved very successful, the insurgents slowly enlarging the rectangle of area they controlled and reaching the suburbs of Tananarive, Tamatave and Fianarantsoa. Razafindrabe, with a headquarters at Beparasy, headed some dozen local sector commands; Radaoroson's command at Mahatsara near Befody was less well structured.[10] Co-ordination was exceedingly difficult, because of the nature of the terrain and because the insurgents possessed no signals equipment. They nevertheless retained the initiative throughout most of 1947, their initial series of attacks being followed by a second, less effective series in October 1947. Their overall situation was, however, weak, being cut off from any international or other support, and evidence of discouragement and weariness had begun to appear as the various groups took heavy casualties and ran out of ammunition and food. Desertions, despite severe punishment in the event of recapture, multiplied. In August 1947 Razafindrabe was obliged to leave Beparasy and Radaoroson found his authority usurped by another insurgent leader, Lehoaha, whose men possessed better weaponry. Further fragmentation followed at the end of the year. The small size of the local garrison had enabled the insurgents to achieve their early successes. To restore their authority the French moved in reinforcements, totalling 18,000, some regiments being re-routed while on their way to Indochina. The units, which arrived between April and July, included three Algerian, one Moroccan and two *Tirailleurs Sénégalais* battalions, a

9 Tronchon, *L'Insurrection*, pp.358–60, sets out insurgent instructions on the restraints to be observed and concoctions to be prepared for these medicines to be effective. Madagascar had originally been based on small local units with as linkages, land, kinship relationships and burial monuments. Religion centred on talismans, small fetishes, seen as symbolizing the unity of an area. They were therefore of considerable significance in securing loyalty. The insurgents' flag was that of the former Merina monarchy, red and white with, superimposed, eighteen stars, one for each of the island's main ethnic groups.

10 Razafindrabe styled himself Marshal and Radaoroson appointed himself Inspector-General. The two had been both MDRM officials and JINA members.

unit of *Coloniale* infantry and a battalion of *Légion* infantry with a squadron of *Légion* armoured car cavalry. With these forces, under the command of General Pellet until December 1947 and thereafter under the much more effective General Garbay, the French mounted an exceedingly severe campaign of suppression, including retaliatory excesses both by the *colons* and the *Tirailleurs Sénégalais*. Initially the French deployed units defensively, experiencing serious problems of training and disease. It was not until April 1948, after the rains, that regiments became fully effective. The insurgents then became fugitives. Radaoroson was killed on 20 July; Razafindrabe was captured on 2 September, dying in hospital five days later; Lehoaha surrendered on 11 November. The last senior insurgent leader, Ralaivao, whose role had been political as well as military, was taken in February 1949, after which fighting came to an end, the last and some of the fiercest, being in the Tanala people's area. Much of the fighting, in which the *Légion* generally played the lead role, was one of night marches in the escarpment forests, often in rain, to mount dawn cordon-and-search operations. In the night marches soldiers had to touch hands to keep line and contact; separation could lead to ambush. Aerial bombing and naval bombardment was used in support of troops wherever possible.

The suppression involved very large numbers of arrests, severity and torture in the questioning of prisoners, summary executions, and the punitive burning and destruction of villages, with rape of women and girls. Both sides appear to have mutilated the living and the dead, and displayed the corpses or sections of them. The repression caused thousands to flee to the forests; many died of starvation or disease. As he became aware of the excesses, Garbay, to his credit, exercised stricter control, but this was somewhat belated. In the last year of the revolt, also, insurgent groups turned against one and other, settling political, religious, community and family vendettas.

THE RESULTS OF THE REBELLION

The total number of deaths will never be known. Only journalists approved by the French were allowed near the operational zones, so few knew of the realities. After the rebellion was over the French administration carried out a careful survey and assessed the total killed as approximately 11,000. A confidential French Army assessment, however, totalled 89,000.[11] De Chevigné, the liberal High

---

11 Tronchon, *L'Insurrection*, p.73, notes that this figure is based on counts of the population of the affected areas before and after the uprising and therefore likely to be more accurate.

Commissioner, de Coppet's authoritarian successor, estimated an even higher total of more than 100,000. The French Army gave no honour award to any of the regiments participating in the operations, an indication of uneasiness. The *colon* population consistently accused de Coppet of weakness, a major cause of his replacement in March 1948. At one point *colon* extremists even plotted to seize power and install a retired general as High Commissioner.

The MDRM was dissolved as subversive on 10 May, with large numbers of its leaders and members detained. JINA and PANAMA were both proscribed. The trials, opening in July 1948, of the political leaders and military chiefs produced confusing evidence and accusations. But it became clear that in a number of cases the MDRM had been a screen for JINA and PANAMA. JINA in particular had produced a number of insurgent field commanders. The overall impression left by the trials is that, while some MDRM officials were involved, many were not but they had lost control. As a party the MDRM denied complicity in the uprising, a denial not accepted by the French. Doctors Raseta and Ravoahangy, both Merina Protestants, veterans of the VVS and the inter-war years' agitation and founder members of the MDRM, lost their parliamentary immunity and were sentenced to death, although Ravoahangy had issued an appeal for calm on 27 March 1947. The prosecution alleged the appeal was a disguised call to arms. Also arrested was the third Malagasy deputy, Rabemananjara, a journalist and another founder of the MDRM; he with nine others were given sentences of heavy forced labour or life imprisonment. In the event, following Communist and some Socialist pressure in Paris, the death sentences were commuted to imprisonment, and all except the main MDRM leaders were released following a general amnesty in 1954. Rabemananjara and Ravoahangy both became ministers in Madagascar's independence government in 1960.

In Madagascar the major political consequence of the uprising was the destruction of the MDRM, bitterness and recrimination among the remaining nationalist leaders, and apathy even among the PADESM, which wasted away. The French moved on to portray the rebellion as one led by the old Merina aristocracy and bourgeoisie, a final fling of the *politique des races*; covert British support for the revolution was also alleged. When nationalism returned to the front of the political stage, in the more liberal era of Prime Minister Mendès-France following the Dien Bien Phu disaster, it was to take a more moderate form – that of Tsiranana's *Parti Social Démocrate* (PSD). This party, which drew its strength primarily from the coastal peoples, was prepared to work with the French towards autonomy and then independence.[12] The rural insurrectionary tradition of *menelamba* and 1947 was, however, to reappear in the unrest of 1972–75.[13]

In France, Communist criticism of the repression of the Madagascar uprising was a minor but noteworthy contributory cause of the 1947 change of the political scene already noted, the end of Tripartism. But one almost paradoxical consequence of the Left-wing activity in Paris was that the generous political support given by the French Left to the Malagasy nationalist leaders made a great impression and eased the path of reconciliation.[14] Rabemananjara, in particular, long retained a sense of gratitude.[15]

The uprising and its repression attracted very little attention outside France, other events, in particular the worsening Cold War situation, occupying the headlines of the world's press.

12 After independence, Tsiranana demanded the release of the 'Three Deputies' – Raseta, Ravoahangy and Rabemananjara – still held in detention in France. On their release all were invited to join the government and the PSD. Raseta, who had always been the most militant and was probably a member of JINA, refused; the other two accepted.

13 Stephen Ellis, *The Rising of the Red Shawls, a Revolt in Madagascar* (Cambridge, Cambridge University Press, 1985), p.159.

14 The Communists, for example, were the only party in the *Chambre* to vote against the withdrawal of parliamentary immunity from the 'Three Deputies'.

15 Charles Robert Ageron and Marc Michel (eds), *L'Afrique noire française: l'heure des Indépendances* (Paris, CNRS, 1992); article by Jacques Rabemananjara, p. 628 'We were in a colonialist gaol and the National Assembly recognized our total innocence.'

6 NORTH AFRICA, 1946–56

Neither events in Indochina nor developments elsewhere in the Arab world had any effective liberalizing effect on French policy in North Africa until Dien Bien Phu. In all three North African territories pressures built up to a point of revolt. Violence first broke out in Tunisia, but before this violence had been settled, revolt had erupted in Morocco. In turn, this had not been resolved before the opening of the Algerian war. It will be simplest, however, to follow the events by territory rather than chronologically.

TUNISIA

In Tunisia, Bourguiba returned to Tunis in September 1949 amid rejoicing crowds. The French Resident-General, Mons, a Socialist who had already effected several reforms, accepted Bourguiba's return at least in part in the belief that Bourguiba might quarrel with the *Néo-Destour*'s more extreme Secretary-General, Salah Ben Youssef. But Bourguiba's status as the nationalist leader was undoubted, particularly after the death of the deposed Bey Moncef in 1948, as his *Néo-Destour* was successfully combining the French-educated Tunisian professionals, businessmen, landowners and an increasing number of skilled workers. He immediately demanded a universal suffrage election for an assembly and government to reconstitute Franco-Tunisian relations on a basis of equality and co-operation. His demands met with some support in Paris from the Socialists but strong opposition in Tunisia from the French *colons*.

The French government reaction voiced by Schuman, the MRP Minister for Foreign Affairs and a new Resident-General, Périllier, was an offer of a move towards independence within the French Union, in effect internal autonomy, an offer made in June 1950. Bourguiba and Ben Youssef welcomed this as a basis for negotiation, and Ben Youssef became Justice Minister in a Tunisian administration formed by another political figure, Chenik, on 17 August. Plans for negotiations with France were announced. These developments heightened the angry and frightened reaction amongst the European *colons*. There was also opposition from the French governor-general in Algeria, alarmed at possible consequences in that territory and from the military, who began to argue that control of Tunisia was essential for the security of NATO. Périllier was obliged to call a political pause; disorder and some rioting followed. In disgust and after vigorous but fruitless representations at the Residency, Bourguiba left Tunisia to seek international support. In February 1951 Périllier put forward a modified administrative reform programme including an ultimate goal of 'co-sovereignty'; these measures clearly indicated that French control was going to be maintained.

France's firmer line was taken a stage further following the Right-wing gains in the 1951 General Election. A new hard-line Resident-General, de Hauteclocque (not to be confused with General Leclerc de Hauteclocque) was sent to Tunis; it was announced that no Tunisian parliament would be created, and that no further constitutional or political changes would be made. Bourguiba returned to Tunis in early January 1952, and in his usual style began tours of the territory to whip up support. He also decided to try to raise the issue of Tunisia at the United Nations, where his efforts were supported by Arab and Asian countries, but blocked by the United States. Ben Youssef left Tunisia in secret also to mobilize support from anti-colonial nations. In Tunisia herself the French authorities banned a conference of the *Néo-Destour* and on 18 January detained Bourguiba, placing him under a loose form of house arrest. The French troops also conducted a number of cordon-and-search operations, in particular in the Cap Bon area, for dissidents.

The detention of Bourguiba sparked off protest that gradually increased in scale to insurgency. Initial protest took the form of a general strike called by the powerful *Union Générale Tunisienne du Travail* (UGTT), which enjoyed American union support, and also clashes between demonstrators and police and gendarmerie in Tunis, Bizerta and Ferryville. In a brush with the military at Sousse a colonel was killed, and in the Gafsa area a pro-French *khalifa* met a similar fate. By March over 800 acts of sabotage had been attempted, all adult male *colons* had been conscripted into security groups and troop reinforcements had been moved into Tunisia from France and Algeria. On 26 March de Hauteclocque – whether supported by Paris or on his own initiative is not known – arrested Chenik and three of his colleagues. Bourguiba was despatched to the Sahara and, following protest demonstrations, large numbers of Tunisians were arrested.

The next month saw a succession of murders of *colons* and Tunisians known to be pro-French. In the summer tension was eased a little by some minor reforms and the release of detainees. But no concession was made on overall French policy, or more correctly the absence of any such policy, despite the comments of Socialist and other critics in Paris. In consequence, a new terrorist campaign opened in October 1952, *colons*, military and police personnel and pro-French Tunisians again being attacked and killed. Among those killed was the heir presumptive to the Bey. The Bey himself refused to co-operate with the French. The timing of the campaign coincided with United Nations General Assembly criticism of French policies in both Tunisia and Morocco; a resolution was passed calling for 'free institutions'. In response to the violence, *colons* formed vigilante groups, overtly to protect themselves and their homes but covertly to exact reprisals. They also issued threatening leaflets imprinted with the mark of a red hand.

In September 1953 a new Resident-General, Voizard, who was a diplomat, arrived with some initial concessions including the release of a number of detainees and the ending of military rule in most areas of Tunisia. In consequence, tensions eased until December when the militant UGTT leader Ferhat Hashed was murdered, almost certainly by one of the red hand groups. The unions called a three-day strike, which the French authorities countered with curfews and troops in the streets of towns and cities. A series of killings followed in the early months of 1954, insurgents murdering collaborators and French military personnel, including the garrison's chief of staff, *colon* vigilantes targeting known nationalists.

The military problem facing the French was difficult. The *colon* population included a number of small farmers in some 4,000 small, scattered properties as well as the *colons* in towns. The garrison – six infantry battalions, two *Spahis* squadrons, some smaller units and 15 gendarmerie squadrons 75 men strong – was inadequate for security, and the Army commander in Tunisia, General Boyer de Latour du Moulin, asked for reinforcements. These, drawn mostly from France and Algeria but including some from West Africa, arrived progressively in the summer and early autumn of 1954; by the end of the year the French garrison totalled more than 40,000. Boyer believed that the Moroccan *goum* system – small units of irregulars, 120 on foot, 60 mounted on ponies and the balance, mule-supply personnel – would be very suitable for security work, and raised six *goums* locally for use in the Algerian border areas.

But May 1954 had seen Dien Bien Phu, with unfolding consequences for France and her territories. In France herself Mendès-France, a known critic of France's policies in North Africa as well as in Indochina, came to power, including in his government a Ministry for Tunisian and Moroccan affairs – though the minister appointed was in fact a Gaullist. Mendès quickly promised to resume negotiations for political advance to autonomy. These negotiations suffered interruption, but, nevertheless, at the end of July, Mendès-France, his minister, and Marshal Juin all arrived dramatically in Tunis. At the Bey's palace in Carthage Mendès pronounced the famous 'Declaration of Carthage'. In this Mendès announced that France fully recognized Tunisia's claim to internal autonomy and was now ready to implement it.

Juin's Algerian background and upbringing have already been noted; he and his wife – also an Algerian *colon* – held virtually all the prejudices of *colon* society. As will be seen later in this chapter, these prejudices were clearly evident in his opposition to the Sultan and nationalists in Morocco during his tour as Resident-General from 1947 to 1951. His presence on this occasion was part of a package necessitated by Paris domestic politics and *colon* pressures. His appearance and prestige as a Marshal were meant to convey that France would still retain military and overall political control. Juin, who had been ordered to accompany the Prime Minister at no notice whatever, was described as being sombre and laconic. He later angrily alleged that alterations in respect of the negotiating commissions in Mendès-France's Declaration for which he had asked, and to which Mendès had agreed, were not in fact included in the final text. Also, as part of the package, was the replacement of Voizard as Resident-General by the Army commander, Boyer, who had earlier issued an offer of amnesty to all who surrendered, except those who had committed murder. This offer achieved little initial success. The Declaration was immediately seized upon by the (still imprisoned) Bourguiba as representing a step towards full independence. This, together with a very real French devolution of control to internal self-government and the recognition of Arabic as the official language, in turn further alarmed the *colons* and their allies in Paris, so exposing Mendès to sharp criticism in the Assembly. The mauling he received made him cautious over Morocco.

The Declaration of Carthage briefly eased tension, and, as a carrot, in time encouraged others to surrender; an effective goad was the high French kill rate – more than 250 with 200 weapons recovered.[1] By late October insurgency had returned, but in November the French

1 Pierre Boyer de Latour du Moulin, *Verités sur l'Afrique du Nord* (Paris, Plon, 1956), p. 91.

offered a new military *paix des braves* amnesty to all who surrendered themselves and their weapons; the offer included re-instatement in civilian life. Twenty-two joint Franco-Tunisian teams were sent to the main insurgent areas – the highland hinterland around Bizerta, Le Kef, Maktar, the hinterland west of Kairouan and Sidi Bou-Zid, Gafsa, the Gabès area and the southern Matmata area. These teams explained the terms which specifically required weapons to be surrendered to French personnel. In an eight-day amnesty period in early December, 2,514 insurgents – including almost all from the two largest groups led by Lashar Chraiti and Sassi Lassoued – surrendered, and 1,958 weapons were handed in; these figures represented 90 per cent of the insurgent strength. Boyer alleged a measure of bad faith from *Néo-Destour* supporters and no support for him in Paris when he exposed them. The total casualties from 1 May to 1 November 1954 were 80 civilians and 34 soldiers or police killed and others injured by insurgents. The total of insurgents killed was 147. Boyer faced continuing *colon* criticism; one leading critic, a retired general, was deported on Boyer's orders.

In the style of Lyautey, Boyer then ordered military engineers to embark on large-scale road construction. Negotiations on the internal autonomy arrangements were completed in June 1955, Bourguiba being allowed to participate, and then to return to Tunis in triumph. In August 1955 Boyer was moved to Morocco, his civil servant successor, Seydoux, was styled High Commissioner rather than Resident-General. Seydoux repeated the amnesty offer with, again, some success.

Once more it appeared that violence was dying down, but the lull was again to be short-lived. For some, notably Ben Youssef, much influenced by Nasser during his exile in Cairo, internal autonomy was a 'step backwards'. His vision for Tunisia was one of a radical Arab-Islamic state in contrast to Bourguiba's assertion of a distinct Tunisian personality; he also envisaged a Maghreb union of Tunisia, Morocco and Algeria. This last round of violence consequently became more one between Tunisians than against France. On his return Ben Youssef attacked Bourguiba, but a *Néo-Destour* Congress supported Bourguiba and expelled Ben Youssef. Despite a formal demand for full independence made by the newly autonomous Tunisian government, which included three *Néo-Destour* ministers in November 1955, violence returned to the country in January 1956. Frustration over the delays in progress to full independence and sympathy with the Algerian insurgents in their war with France incited a number to arms. Several areas were affected, in particular the Matmata mountains. Some 20 groups of insurgents, followers of Ben Youssef each about 30 strong, were involved. One, led by Tahar Lassoued, an insurgent leader who throughout had rejected all the amnesty offers, styled itself the 'National Tunisian Army of Liberation'. The French replied with sweeps by ground troops supported by artillery and aircraft; *colon* counter-terrorist assassination squads and vigilante groups also re-appeared. Some 200 insurgents were killed, as were four French soldiers and a small number of civilians. Following the murder of two French farmers, Seydoux's car was stoned and a crowd of *colons* sacked the American Consulate-General and Information Office.

The end came in March 1956, when the Mollet government was faced with the need to recall reservists and extend conscription to provide the 400,000 soldiers required for the worsening situation in Algeria. Mollet conceded full independence to Tunisia after only a short period of negotiations. French traditional attitudes and pride were met by the concept of 'interdependence', which served very briefly to disguise the reality. In the elections that followed, Bourguiba's *Néo-Destour* and its allies and supporters won a complete victory. In the following year the monarchy was abolished, Bourguiba becoming President of the Republic, in marked contrast to the constitutional developments in Morocco.

Just before the election – but with the likely result clear – the Tunisian government appealed for an end to the insurgency, adding a warning that the amnesty would not be extended after independence. This appeal secured order just after formal independence; further troubles were a product of the Algerian war and are considered later. Under the independence arrangements France secured rights at the naval base at Bizerta, a garrison, and for a transition period French military control over the southern border areas. The garrison was argued to be necessary for the safety of the *colons* and as a screen for Algeria. But these arrangements led to a dispute later in 1956 when Bourguiba sought the withdrawal of French troops and announced that Tunisia would establish its own diplomatic representation and its own armed forces. The French government objected strongly but had no power to prevent this. Negotiations broke down.

Thousands of *colons* left Tunisia, to its economic loss, an emigration that could have been averted if the French had earlier shown a willingness to compromise.

MOROCCO

Events in Morocco reflected the same French inability to understand Arab nationalism; in Morocco Sultan Mohammed V saw himself faced with the growing strength of his rivals, the *Istiqlal* party leaders, now drawing wider support from the lower-middle classes in the cities and towns. At first, however, hope seemed to lie in the policies of the French Resident-General Labonne, who from the spring of 1946 possessed a rare appreciation that the political clock could neither be put back nor stopped. On his arrival he released a number of political detainees and announced a programme of rapid social, educational and economic development, together with improved labour conditions, all to the fury of the *colons*. Although his programme was attacked as inadequate by both the *Istiqlal* leaders and the Sultan, hopes of progress and change lasted until 1947. These were to end with three events in 1947: a bloody riot in Casablanca, a nationalist speech by the Sultan, and the replacement of Labonne by General Juin.

The Casablanca riot of 7 April 1947 was almost certainly the result of the molestation of an Arab woman by a black *Tirailleur Sénégalais*, but 83 people were killed, with many more injured. The event, in particular the very late arrival of the police, resulted in allegations of police complicity and led the Sultan to omit all favourable reference to French rule from an important speech he was due to make in Tangier, although the text of that speech had been issued in advance to the press. The controversial parts of the speech referred to the legitimate rights of the Moroccan people, and his desire to strengthen bonds with the Arab League, a clear reference to full independence. The speech received immediate acclaim in Morocco. The Sultan also enhanced his credentials as a nationalist leader by overtly criticizing the *caid* policy. This involved rupture with the *grands caids*, some of whom had been traditional supporters, but it defused *Istiqlal*.

The immediate French reaction was that authority must be re-asserted. Labonne was recalled and his successor appointed, arriving in early June. Juin was an 'old Moroccan hand', a *vieux Marocain*. He had first served in the territory on his leaving Saint-Cyr in 1912; he served further in Morocco in the First World War (when not on the Western Front with Moroccan troops), and then in the campaigns of the 1920s and 1930s. He had commanded Moroccan troops with distinction in Italy in 1943–44. But although he had at one time been Military Assistant to Lyautey, he did not have Lyautey's understanding that policies must advance and develop. He and his wife saw Morocco in terms little advanced from the traditional paternalist *politique des races*; protection of the Berbers against an Arab-based nationalism was now seen by Juin as ever more necessary. In addition, as time passed, Juin began to be concerned with the effect of any emancipation of Morocco on his native Algeria. Juin's letters of instruction, drafted by Bidault, the Foreign Minister, with the approval of Ramadier, the Socialist Prime Minister, enjoined Juin to inform the Sultan that political demands of the type made by him at Tangier were not acceptable, and, if maintained, the Resident-General had power of deposition.[2] These instructions were not discussed by the rest of the French Cabinet nor did President Auriol, although *ex officio* also President of the French Union, know of them. Auriol only learned of them, to his extreme annoyance, in 1950 when he at once ordered their revocation.

On his arrival Juin talked, somewhat vaguely, of a final stage of a French-style 'independence, as an Associate State within the French Union, very many years away in the future; in 1949 he proposed the 'co-sovereignty' concept as a shorter term aim. For the immediate 1947 situation Juin envisaged co-operation with moderate nationalists only. This co-operation he hoped to secure from new elite groups to be thrown up following economic development, the securing would be by means of an appeal to a carefully tailored democracy of a regional and, later, a national assembly. The Sultan saw this as inevitably weakening his own power and authority and opposed the proposals, enabling Juin to portray him as an oriental despot. The style of Juin's arrival in a warship, and his paying of his ceremonial visit to the Sultan grim-faced and in full uniform, booted and spurred, foreshadowed the new *politique du sabre*.

Juin had some good senior officials, but came to lean excessively on one of dubious qualities, Boniface, his Director of Political Affairs and later administrator of the Casablanca area. Boniface was a firm believer in the Berber policy and also an Algerian *colon* who disliked young, educated Moroccans. Juin himself would often speak of Paris politicians, particularly those of the Left, in terms of open contempt and, when faced with argument he did not like, would fall back on an attitude of military authority or a threat of resignation. The social life of the Residency centred around the French; Moroccans, particularly the young and educated, seldom figured.

Predictably, dialogue between the Sultan and Juin was from the start formal, by the end of 1950 confrontational, at times openly hostile, with Juin becoming increasingly convinced that the deposition of the Sultan would be necessary, sometimes so hinting to the Sultan himself. The Sultan put forward the nationalist case on a number of specific issues, Juin's proposed changes in urban administration, candidates for *caid* appointments, and the teaching of Arabic rather than

2 Evidence for this is clearly set out in Charles-André Julien, *Le Maroc face aux impérialismes, 1415–1956* (Paris, Editions J – A, 1978), pp. 205–7.

French. He met with little success on these issues, and no success whatever on any issue of major policy, the Sultan seeing only too clearly that Juin's proposed co-sovereignty would mean the extinguishing of any true nationalism. In turn Juin's suspicions of the Sultan were heightened as a result of a visit by the Sultan to France in 1950. In the course of this visit the Sultan called for an end to the Protectorate treaty, tried to win Paris political support and to undermine Juin. The Sultan returned to a tumultuous welcome.

In response Juin, abetted by Boniface, fell back on the *grands caids* policy, finding a willing supporter in the wealthy but monstrously corrupt figure of Thami el Glaoui, Pasha of Marrakesh, who was happy to portray the Sultan as the tool of the 'Istiqlalo-Communists' and unfit for his office. In support of him was Abdelhay el Kettani, who could claim descent from the Prophet, so combining a claim to spiritual authority with warrior chieftaincy and a long family vendetta against the Sultan. Other Berber chieftains, some for reasons of perceived advantage, others genuinely critical of the less attractive aspects of the Sultan's political and personal style, supported him in a 'Movement of Opposition and Reform'.

On 12 December Juin personally ordered out of a meeting of the Second College of the *Conseil du Gouvernement* Laghzaoui, a leading *Istiqlal* critic. Other *Istiqlal* members followed in sympathy – and were given a reception by the Sultan. Juin deployed troops and tanks in the streets of Rabat. On 21 December Glaoui openly attacked the Sultan and *Istiqlal*, and a bitter public wrangle ensued. In January 1951 Juin demanded that the Sultan denounce *Istiqlal* practices, remove their members from his entourage and reaffirm his loyalty to France, in a veiled threat also hinting at deposition. The Sultan demurred.

After a visit to Washington, where he aggressively defended French policy, Juin resumed his pressure on the Sultan. At this point events moved into early phases of disorder as thousands (one estimate was 250,000) of Berber horsemen, retainers of the *grands caids*, began mass moves into Rabat and Casablanca. It seems that some were bribed by sugar and feasts, others genuinely resented the tribute that the Sultan exacted from their *caids*, ultimately from them, and yet others had little idea of why they had been ordered out. Juin was able to present Paris with a picture of himself holding the balance between a spontaneous Berber protest and the Arabs; he expressed anxiety for the life and safety of the Sultan. The Sultan appealed to President Auriol, who disliked Juin and disbelieved the picture presented. But angry though Auriol was, the Paris political system prevented presidential intervention and he was obliged to advise the Sultan to concede.

Overall the events very quickly served to draw Berber and Arab together, the Sultan refused to sign any of the co-sovereignty decrees and the last months of Juin's proconsulate were ones of uneasy calm. As part of his project of countering nationalism with a new legitimacy from revived popular assemblies, and despite the opposition of both Sultan and *Istiqlal*, a July 1951 decree authorized new bodies. These were, however, again dominated by the *caids*.

Juin was required back in France for a major NATO command, but he made it a condition of his acceptance of this command, to the point of threatening refusal, that another *vieux Marocain* general, Guillaume, should be his successor, and Boniface's appointment extended. After an initial refusal, claiming that Juin was becoming a French General MacArthur, Auriol again gave way. Guillaume, elderly and unfit, pursued essentially the same policies as Juin, and tension in consequence heightened. In the next year, after *Istiqlal* had strengthened its following at home and acquired more friends at the United Nations, the Sultan in March asked Paris for changes from a protectorate to a new treaty relationship; in September this was refused by the Pleven right-of-centre government's Foreign Minister, Schuman.

The next major eruption onto the streets was two days of rioting in Casablanca on 7–8 December 1952, in which approximately 100 people were killed. The riots were sparked off by the murder of Ferhat Hashed, the Tunisia trade-union leader. Rumour wildly magnified the small number of Europeans killed. Some 2,000 police and 3,000 troops (*Spahis, Tirailleurs, Chasseurs d'Afrique* and *Légion*) had to be deployed all under the direction of Boniface. Smaller riots took place in other cities. Mass arrests of *Istiqlal*, Communist and trade-union leaders followed. Most were brought before the courts of the local *pasha* and given prison sentences. *Colons* thought to be sympathetic to the nationalists were deported.

Conflict was now inevitable. Ranged against the Sultan and his widening groups of supporters were the traditionalists in the French administration and the police, the *colon* settler population and a number, already beginning to dwindle, of Berber chieftains led by Glaoui, all supported in Paris by Bidault, once again Foreign Minister, and Juin, now with the enormous prestige of being the only living Marshal of France.[3] Juin occasionally revisited Morocco, on one occasion attending with Guillaume a mass rally of Berber ex-servicemen; but the liberal Catroux was forbidden to enter the protectorate.

3 On 29 June 1953 Juin, on election to the Académie Française, chose to mark the occasion with a highly paternalist defence of French policy. Accompanied by Glaoui as his guest of honour, Juin went out of his way to insult holders of more liberal views.

On 20 March 1953 Glaoui, supported by a number of *caids* and a little later by Kettani, openly demanded the abdication of the Sultan, arguing that both Mohammed V and the *Istiqlal* were Communist-linked. In Paris the Mayer government was collapsing and acted as only caretakers for most of June, unable to pre-empt a crisis. In early August, Glaoui, stage-managed by Boniface, visited several cities, attracting huge crowds and calling for the deposition of the Sultan.

Once again the streets of Moroccan cities appeared spontaneously to be filled with armed Berber horsemen. On 12 August the Laniel government, distracted by mass public-sector strikes in France and with the country semi-paralyzed, agreed to Guillaume's demand. One junior minister, the future President Mitterrand, resigned in protest over Maghreb policy in general. After he had spent a period in Corsica, the French made repeated and unsuccessful efforts to persuade Mohammed V to abdicate formally. The Sultan's cousin, Ben Arafa, an old man willing to serve the French, was installed as Sultan, but no Moroccan of any repute rallied to him. Official rhetoric spoke of a 'revival of Franco-Moroccan friendship', but neither the rhetoric nor the creation of a new Council of Moroccan viziers and French officials, designed to implement co-sovereignty, won any support. Troops had to secure the main cities, and to present the deposition as a result of popular protest; the armed Berber horsemen also remained. The general reaction was that of a people stunned, with only minor street protests, with the exception of Oujda, where a clash between supporters of Mohammed V and the local Europeans resulted in the deaths of *colons* and *Légion* soldiers.

It is most useful next to set out the succession of events and then proceed to offer an analysis of some of the main features of these events. The succession itself needs to be set in the context of events unfolding elsewhere, the strident voice of Nasser in Egypt and disaster in Indochina. Mohammed V quickly became the hero of the nationalists, now acquiring, despite exile, mass support. What had been a manipulated pull-devil pull-baker conflict between the Residency and the Sultan's palace moved to a general popular revolt. A number of leading Moroccans resigned from government posts. As 1953 drew to a close, overt terrorism and sabotage opened, with assassination attempts made on Ben Arafa (twice), Guillaume and Glaoui, the killings of Moroccan loyalists and a few *colons*, and destruction of French farms, factories, shops and homes. In view of the violence, a parliamentary mission was sent to Morocco in January 1954; its report was critical, but more of the execution of policy than of policy itself.

As a result of this criticism François Lacoste, a diplomat, was appointed by the Laniel government in June 1954 to succeed Guillaume. The appointment was made in the shadow of the Dien Bien Phu disaster. The Laniel government fell, to be replaced by Mendès-France. He at this point appeared to hope for some form of negotiated settlement, but he was strongly advised to be cautious by Juin. Lacoste, on the ground, found himself constrained by the combined forces of the military, the administration and the *colons*; his own personality, bureaucratic and lacking in imagination, could offer no solution. To complicate matters, General Duval, the commander at Sétif in 1945 and now the Army Commander in Morocco, was reputed to be planning a coup if Mohammed V was restored – an allegation in fact untrue. Terrorism, arson and sabotage intensified, notably in Fez, Petit-Jean and Port Lyautey. A French general was seriously injured in Glaoui's own Marrakesh. *Légion* reinforcements had to be despatched from Algeria. From 1 July 1954 to 30 June 1955, 41 Europeans and 254 Moroccans were killed, with many more injured in terrorist attacks. The new wave of arson, sabotage and killing was met by a *colon* counter-terrorist campaign conducted by the *Organisation de Défense Anti-Terroriste* (ODA-T). On 1 November the Algerian insurrection opened.

Mendès-France became increasingly frightened by the Moroccan situation but confused over what policy to pursue. He was therefore not able directly to take the situation any further before he was forced to resign on 5 February 1955. His resignation was due to a variety of causes, of which the worsening situation throughout North Africa was only one. The others were domestic; the MRP's resentment over Mendès's opposition to the European Defence Community project and his willingness to talk to Moscow, a scandal over leaked defence documents and his personal anti-alcohol campaign. Mendès, however, had indirectly made a substantial contribution through his Tunisian policy; this prepared the way for change under the next government, that of Faure.

A liberal-minded diplomat, Grandval, was despatched to Rabat as Resident-General in June 1955. On his arrival Grandval quickly released a number of detainees and commuted death sentences imposed upon others; he dismissed a number of 'old Moroccan hand' officials and had arrested a number of known *colon* counter-terrorists. Grandval unwisely, at the request of General Koenig, however, appointed a scheming hard-liner to be chief of intelligence, with the result that his enemies had intelligence while he did not. But these actions, the knowledge that Grandval was prepared to allow Mohammed V to return and to end formal protectorate rule, together with the 'Mers

Sultan incident', a nationalist bombing outrage in Casablanca in July, all led to a bloody *colon* reaction. This included random firing from car windows on Moroccans, which Duval appeared unwilling or unable to restrain. Another general, Franchi, at the head of a *Légion* contingent, restored order. Clashes and bloodshed followed in Marrakesh and other cities. In Paris Grandval's developing contacts with moderate nationalists were sharply criticized within the Cabinet by Koenig and from outside by Juin.

Worse followed in August, at the time of the second anniversary of the Sultan's deposition. On 18 August severe rioting in Khenifra was suppressed by the *Légion*; aircraft also fired into columns of Zaian Berbers moving in from the mountains to support the rioters. On the twentieth, violence erupted throughout most of Morocco. This violence highlighted the divisions, traditional and contemporary, among the Atlas Berbers; these will be examined later. On this occasion a number of Berber chieftains urged their followers to massacre the *colons*. Several score were killed, in the worst single instance at Oued Zem 49, including women and children.

Pleas for restraint made by the more moderate nationalist politicians were unheard. Drastic retribution at the hands of the *Légion*, parachute units and the *Chasseurs d'Afrique* followed; the official figure of 700 killed is a minimum.

Grandval's policies were seen as the cause with, behind them, Mendès-France. The intensity of *colon* feeling against Grandval exploded when he was obscenely and roughly handled at the funeral of Duval, who had been killed in an air crash. *Colon* rumour alleged murder by Grandval; another known hard-line general, Miquel, was cheered. In response to this pressure and at the instigation of Juin, General Boyer was selected to succeed Grandval.[4] Although also a *vieux Marocain*, Boyer had a much clearer understanding of the realities of the situation and wished to end the *caid* policy, but it was now too late. In any case Boyer had received a blunt briefing from Juin and he promptly surrounded himself with hard-line officials. But the *quid pro quo* of his appointment was the opening of discussions at ministerial level with Moroccans, including nationalist leaders, at Aix-les-Bains.

These discussions presented a confused pattern. Boyer's preference was to restore order with firmness and force, and if possible retain

4 Faure remarked to a Cabinet colleague who objected to this appointment, 'I had to appoint a soldier, Juin insisted'. Julien, *Maroc*, p.215. Julien also records the soldierly terms in which Juin briefed Boyer (p.240), quoting from Claude Paillat, *Vingt Ans qui déchirent la France, II, La Liquidation 1954–1962* (Paris, Laffont, 1972), p.251.

Ben Arafa. Si Bekkai, a distinguished former Moroccan officer of *Spahis* who supported the return of Mohammed V, attempted to mediate between the French and the disputacious Moroccan factions. Boyer, in turn, sought the help of another, more senior, Moroccan officer serving in the French Army, General Kettani Ben Hammou. Mohammed V agreed with an arrangement by which Ben Arafa would be replaced by a Council of the Throne. One purpose of this was an attempt to present the question of who was to be Sultan as a purely local domestic one, and not a consequence of French policy. Boyer, supported in Paris in the Cabinet by the Defence Minister, Koenig, and locally by the *colons*, hoped Kettani would serve on the Council and mediate between traditionalists and nationalists in favour of the former. Kettani, however, refused to become involved.

The stalemate over membership lasted until late September, Boyer contesting any arrangement that he thought would permit Mohammed V's return. But the Faure government finally summoned sufficient courage to order the retirement of Ben Arafa to Tangier, sweeping aside any conditions and refusing Boyer's protest request to resign. Ben Arafa departed on 1 October. There followed a period of bitter political activity in Paris, in which five Social Republican (hard-line) ministers, including Koenig, resigned from Faure's cabinet in protest against the government's policies in Morocco and Algeria. This activity was matched by agitation, rallies and demonstrations by the *colon* population in Morocco, countenanced by Boyer. On 15 October the Faure government gained a partial victory with the appointment of a Council to the Throne in which were two moderate nationalists; this Council a few days later appointed another moderate nationalist as Prime Minister; the return of Mohammed V was a 'hidden agenda'.

The reality of the situation, however, was not the political activities in Paris or Rabat but the opening on 1 October of a new and very much more bloody insurgency campaign in the Rif and Middle Atlas in which small posts were attacked, their garrisons and *goumiers* killed and weapons stolen. In July a 'Maghreb Liberation Army Co-ordinating Committee' had been set up, the planning of this uprising being a main purpose. A Moroccan Liberation Army, ALM (*Armée de Libération Marocaine*), claiming to be some 2,000 strong but in reality only 700, proclaimed its existence a few days later. Riots occurred in Marrakesh and Rabat; terrorism returned to Casablanca. Koenig's successor, General Billotte (who had never served in Morocco) sent a division to Morocco, bringing the total number of troops to more than 105,000.[5] Billotte was, however, openly snubbed by Boyer while visiting the territory.

French policy had now collapsed. Its total failure was highlighted first by desertion of Moroccan soldiers and then by polite but firm refusals of Moroccan units in Algeria to continue to serve. Also fatal was the decision by Glaoui, who had distrusted the Council of the Throne project, that it would be prudent to change from France to the winning side and join in the demand for the return of Mohammed V. Despite warnings grim and desperate from Juin, the Faure government again gave way and the Sultan's return was sanctioned. Catroux, whose views were known to be totally different from those of Boyer and Juin, was used by Faure as an intermediary. On 5 November the Sultan signed an agreement promising to work with France towards an independent Morocco linked with France within a framework of interdependence. Boyer resigned and was replaced by a functionary, Dubois, the fourth Resident-General of 1955. The Sultan arrived back in Morocco on 19 November amid wild popular rejoicing. He attempted, with a measure of success, to form a broad-based government of national unity. Glaoui made a grovelling submission, an event very well publicized.

There were, however, to be several further rounds of fighting. Other Berber chieftains and *caids* who had supported France were not as fortunate as Glaoui. Many, on their way to make submission to the Sultan, were brutally attacked, a number being killed. Dubois ordered French military commanders not to intervene although aircraft observation kept the Residency informed of what was happening. Elsewhere similar individuals and groups were mutilated or killed. The Sultan then issued an order to end terrorism, but this did not prevent the brutal killing of 19 relatives and supporters of Glaoui in May 1956.

In Paris the Faure government dissolved the French legislature – over a proposed change in electoral procedure – on 29 November. Behind the resignation, however, were events in Algeria and specific allegations that Faure was giving Morocco away. There followed a General Election campaign interregnum until, after the election, the Mollet government took office on 5 February 1956. It was at last realized in Paris that the only way to preserve any French influence and economic links was to accept the end of the protectorate; the Council of the Throne project was not going to succeed or even buy

5 For comparison, the maximum number of British and locally recruited African military units committed at the height of the Mau Mau Emergency in Kenya totalled 14,000.

time. Final details of the negotiations for Moroccan independence were completed in February and March, the concept of 'interdependence' again being used to save French face. France was also to be allowed to retain troops in Morocco until 1960.

It was some time, however, before military operations ceased, despite the return of the Sultan. By the end of 1955 a 30-kilometre-deep zone had had to be evacuated along some 150 kilometres of the border. The insurgents, now several thousand, had linked with Algerian insurgents and were attacking the Beni Snassen; a particularly violent series of attacks was launched in the Rif on 29 December. General Agostini, the French commander, had to deploy a force of 15,000 men to clear the area. But his Moroccan personnel deserted in large numbers, and the *goumiers* had to be disarmed and withdrawn by lorry; for totally reliable units Agostini could only count on the *Légion*. Large areas of territory remained without any surviving French control, administration collapsed and taxes were uncollected. The situation only began to improve in February 1956, when the Spanish authorities agreed to cease providing refuge and bases. In early 1956 a small number of hard-line militants, opposed to negotiation with France, met violent deaths. Moroccans blamed French counter-terrorism but the reverse seems more probable.

Thereafter military operations reduced in scale. Some sharp clashes between French forces and hard-line ALM groups occurred on the Moroccan–Algerian border; a deal was eventually struck by which France agreed not to use Moroccan territory as a base for operations against Algeria, and in turn was allowed to use her forces to prevent Moroccans joining the Algerian insurgents. There was also a series of anti-French riots in a number of Moroccan cities, anti-French feeling being heightened by the developing Algerian conflict and, later in the year, the Suez crisis and hijacking of the Algerian leader, Ben Bella.

Analysis of the events from 1951 to 1956 reveals a number of interesting features. The whole legality of the Sultan's deposition appears doubtful. The Paris *Cour de Cassation* had in 1934 ruled that Morocco possessed internal autonomy. The deposition arrangements directed by Paris in the name of 'sovereignty' represented intrusions into that autonomy. The appointment of Ben Arafa as Imam without election by the *oulema* was illegal, and the signatories of the *beia*, oath of allegiance to the Sultan, signed under duress.

Police methods appear to have been very severe. Many policemen were Corsicans of doubtful standards. After the exile of the Sultan, interrogations that followed the widespread arrests were brutal, torture being used on occasions. Examples included the reinstating of an inspector in one of a number of special anti-terrorist units who had been suspended for '*la manière forte*' by a magistrate; his professional organization secured his return to duty. Worse were the excesses of one police officer, Garcette, whose torture styles included the usual range of contorted hangings, electric shocks and immersion in water as well as beatings and maimings. A few known *Istiqlal* members also disappeared, almost certainly deliberately eliminated. Death sentences were imposed for terrorism, December 1954 seeing a record 15 for the Oujda killings and six in Casablanca. The *colon*'s ODA-T was supported by both *colon* vigilante groups and a new Berber *garde civile* who on many occasions supplemented their pay by pillage. The activities of the vigilante groups were often ignored by the police, gendarmerie and the Army.

The French military security forces consisted of regiments of the largely white *Chasseurs d'Afrique*, of the *Légion Etrangère*, and locally recruited *Tirailleurs Marocains* and *goums* irregulars. The *Tirailleurs Sénégalais* were withdrawn from Morocco in the early 1950s. As discipline broke down the French were ever more dependent on the *Légion*, whose regiments retained few scruples. At Port Lyautey in August 1955, for example, Moroccans were corralled into the market place and there clubbed and beaten. The desertion problem was one that principally affected the *goums*; only 1,080 Moroccan *Tirailleurs* and *Spahis* deserted between June 1954 and March 1956. The *goums* were, however, vital for the maintenance of French administration in the mountain areas.

At the Residency and military command levels, from Juin onwards, may be seen the familiar contempt, at times disobedience, of Paris of senior officers, a pattern to be repeated in Algeria. At lower levels the protectorate provincial administration declined from their pre-war standards and lost contact; one reason for this appears to have been the appointment of a number of *colon* Algerians in their ranks.

The spread of nationalist ideas among the Middle Atlas Berbers and the consequential *goumier* desertions and collapse of French Berber policy had begun before the deposition, but was much intensified by it. This was not primarily due to any affection for the Sultan, though as *Imam* he enjoyed respect. Nationalists found supporters, notably including womenfolk, among the '*lef*', clans opposed to the local *caid* and his followers, whose exactions, after the deposition, had become unbearable. These exactions remained unchecked by the French authorities, bound as they were to the established order. Women rallied to the support of the Sultan, seeing him as bringing emancipation; they were to be seen in the crowds, they were also at work in homes applying pressure upon Moroccan officers and officials. Traditional ethnic divisions remained, however, and were evident in the 1955 uprising. The Guezenia, Bou Yahia, Mernissi and later the Beni Snassen provided the men, other communities sometimes providing the leaders of military capacity; the Oued Zem killings were the work of hitherto pro-French Zaian and Ait small communities. The Beni Ouraghiel did not participate. Some Algerians also figured.

Who were the earlier urban insurgents? They were not members of any party but were evidently 'small men' – farmers, traders, workers, rather than the intelligentsia; they organized themselves into small local cells, adopted *noms de guerre* and after an attack disappeared into the crowd. A member of one group, interrogated as to why he killed, replied, 'Because it was the will of God.' Others spoke in simple terms of patriotic nationalism; one remarked to a Frenchman, 'We are doing what you did to the Nazis.' The *Sûreté* found it very hard to recruit informers. The Ammeln, of the western Anti-Atlas, were conspicuous in their support for *Istiqlal* and provided a number of the urban terrorists.

The members of the militant – unofficial – *colon* counter-terrorist groups were generally under forty, many were Corsicans or Spaniards and Italians of the artisan class; they were funded as necessary by local *colon* industry and trade. The alleged, and almost certainly true, identities of the members of one particularly ferocious group (at least 12 murders to its record) tells its own story – seven policemen of whom one was the leader, a German miner, a metal beater, a barmaid and one professional man.[6] The counter-terrorist groups' most spectacular coup, the work of ODA-T, was the killing of the liberal editor of *Maroc Presse*, Lemaigre-Dubreuil, in June 1955. The group arrested for this murder were quickly released for specious reasons but in reality in the face of *colon* pressure.

The *colon* media and, on occasions, rumour and hysteria worsened matters. Four leading papers all supported a hard line, vilifying the Sultan and the nationalists, supporting the *caids* and demanding full assertion of French interests. The *colon* population itself had grown from the 290,000 of 1945 to nearly 450,000.

French policy in Morocco attracted overseas criticism. Juin aggressively defended his policies during his visit to Washington in January 1951, scandalizing the State Department, who made it clear they would not support any deposition of the Sultan; this worried the Quai d'Orsay, but not Juin. Serious UN criticism of French policy in Morocco

6 Julien, *Maroc*, p.415.

began in December 1951, but was deflected by the United States. The same American support followed further UN attacks on France after the December 1952 rioting, and was maintained by the new Eisenhower-Dulles administration at the time of the deposition of the Sultan, despite the furious Arab and Communist world reaction. Britain followed the American lead. The American business community in Morocco, however, were frequently openly anti-French. Mendès-France's concessions in Tunisia bought time, and from the outbreak of the Algerian uprising Morocco became subsumed into wider international criticism of French policies.

Juin had a soldier's working relationship with General Varela in Spanish Morocco. But after Juin's departure and the death of Varela relations collapsed. The next Spanish High Commissioner, General Valino, was anti-French, a consequence of French support for the Republicans in the Civil War. Spanish policy, too, was to woo the Arab world. Valino refused to recognize Ben Arafa. Despite a French naval demonstration he supported a demand for the return of Mohammed V signed by a very large number of *caids* and *pashas*. He then arranged for General Franco in Madrid to receive a delegation from this group at a well-publicized ceremony, to the fury of the French government. In 1954–55, Valino on a number of occasions allowed insurgent groups to take refuge in Spanish Morocco, ordering his own frontier troops to withdraw 16 kilometres from the border. The MLA established its base in the Spanish zone. French 'hot pursuit' operations worsened relations still further until a Franco-Spanish agreement in February 1956.

In respect of Morocco's post-independence structures, the events of 1947–56 immensely strengthened the dynasty and Sultanate, in marked contrast to the pattern in Tunisia. Of the Sultanate's two rivals, the *caids* were ruined as a political force and *Istiqlal* overshadowed. As early as 1952, even before the deposition, French politicians had noted how the beleaguered position of the Sultan, rather than the oratory of the nationalist politicians, was becoming the focus of attention. In the government formed at his restoration, Mohammed V chose to play the role of political broker, and in so doing was able to administer a check to the ambitions of *Istiqlal*. This government was headed by Bekkai, and although *Istiqlal* received nine portfolios they did not include the key posts and several militants of the past received no appointments at all. The Sultan, perceived so wrongly by the French as militant, secured for them a moderate rather than a militant regime with which to negotiate the independence settlement. In 1957 the Sultanate became a kingdom.

Restoring the provincial administration to order from the total anarchy into which it had fallen proved more difficult. Many *pashas* and *caids* were discredited; the fate of a number has already been noted. Local *Istiqlal* militants harassed their work, and also that of French officials who tried to assist them, some with only lukewarm enthusiasm. In December 1955 the Sultan's government reorganized the administration by appointing 15 new regional governors, to replace the former *caid* system. *Caids* and local dignitaries who had supported the Sultan were rewarded with civil servant status. Traditional rural landowners, new landowners who took possession of abandoned *colon* estates, and the new civil servants formed the pillars of the new establishment; aid and development projects for smallholders and poorer peasants were to complete the legitimization. Within 18 months and with the exceptions of the incidents of violence noted earlier, the country was slowly returned to order.

The legitimacy of the royal authority was also able to build new 'Royal Armed Forces', drawn from the French colonial regiments, *goumiers*, Spanish units and some members of the Algerian insurgent *Armée de Libération Nationale* (ALN). Until 1957, however, they had to contend with some 4,000 members of the ALN operating with the FLN in the Algerian border areas; they drew on French military support and local knowledge. As in Kenya, the continued presence of the troops of the outgoing colonial power underpinned the regime at the delicate point of transition.

The independence of Morocco made little impression on the indifferent mass of French public opinion. The *colon* farmers and small businessmen who fled the country arrived in unspectacular trickles attracting little media attention. Few conscripts served in Morocco. The rhetoric of 'interdependence', the interim continuing presence of French troops and interim existence of some of the regiments of *Tirailleurs Marocains* (the last only disbanding in 1964–66), and the continued residence of a number of the *colons* obscured, for a while, the reality. Many large business interests and trading patterns remained little affected. Among the more politically sophisticated, Moroccan independence if anything hardened views, not only on the Right, on the necessity of retaining Algeria. The security operations in Morocco never seriously troubled the French conscience, despite critical press articles and occasional criticism by politicians.

Perhaps only in one respect was French political culture markedly affected by the loss of Morocco. As in Tunisia, Morocco's independence confirmed many in their suspicion of the United States. This emotive scapegoating was another step towards the later general acceptance of the virulent anti-Americanism of de Gaulle. Of American interests and activities in Morocco, the normally scholarly and liberal General Spillman wrote describing the Americans present at Duval's funeral, 'As for the Americans, their faces reflected their total disdain for those olive-skinned Europeans so unkempt in their appearance', adding in a footnote, 'For Americans, all Frenchmen born south of a line Nantes –Lyon belong to the olive-skinned races, a designation which unites in the same disdain all the Mediterranean European peoples, but not the Arabs, the petroleum barons.'[7] Spillman's views were already shared by many, with numbers to increase in the next few years.

ALGERIA TO OCTOBER 1954

Tunisia and Morocco were, however, to be totally overshadowed by the drama that had already begun to unfold, exponentially, in Algeria on 1 November 1954. Since the Sétif events both the economic and social and the political conditions in Algeria had worsened sharply; these conditions were also to mould the form of revolt when it erupted.

The economic and social changes were largely exacerbations of unfair structures dating back to the 1920s and 1930s and even earlier. Perhaps singly the most important development was the increase in Algeria's Moslem population from the 5 million in 1926 to the 8½ million (with another 250,000 at work in France) of 1954. Of this population over 90 per cent were illiterate; in 1954 there were only 859 in post-secondary education. The increase was reflected by the massive growth of the Moslem urban population, thousands living under-fed, under-employed or unemployed in shanty suburbs, *bidonvilles*, of the Algerian cities and towns.

On the land the process, begun at the turn of the century, of the buying out of European small farmers by large estate-owners, had continued. This had in practice vacated some poor-quality land and town property in the interior which Moslems had occupied in one fashion or another. But the process had had more serious implications for the future. Many of the big *colon* estates were exceedingly prosperous, profiting from the growing of vineyards, the mechanization of cereal agriculture, and the expansion of fruit and vegetable growing. But as prosperous estates farmed by Moslem labour they reduced the density of the Europeans on the ground, and appeared ever more attractive targets for the deprived and underpaid work force. At the same time the *colon* population, a number now in the second or third

---

7 Georges Spillman, *Du Protectorat à l'Indépendance* (Paris, Plon, 1967), p. 222.

generation, began to feel a new identity with a specific local culture, French but a different French, exuberant, *méditerranée et demie*. The captivating scenic beauty of much of Algeria strengthened this local culture and attachment to the territory. The *colon*-dominated media reflected their culture, to the resentment of the Moslem majority.

Colon political rhetoric, and that of their allies in Paris, stressed the economic linkages between Algeria and metropolitan France, claiming that these were vital for the prosperity of both and any severance would be catastrophic. In fact, France's trade with Algeria equated roughly with her trade with the Saar; in 1954, 6.7 per cent of Algeria's exports went to France, 11.3 per cent of France's exports went to Algeria. After 1945 capital investment had not been great; France had to subvent the Algerian budget. Half of Algeria's exports to France was in fact wine; this, together with phosphates and minerals purchasable elsewhere, was not vital to the French economy.[8]

Colon success and profitability, too, stood in marked contrast to Moslem peasant agriculture, where production hardly increased at all, and in some sectors actually fell. The population increase led inevitably to land parcelling and sub-economic holdings. Yields stagnated and soil was degraded, no capital was available for development or mechanization, and there was no internal market from which capital could be formed. The process of immiserization in the towns was therefore matched by the reduction of the rural peasantry to a proletariat, impoverished, under-nourished and with a high infant mortality rate. The gap between the modern *colon* and the traditional Moslem economies was almost total. For these economic conditions the *colon*-dominated Algerian government appeared to have neither strategy nor even interest.

Two social conditions, also with origins in the 1920s and 1930s, were to affect the leadership of later protest and revolt. First, the traditional Arab aristocracy had largely disappeared; as a possible political force it had been destroyed by the French. Second, the number of educated Moslem *évolués* was exceedingly small – in 1954 only 354 lawyers, 185 secondary teachers, 165 professional medical men and 28 engineers, with only 6,260 children in secondary education. Of greater significance in forming the demands and style of the revolt

8 Charles-Robert Ageron, *Modern Algeria* (trans Michael Brett) (London, Hurst, 1991), chapter vi, provides an excellent survey of Algeria immediately prior to the outbreak of the revolt. Greater detail also appears in the classic work on the Algerian war, Alistair Horne, *A Savage War of Peace: Algeria 1954–1962* (London, Macmillan, 1977), chapter iii. The trade statistics and the comparison with the Saar appear in Jacques Thobie and others, *Histoire de la France coloniale*, vol. II (Paris, Armand Colin, 1990), pp.508–9.

was the experience of labour or soldiering in France, an experience gained by more than 2 million Algerians by 1954.

The political developments were simply the other side of the same coin. Some minor cosmetic reforms followed Sétif; in particular, the number of representatives sent to the Paris legislature by the Moslem Second Electoral College was raised to equal the number sent by the French First College. But the first (1945–46) French Constituent Assembly did not discuss Algeria's constitutional arrangements at all, and all that was achieved in the second (1946) was a limited increase in the number of Moslems eligible to vote in the French College. In this Assembly political moderates of Ferhat Abbas's new *Union Démocratique du Manifeste Algérien* (UDMA) Party were taken to task for not being sufficiently French, while the integrationist followers of Dr Ben Djelloul represented virtually nobody other than themselves.

The Fourth Republic's first Assembly, elected in November 1946, much influenced by Bidault, reverted to a slightly modified version of pre-war Algeria, formalized in a *Statut de l'Algérie* enacted in September 1947. Under this legislation Algeria was described as a group of provinces possessing a civil identity, certain local institutions and fiscal autonomy; her administration was to be headed by a governor-general and a council of government of six, of which two were nominated by the governor-general, the president and vice-president of the new Algerian Assembly, and two elected by that Assembly. The Assembly itself was a revamped version of the *Délégations Financières* (which had in fact been renamed *Assemblée Financière* in 1945). But even here Paris stipulated approval for the Assembly's measures and could require these to be secured by a two-thirds majority. As the Assembly was elected on the basis of the equal number of members, now extended to 60 from each College, *colon* domination was again ensured.[9] Other reforms in the *Statut* provided for elected local councils, the recognition of Arabic as an official language with French, and the enfranchisement of Moslem women as electors for the Second College.

The political fall-out from this new *Statut* was, inevitably, unfortunate. The *colons* regarded the changes as excessive, the Moslems withdrew from the Assembly in protest at their meagre scale. In municipal elections that followed, both communities elected parties opposed to the *Statut*, the *colons* for their *Union Algérienne* and the Moslems for Messali Haj's new, militantly nationalist *Mouvement*

---

9 The 1947 figures are instructive. The first College comprised 464,000 *colons* and 58,000 Moslems; the Second College, 1,300,000 Moslems. Population figures at the time were 922,000 Europeans and 7,860,000 Moslems: Ageron, *Modern Algeria*, pp.104–5.

pour la Triomphe des Libertés Démocratiques (MTLD), a result that led to the Algerian Assembly elections being deferred. The Ramadier government reacted by replacing the Governor-General, Chataigneau, by Naegelen, a strong nationalist. Naegelen was the personal selection of Mayer, who had close links with the *colon* community, in particular Henri Borgeaud, whose vast personal empire included vineyards, cigarette manufacture, banking, transport and a number of industrial enterprises. Naegelen directed the French administration to manage the elections; this was achieved so successfully that out of the Moslem College's 60 seats 41 were gained by government-favoured candidates, referred to derisively as *'beni oui ouis'*, in comparison to nine won by MTLD, eight by UDMA and two by independents. The techniques of management of the Second College elections varied from pre-prepared ballot boxes taken off for counting, ballot boxes being filled with false votes, polling stations menaced by police, soldiers or even tanks, and the simple announcement of winners not accompanied by voting figures. MTLD candidates and meetings were harassed and arrests made. Other elections that followed in the years 1947 to 1954 were similarly managed by Naegelen and his successor Léonard, to the gratitude of the *colons*. The Moslem population was forced to accept that there could be no constitutional path to reform, and the UDMA lost its appeal to any audience other than the small elite.

Behind this political façade continued the covert revival of Islam, taught in the Koranic schools and Moslem associations, that had begun in the 1930s; events elsewhere in the Arab world, particularly in Egypt, stimulated the revival further. To Islam, and as a consequence of the evident failure of peaceful attempts at constitutional reform, came to be added an ideology of revolution, Marxist-inspired and initially directed by the MTLD. To rouse the masses this party developed a territory-wide organization of party officials, unofficial courts and fund collectors; the organization was based on five, later six, zones (later called *wilaya*), circles and sections. A secret underground section *Organisation Spéciale* (OS) was tasked to prepare armed revolution. The OS eventually totalled more than 4,000. French police discovered the OS in 1948 and made a number of arrests; some of those arrested later made dramatic escapes. Later the OS was re-formed in Egypt. The difficulties facing Messali and the MTLD, however, proved too great for cohesion. Messali himself was ordered to live in France and a liberal mayor of Algiers, Chevallier, persuaded some of the less militant members to enter the city's administration. Crisis point was reached in July 1954 when the party split into three. Messali unwisely allowed a personal clique to elect him party president for

111

life, but the party's legal Central Committee decided to join a coalition with other groupings of more moderate views. A third faction, encouraged by the news of Dien Bien Phu and the concessions by France that had followed insurgency in Tunisia, resolved to continue the planning of a revolution.

This third faction called itself the *Comité Révolutionnaire d'Unité et d'Action* (CRUA), and was led by the 'historic nine' who conspired in secret in France, Algeria, and on one occasion under cover of a World Cup football match, in Switzerland. None of the nine were educated *évolués*. Their chairman, Mohammed Boudiaf, was at thirty-five the oldest; he had had his education cut short by tuberculosis. His role was to be the link with three members tasked to raise support in Cairo. These three were Ahmed Ben Bella, a former and much decorated French Army warrant officer, Mohammed Khider, a former deputy in the Algerian Assembly, and Hocine Ait Ahmed, a Kabyle. In Algeria, Mostafa Ben Boulaid, a miller who had also served as a French Army sergeant and had already the nucleus of a local insurgent group was tasked with the Aurès. Larbi Ben M'hidi was allotted the Oran area, Rabah Bitat Algiers, and the twenty-year-old Mourad Didouche the north Constantine. The leading fighter at the outset, though, was the ninth member, the Kabyle Belkacem Krim, the son of a loyalist *caid* who had been leading an effective partisan group of some 500 active members, supported by some 2,000 more 'part-time' or food-providing followers, in the Kabyles since 1947. Of these Ben Bella, Ait Ahmed, Boudiaf, Bitat, Boulaid and M'Hidi had all been members of the OS. Their plans provided for a political front, the *Front de Libération Nationale* (FLN), which would command a resistance army, *Armée de Libération Nationale* (ALN) to be supported in the field by weapons and propaganda from Egypt. Their aim was to launch a nation-wide insurrection on the night of 31 October–1 November 1954. They hoped to catch the *colons* off guard, the night being the feast of All Saints (*Toussaint*) always celebrated by the Catholic *colons*.

THE FIRST MONTHS OF THE WAR

The FLN drew chiefly on the Viet Minh as a model for organization, with also some ideas from the French Resistance. The leadership remained collective despite all the difficulties of communication within Algeria and beyond. Fighting groups were small in size at the outset; only the leader knew the identities of any FLN members other than those in the group. Operations were directed by a zoned *wilaya* command which acted on the orders of the CRUA. Its overriding strategy, an important binding factor in itself, was that of fighting on to full independence and victory, but in one aspect of strategy the FLN differed significantly from the Viet Minh. The Viet Minh had sought primarily to clear and then hold territory, area by area, starting in the Viet Bac of north Tonkin. The FLN's aim was, even from the start, more political, to create everywhere a general atmosphere of fear at home and to appeal to world opinion abroad. It was recognized that the ALN was too weak to hold and secure a firm base area. Accordingly, in the FLN tactics the teaching was to strike and then disappear. If disappearance was not possible, groups should hold on for reinforcement, but frontal combat was to be avoided. Targets selected were large *colon* estates, French military personnel and security posts, and Moslem loyalists. Orders not to attack European women and children were disregarded from the outset, an indication of the passion and hatred of the campaign; terror and cruelty also complemented traditional concepts of a religious war. Some of the FLN's weaponry had already been seized from the French, who had hidden firearms from the Germans in the war and kept records better known to dissidents than themselves; some also had been taken from American units, equally negligent, and some had arrived from Spanish Morocco. The bulk of the ALN weaponry for the first years of the war was, however, sporting guns. Bombs were manufactured in secret in pharmacies or cellars.

Direct recruitment was by word of mouth and contact; it tended to follow success and was concentrated in areas where French administration was thin on the ground. Increasing numbers of better-educated Moslems joined. The close-knit family ties of the Moslem communities also assisted recruiting: if one member of a family was involved the whole family was seen to be so also, thus leaving other members with no option but to become active members. Even young shepherd boys were included – to act as sentinels watching out for French columns. Women, however, played a lesser role than in the Viet Minh, partly on account of Moslem attitudes and partly because the FLN never held any secure base area. Their combat service was largely in towns, in particular Algiers.

The FLN also succeeded in establishing a cell structure, the *Organisation Politico-Administrative* (OPA), in settlements, villages, and small towns and in some of the cities that extorted or collected funds at fixed rates, amassed supplies and intelligence, and disseminated propaganda. This six-member cell structure amounted to a local government in the large areas of hinterland in which there were no French troops, collecting money and administering justice. An initial setback was the opposition of the other MTLD factions to the revolt. But the ground, fertile enough, was prepared still further by an FLN proclamation calling for a mass uprising to support a national struggle for a free, independent Algeria. This manifesto was disseminated in secretly printed leaflets and by Cairo radio. Interestingly, the manifesto did not specifically mention Islam or suggest that the revolt was one of religion, nor, despite the Viet Minh influence in organisation, was there a reference to Marx, Lenin or Communism. The revolt was and remained essentially one of gut-reaction anti-colonial nationalism, and the belief that the overthrow of the whole colonial system and its values could only be achieved by violence, that violence itself both justifiable and purifying. These sentiments were expressed later in articulate form by the Martinique writer Fanon, who served as a doctor with the FLN from 1956 to his death in 1961. Unlike the Viet Minh, the FLN never evolved an ideological blueprint for the territory once liberated; when it was anti-bourgeois it was so because the bourgeois were seen as Bao Dais who might compromise with the French, not because of their status as a class.

The three of the nine sent to Cairo to secure Egyptian support, the nucleus of the future 'external FLN', found Egypt's help disappointing, being limited to strident propaganda. Their apparent failure was to cause growing friction with the insurgents fighting at home.

Overall an asset for the FLN and always a major difficulty for the French was the terrain of Algeria, particularly in the north, where most of the war was to be fought. From west to east run a chain of large mountain ranges, the Ouarsenis, the Kabyles, the Hodna, the Aurès and the Nementcha, with numerous other smaller hill ranges. Only a very few roads entered the mountain areas; scrub-covered hillsides provided ideal cover for ambushes. In summer the mountain ranges remained almost unbearably hot, while in winter cold temperatures and icy winds could make conditions as difficult and miserable as any theatre of war in central Europe.

The French authorities in Algeria were not fully prepared to meet this challenge. It had suited everyone – the Paris politicians, the *colons* and, until it was ready to strike, the FLN – to present an appearance of serenity. The activities of Belkacem Krim and a rising scale of incidents of violence in eastern Algeria on the Tunisian border in 1954 had provided clues that some trouble was brewing. There had also been signs of danger on the Moroccan border. From September 1953 sporadic attacks on *colons*, railway sabotage, arms thefts and occasional killings of military personnel had taken place. On 26 October

Vaujour, the police Director of Security, concluded that violence would break out to coincide with a UN debate on French policy in Morocco early in November, but his warning resulted in only small-scale local preparations and precautions.[10] Of the nine, Ben Bella's identity was well known, but most of the others were not identified at the time. Several different intelligence organizations were studying different areas of unrest; their reports were not properly collated and, therefore, not properly presented and assessed. Algeria's garrison totalled 65,000 men, but these were mostly in training and administrative units. The best troops were from a division originally assembled for Indochina, just beginning to arrive in October; other units were regarded as questionably loyal after return from Indochina. The despatch of regiments to Indochina and Tunisia had reduced the total of fit men in combat-ready units to 3,500, together with some 2,000 gendarmes. The French Army, too, was lorry-bound when mules and horses were needed – until helicopters were sufficiently developed. The response that could be provided, then, to the initial outbreak of killings and bombings on 1 November was limited. But as could be expected from so hurriedly assembled an organization, the ALN's initial *Toussaint* strike was also not very impressive, marred by premature firing, last-minute defections and bungling. French civilians (including women) were attacked and killed, as were three French military personnel: some sabotage damage was effected. Such success as there was, was in the Kabyles and Aurès; in the west the French annihilated an ALN detachment.

On 6 November, in Operation *Bitter Orange*, the French dissolved the MTLD; a number of its known leaders were detained and subjected to severe interrogation. In this unwise move the French alienated potential *interlocuteurs*, driving many straight into the FLN camp. The French military reaction was almost as inept. The Army Commander, Cherrière, at first believed he was faced with only a small-scale tribal revolt. He sent his effective units into the Kabyles and Aurès and sought reinforcement, which in the form of an elite airborne division arrived quickly. Elsewhere MTLD activists were rounded up in Algiers and Oran; These were often also FLN, or under interrogation revealed local FLN members. The most notable arrested was Bouadjadj, the ALN chief in Algiers; the movement thereby received the first of several sharp reverses. Worse was to follow after the arrival of the airborne division, whose combat group commanders had Indochina

10 François Portheu de la Morandière, *Soldats du Djebel* (Paris, Société de Production Littéraire, n.d.), pp.20–2, article by General Lenormand.

experience. One of these groups in a sharp battle in the Aurès killed 23 ALN members, among them being Grine, a very experienced leader, and captured a further 18. Another group killed Didouche, one of the 'historic nine', in the north Constantine. In February Ben Boulaid, another of the nine, was captured, and a month later a third was taken when the French forces caught Bitat. Boulaid, interrogated skilfully, exposed the FLN military organization.

At the same time the difficulties of the campaign were emerging. The winter of 1954–55 was a miserable experience alike for insurgent and French soldier, the majority on both sides poorly equipped and trained. The French found intelligence increasingly hard to obtain as the FLN's campaign of terror was slowly spread among loyalists by means of disembowelling or mouth and throat slitting. Columns would be sent into the mountains on grandiose sweeps such as Operations *Véronique* and *Violette*, arresting scores of people whom no one knew how to screen or even hold, and proving generally fruitless even with air reconnaissance, while small groups of insurgents would execute or engage in minor sabotage or destruction of vineyards or orange tree groves, and then slip back as ordinary peasants into their communities. Outlying farms and forest stations had to be given sub-units for defence. The French, too, were prone to attribute Viet Minh skills and techniques to the much less sophisticated FLN. Political considerations forbade bombing; official military policy was *répression limitée*, and many French commanders felt they were fighting with their hands tied. FLN members caught could, for example, regain liberty or escape with only a light sentence if defended by an able lawyer.

This *répression limitée* and the difficulties facing the French Army enabled the FLN to recuperate and rebuild its network. A steady stream of recruits joined, particularly in the Kabyles and the Aurès and from early 1955 the Nementcha range. The recuperation was assisted by the poverty and deprivation, the OPA's internal and Cairo external propaganda offensives, indiscriminate arrests and French official rhetoric, heavily endorsed by the *colons*, that there could be no possible prospect of political change until law and order had been firmly restored.

This rhetoric, was, as before, the result of the Paris political situation. The Mendès-France government, already alleged to be weak over Tunisia and suspect over Morocco, had to fall back on the conventional policy of the restoration of order, full implementation of the 1947 *Statut*, and Algeria remaining part of France. It only survived a November 1954 confidence motion with the support of the pro-*colon* lobby. Mendès's Interior Minister, Mitterrand, did however order the *répression limitée*, ignored increasingly, and the fusion of the Algerian police with that of the metropole, a fusion more theoretical than practical.

Early in 1955 Mendès despatched to Algeria as governor-general a gifted Left-wing Gaullist academic, Soustelle, tasked to a policy of reform with, initially, honest elections. *Colon* reaction was frigid.

Before Soustelle had even arrived in Algeria, however, the *colon* lobby had turned against Mendès and played its part in the latter's fall. Soustelle surrounded himself with liberal advisers and set out proposals for reform. The philosophy behind these reforms was said to be integration. But the actual measures were cautious, reflecting *colon* and military suspicions. They were limited to providing improved Moslem representation in central and local government and the administration, education was to be expanded, especially the teaching of Arabic, and public works and agricultural development projects set in hand. Although Soustelle extended secret feelers to Messali Hadj and Ferhat Abbas and engaged in a dialogue with other moderate nationalists, he never dared offer any acceptable solution. Some MTLD members were released, but of these many promptly joined the FLN. The Faure government sent a further 10 battalions of troops, bringing the garrison to over 110,000. Able generals with Indochina experience such as Allard and Beaufre arrived and, highly important for the operational zones, a few helicopters began to appear. A formal state of emergency for the Aurès and Kabyle areas was declared in April 1955, extended to all Algeria in 1956. The first internment camp opened at Khenchela in 1955; others, graded according to the militancy of the detainees, followed. In June the government sanctioned military tribunals for the trial of captured insurgents.

Perhaps the most encouraging feature on the Algerian scene, though, was Soustelle's most imaginative practical measure. This was a return to an honourable French Army tradition, including the protecting of Moslems against *colon* abuse, that of direct military administration in troubled areas. Beginning in the Aurès, *Sections Administratives Spécialisées* (SAS) were established; it was seen as the counter to the FLN's OPA cell system. The sections operated in small teams, almost all Army officers, tasked to restore order and initiate rural development work, adult literacy and primary education, feeder roads, market and irrigation schemes, preventive medicine and dispensaries. When well-run, which was almost always the case, these proved enormously successful and popular, the system being extended to a total of 800 centres involving 5,000 personnel over the next four years. They suffered, however, from four difficulties: *colon* opposition, especial targeting by the FLN, the fact that months or years of careful confidence-building could be ruined by a ruthless punitive sweep operation, and the fact that much of the Army believed that they, and any others who tried to befriend the Moslems, were at best misguided and sentimental, if not actually Communist and subversive. Back-stabbing allegations behind closed doors were frequent.

THE WAR IN 1955 AND 1956

Despite the French Army's efforts and because there was no apparent political solution, the military situation slowly but steadily worsened during the summer of 1955. Violence, sabotage and killings spread over all North-east Algeria. The FLN in the north Constantine area became able to field larger bands of insurgents, up to 50 in number though elsewhere groups remained small. More and more loyalists were butchered, usually by nose or throat-slitting, castration or disembowelling, often unhurried. Throat-slitting, the method of killing animals, was especially humiliating and often preferred. Smaller numbers of *colons* and soldiers were also killed. In response, Army commanders increasingly ignored the *répression limitée* instructions, turning to bombs, rockets, the 'collective response' destruction of Moslem settlements, and on occasions reprisal executions of 20 or more of their inhabitants. The cycle of rebellion and repression gathered speed; two of Soustelle's closest liberal associates left Algeria in disgust. In Paris Soustelle's integration project began to arouse fears of an Algerian deputy group holding a balance of power; in Algiers Soustelle's reforms were deliberately delayed in the local Assembly by the *colons*.

It was in these circumstances that on 20 August occurred one of the major events of the war, the massacre of 71 Europeans and 61 Algerians, the latter not necessarily loyalist but simply known to oppose violence, in the Philippeville and Constantine areas. The killings were the result of deliberate decisions by the FLN's *Wilaya* 2 led, following the death of Didouche, by Youssef Zighout and Lakhdar Ben Tobbal, the latter well-versed in revolutionary theory. The massacres were initiated by ALN regulars who, at the scene of the worst of the butcheries, a mining town near Philippeville, incited the local Moslem men to join in, some of these being long-serving and trusted employees, so adding to the horror. Their efforts were supported by *muezzins* from the mosque and ululating women. Deliberately, to inflame hatred, the most revolting mutilations and disembowelling were perpetrated against men, women, old, young and infants; houses were described as drenched in blood. In the streets Arab children danced with joy, and kicked any Europeans not quite dead. As was also calculated by Tobbal, the reprisals were equally horrifying, with French soldiers as revolted by the carnage as were the *colons*, and August heat further inflaming passions. Groups of Moslems were herded together and gunned down by regular soldiers and *colon* vigilante parties alike. No reliable figures are available; the French admitted 1,273, the FLN claimed over 12,000 – 2 to 3,000 is more probable.

Philippeville had two major consequences. The event gave the FLN a much-needed boost in morale and recruitment. Even more important, the event opened up an abyss between the two Maghreb communities, mutual fear was replaced by mutual terror and hatred, fanned in the case of the *colons* by the local *colon*-controlled press. The supposedly reliable Moslem deputies in the Algerian Assembly, almost certainly under personal threat, unanimously rejected any form of integration. But the gesture was matched by some disillusioned *colon* liberals such as Chevallier. Nauseated and embittered, Soustelle too turned to a policy of firmer repression, believing that no negotiation with the FLN, or with any who might have links with the FLN, was possible. From being a distrusted liberal he became the darling of the *colons*.

On the wider world stage the FLN were able to capitalize on their success in being invited to attend the Bandung 'Third World' Conference of April 1955 and by ensuring that Algeria was discussed specifically for the first time at the United Nations in November. The French delegation withdrew in protest. In Paris the Faure government, reiterating the usual 'pacification first' policy, was bitterly criticized over Algeria in the *Chambre*. Faure, a Radical, was the especial target of his more liberal fellow Radical Mendès-France, as well as the target of both the political Right, now reinforced in voice by the Poujadist populist movement who blamed him for the loss of Morocco, and of the Left. At the end of November he was defeated in a vote of confidence and until February 1956 France was plunged into unedifying electioneering and political bargaining in which extremists of both Right and Left, together with the populist Right Poujadists, all made considerable gains, reducing the prospects of stability for any Centre-Left government. The new Prime Minister, Mollet, and his successors had to cobble majorities together from groups in the political centre in which the Socialists were pivotal. But these precarious majorities had to include the MRP or the old Right if they were to survive against the Communists and Poujadists; although Mollet was a Socialist his policy had, therefore, to be cautious.

119

In any case it was clear that French public opinion still nurtured the belief that Algeria could and should remain in some form part of France; even those who favoured negotiation saw a solution within this frame. Right-wing politicians even talked of a need to reconquer Tunisia and Morocco; others in writing averred that Algerian nationalism was as factious and insignificant as Breton or Corsican nationalism. In March 1956 even the Communists voted for the special powers Mollet sought to re-establish order and to introduce democratic reforms. Mollet's own preferences were for Soustelle's reforms as likely to be the maximum feasible for the moment, and overt discussions with acceptable Moslem leaders together with secret overtures to the FLN with perhaps new local elections and negotiations to follow. He also selected a new Governor-General, the liberal though now very aged Catroux. But on a visit to Algiers, rashly publicized in advance, Mollet was insulted and pelted with rotten fruit, and Catroux declined the thankless task. Mollet's visit in February 1956 was significant as the first overt display in Algiers of demagogue-inspired *colon* street power, the most vocal personality being a bar owner, Ortiz. The demonstrators were supported in France by Poujadist ex-servicemen such as Le Pen.[11] The demonstrations were followed by a general strike. Mollet was obliged to back-track. He appointed Robert Lacoste, a Socialist Minister, as Governor-General, the appointment soon elevated to Resident-Minister. Such reforms as Lacoste and Mollet were able to effect were limited in scope while the Algiers *colons* drew the obvious lesson in respect of their street power.

Massive reinforcement of the French garrison continued under Mollet, the need emphasized by some unreliability in Algerian *Tirailleurs* units and the departure of the Moroccans. Two decrees, one in August 1955 and one in April 1956, provided for the recall of first the 1953 and then the 1952 conscripts, and the extension of obligatory national service from 18 to as much as 30 months (36 in the case of *colons*) if necessary, with a whole two-year period in Algeria. By August 1956 the French Army in Algeria totalled 390,000, later to rise to a peak of 415,000 in the autumn of 1957. This total represented a withdrawal of some 200,000 men from the labour force of metropolitan France and an extra 300 million francs on the military budget. Of these 415,000 troops, some 390,000 – 86.1 per cent – were French, 5.1 per cent each of foreigners (the *Légion*) or North

---

11 Horne, *A Savage War*, p.148, notes that the demonstrators included ex-servicemen deployed by a co-ordinating committee, the extreme Right-wing *Association des Elus d'Algérie*, Ortiz's *L'Action* group and another Right-wing organization called *Union Française Nord-Africaine* (UFNA), and a student group led by Lagaillarde.

Africans, and 3.7 per cent Black Africans. In addition, there were approximately 100 light, 90-strong *gardes mobiles* static defence companies, 9,000 gendarmes, 30,000 airmen and 6,000 naval personnel.[12] Finally, there were *colon* vigilante *Unités Territoriales*; these soon came to play political roles.

In 1956 General Lorillot, who had replaced Cherrière, introduced the system of *quadrillage* to try to contain the ALN. This system, drawing on the 1920s experience of Beaufre in Morocco, was a mix of static garrisons and mobile pursuit groups. The static garrisons formed a network of detachments of 60 to 100, supplied by metropolitan conscript or North or Black African units. These also recruited and provided cadres for linked local auxiliaries, *harkis*, who wore some of the parent regiment's uniform, and were later to look to that parent regiment for protection. These *harkis*, some of whom were horsed, totalled 26,000 by the end of 1956 and offered much local topographical expertise. For *quadrillage* three types of zones were created. In *zones interdits*, usually remote, the entire population was moved to create a free fire zone. In *zones de pacification*, movement was checked and controlled, lists of inhabitants were kept and all had to carry an identity card with a photograph; and in *zones d'opérations*, the major population centres, the garrisons awaited opportunities to track down or cordon and search. In time *quadrillage* became very effective.

Prices had, however, to be paid both in the heavy manpower requirement and also the resentment aroused in communities which had lost homes and crops and which were obliged to live in cold, insanitary camps on meagre rations. Many fled to Morocco or Tunisia or joined the FLN. The pursuit groups were, as in Indochina, mostly drawn from elite *Coloniale* and *Légion* regiments and would sortie on pursuits that could last for days, sometimes weeks. They really only became fully effective in the difficult terrain of Algeria with the arrival from 1958 onwards of big troop-carrying helicopters. Construction of a stop line of wire and minefields parallel to the Tunisian border was also begun to prevent the use of Tunisia as a base and refuge. The capture of a haul of FLN documents at the end of 1955 proved a considerable intelligence success for the French.

Lacoste initially hoped that by dissolving the Algerian Assembly and reforming local government, in both cases to provide for greater

12 These figures are taken from Colonel P. Carles, *Des Millions de soldats inconnus* (Paris, Lavauzelle, 1982), p.176. The Navy operated a surveillance system of all ships approaching Algeria, especially any which had sailed from Middle East or Yugoslav ports. Very large quantities of weaponry were seized.

Moslem representation, a middle-class moderate nationalist group would emerge. Military pressure and military needs, however, skewed this policy, and SAS detachments in practice provided local authority; eventually, in December 1956, all elected councils were disbanded. More usefully, wages were raised, some land reform measures attempted, school opportunities for Moslems improved and the public service directed to reserve half of all vacancies for Moslems. Lacoste also increased the number of departments in Algeria to twelve, so providing greater influence in Paris; for the future he envisaged a cantonal Algeria of self-governing regions, each with a common electoral roll for a national Assembly. This project in some measure reflected traditional military Kabyle policy, but legislation to achieve it was in any case overtaken by events.

These measures totally failed to contain the FLN, whose activities in 1956 extended westwards to the Moroccan border, and into the major cities and towns. Success endowed the FLN with *baraka*, good fortune, in Moslem eyes. Improved ALN organization provided for some 8,000 full-time, regular, paid and uniformed *moujahidines* insurgents with approximately 20,000 auxiliaries – part-time *moussebilines*, and intelligence and stores-gathering supporters, *fidayeens*. Numbers increased, recruits now including a few Europeans, mostly Communists, and a number from the Algerian Jewish community. A field military structure of 350-strong battalions (*failek*), 100-strong companies (*katiba*), and 35-strong sections (*ferka*), developed. The usual battle unit was the *katiba*. New recruits were required to kill as proof of their motivation. After Bandung, money started to arrive from several sources. Conduits for men and supplies were extended by either terror or persuasion to include members of Moslem councils of elders, the *Union Générale des Travailleurs Algériens*, the *Union Générale des Etudiants Musulmans Algériens* and the underground Communist Party, which had disassociated itself from the French Communist Party. Those who refused to identify with the FLN were killed, usually after mutilation. Some of the former MTLD leaders had joined the FLN in Cairo, and Ferhat Abbas, his moderate past notwithstanding, had also come out in support. The FLN had by now almost marginalized Messali Hadj despite his attempt to revamp his faction of the MLTD under the new title of *Mouvement Nationaliste Algérien* (MNA). At one point in 1955 the MNA, under a chieftain named Bellounis, fielded its own partisans in a 500-strong group in eastern Kabylia. But the group was surprised by a *Wilaya* 3 FLN force and virtually wiped out, though Bellounis escaped. Thereafter the MNA counted for little.

In quantifiable terms, in the first two years of the fighting the FLN had killed more than 500 members of the French security forces, at a cost to themselves of approximately 3,000. They also had inflicted immense danger on the *colon* agricultural economy, with the destruction of estates and crops and the killing or stealing of animals.

Despite these successes, however, the FLN had its own internal tensions, both at the top between the 'internal' and 'external' leadership and at local *wilaya* leadership levels, particularly in *Wilaya* 1, where Ben Boulaid's successor proved incompetent and was executed by his own men. Ben Boulaid, who had made a successful escape, briefly resumed the leadership until he was killed in a French special forces operation.[13] To resolve these differences and in a remarkably bold gesture, a secret conference of 16 FLN leaders and a number of followers was held, almost under the noses of the French, in the Soummam Valley in the Kabyles in August 1956. Difficulties in arranging the Congress prevented the attendance of the Cairo 'external' leadership, so providing the 'internal' leaders with their chance to set their stamp on the FLN. A new and particularly able 'internal' leader was Youssef Ben Khedda, a pharmacist and former follower of Messali Hadj, who had joined the FLN in 1955. The meeting also represented the ascendancy of the Berbers over the Arabs in the FLN. The conference re-asserted the principle of collective political leadership by establishing a National Council of the Algerian Revolution (CNRA), of 34 members all elected at the Congress, together with a small, five-man Committee for Co-ordination and Execution (CCE). Propaganda was revamped to negate French official propaganda and isolate France before world opinion. The military strategy was to be a mix of combat attrition and economic destruction, in France as well as Algeria. For the ALN, the FLN's fighting units, a general staff with Belkacem Krim as its head was appointed, his lieutenant Oumrane being tasked to command in the Algiers *Wilaya* 4 area, the city itself becoming an autonomous zone. Each *wilaya* was to be headed by a commander and a committee responsible for both military and political action. Under the commander, each *wilaya* and its sub-divisions – *mintaka* (regions), *nahia* (zones) and *kisma* (sectors) – were to have specific officers appointed for political, military and intelligence work. Decisions, in theory, were collective. The field unit structure was also formalized, with NCO and officer ranks up to colonel. The war aims

13 Alf Andrew Heggoy, *Insurgency and Counter Insurgency in Algeria* (Bloomington, Indiana University Press, 1972), p.118. One argument holds that Boulaid's escape was facilitated by one of Soustelle's liberal advisers so that he could be used for negotiation and that Soustelle's harder policies, after Philippeville, returned him to the FLN.

of the FLN, an independent democratic, socialist Republic of Algeria, were firmly re-stated; there was to be no *bourguibisme*, the peaceful acceptance of concessions, as a base for further demands. The event as a whole can be seen as confirming the FLN's status as a mass movement. At the conference, the most forceful figure was Ramdane Abane, who had pulled together the FLN in the Algiers *wilaya* after the capture of Bitat. Intelligent and self-educated – he had studied Marx and Lenin while in prison – Abane's dominance, however, aroused suspicions of personal ambition, later to have fatal consequences for him.

The position of the 'external' leaders was to be still further weakened. The Mollet government's covert attempts to parley with them, at meetings in Rome and Belgrade, failed, and on 22 October the four principal members of the 'external' leadership, Ben Bella, Ait Ahmed, Khider and Boudiaf, were all taken by the French. They were flying from Egypt, over Algeria, to Morocco in a Moroccan aircraft. They aimed to seek Moroccan support for their 'external' leadership and their trip was known to French intelligence. The machine's pilot was French and he obeyed a local French military order to land his aircraft at Algiers, where the four passengers were all arrested. This sleight of hand, which Mollet and Lacoste dared not disavow, aroused very sharp international criticism and, strengthening as it did the hardline 'internal' leadership, finished any prospect of further negotiations between Mollet and the FLN.

Frustration at their failure to end the campaign and the absence of any real policy led the French to look for scapegoats elsewhere. The virulence of Radio Cairo's propaganda, which the French tried unsuccessfully to jam, suggested an easy target: Nasser's Egypt must surely be to blame. This blame was incorrectly also extended to allege massive weapon provision by Egypt, a misconception increased by the detention on 16 October of a ship off the coast of Spanish Morocco in which were found some weapons loaded in Alexandria. France was surprisingly united (in contrast to Britain) on the propriety of attacking Egypt and attempting to remove Nasser. Only the Communists and a handful of extreme anglophobe Poujadists opposed the action. It was seen as a French national re-assertion, much needed after Dien Bien Phu and American and UN criticism. It was believed that the removal of Nasser would prove a fatal blow to the FLN. In this belief two parachute regiments were despatched to the Anglo-French invasion force that was assembled in October 1956 following Nasser's nationalization of the Suez Canal in the summer. In the event, only one regiment was dropped, the French commander, General Gilles, directing operations from a flying command post; the other regiment arrived by sea. Both secured their immediate objectives before the United Nations ordered the Anglo-French operations to cease. Another French policy had come apart, but the reaction in France was far from one of blame. Mollet claimed he was defending not just French Algeria but all of Western democracy against a dictator. He secured a massive vote of confidence in the *Chambre* in December, only Faure, Mendès-France and the Communists dissenting.

The French Army made a determined effort, and one necessary politically, to provide the conscripted soldier with a better life than that experienced in Indochina. Food, uniforms, amenities, medical services were all much improved; Moslem *Tirailleurs* and *Spahis* received special rations. The amenities included transistor radios, later to prove significant. Extended service, separation and in some areas danger allowances were paid, though for an ordinary conscript's pay of less than £10 per month was poor reward. Wives and families of regulars sometimes joined their husbands if these were serving in towns. The desertion rate was much lower than in Indochina.

But nevertheless morale in the French Army at the end of 1956 was still at a very low ebb. The elite parachute units returned from Suez determined that there should never be another failure. The units were disciplined and dedicated down to soldier level, a mirror image of the Viet Minh against which their cadres had fought. The massive call-up of reservists had led to fracas and demonstrations, including women lying across railway lines, at 15 training centres in France.[14] A spectacular FLN success, the killing, in some cases unhurried, of a 20-strong platoon of recalled *Coloniale* reservists in an ambush near Palestro in May 1956 had not only further affected morale but had also started the first general questioning about the war in France, especially amongst the millions with relatives serving in Algeria. *Quadrillage* life in either old urban barracks or new improvised breeze block forts and watch-towers, too hot in summer and too cold in winter, was uncomfortable even when not accompanied by fear of attack or ambush. Ill-concealed contempt from members of the elite pursuit units added to discontent.[15] Fear often led *quadrillage* units to be very cautious in their patrolling. In the mountain areas where

14 Morandière, *Soldats du Djebel*, p.60. In the event many, but not all, of the Communist conscripts totally changed their views in Algeria, becoming some of the most severely repressive of the military personnel.

15 Carles, *Des Millions*, p.195, notes elite soldiers' language in Algeria. Conscript units were referred to disparagingly as 'the soldier-voters', units in *quadrillage* roles as the 'lead bottoms'.

the rugged terrain remained very much in favour of the insurgent, *quadrillage* units spent much time in road construction. These, when completed, enabled pursuit unit troops to arrive in armoured personnel carriers escorted by armoured cars.

By the end of 1956 the real failure of French policies in North Africa was evident. Tunisia and Morocco had attained independence in circumstances that had proved humiliating for France. Despite nearly half a million men under arms and expenditure of £1 million per day, the Algerian war was intensifying. More than 1,000 Europeans, either military personnel, officials or *colons*, had been killed, together with some 6,000 loyalist Moslems. Serious criticism of the war in France had opened, the Socialist Party calling for a cease-fire and negotiations. An opinion poll in July 1956 recorded 45 per cent of those questioned to be in favour of negotiation with the FLN. France herself was under mounting attack at the United Nations; her relations with the rest of the Arab world were soured. The withdrawal of so large a proportion of both her Army and Air Force from NATO roles had weakened her voice in NATO councils, in turn strengthening anti-NATO sentiment in France. The more correct argument, that France was only able to denude her own metropolitan strength to fight a peripheral war thanks to the luxury of NATO membership and much NATO equipment, while other NATO forces secured her continental defence, was hardly ever voiced – in France. The clouds of self-delusion remained; there could be no political or military solution to the problem within the frame of the Fourth Republic, even when the government was led by an otherwise militant Socialist and pacifist such as Mollet.

7 ALGERIA, 1957

Both the FLN and the French entered 1957 determined to intensify the struggle by means of new strategy, new tactics and new leaders.

For the FLN, the last months of 1956 had seen ever-renewed emphasis on killings specifically designed to set the communities apart, in particular the torturing and killing of loyalists and all their families, and of the killing of *colon* families including *colon* children. New leaders, notably Mohamedi Said who succeeded to the leadership of *Wilaya* 3, and his chief field commander, Ait Hamouda, better known as Amirouche, were men of the most ferocious cruelty, in the case of Amirouche to the point of derangement. Oumrane and Abane in *Wilaya* 4 with their local Algiers City subordinate, Saadi Yacef, were almost their equals. For recruitment of followers the OPA remained the agent. The goad continued to be terror; the FLN made little attempt to recruit by means of promise of a better social order. But the carrot of the movement's own clandestine radio broadcasts and news-sheets served also to maintain enthusiasm by keeping the Moslem public informed on the progress of the war. Funds from a number of Arab and other countries facilitated the purchase of weaponry, though the transmission of these weapons into Algeria itself remained very hazardous.

THE BATTLE OF ALGIERS

Events and strategic theory combined to lead the FLN to switch from the country to the cities, in particular Algiers, for their main effort in late 1956 and early 1957. By mid-1956 the FLN had gained control of the Algiers Casbah with its 80,000 Moslem inhabitants, and partial control of other areas; killer squads of three or four assassinated supporters of Messali and police personnel. In June 1956, under very strong *colon* pressure, Lacoste refused final pleas for mercy in respect of two FLN members, one a cripple, convicted of murder. Both were guillotined. In reprisal, Yacef's Algiers City FLN killed 49 Europeans in three days of shootings. This was followed two weeks later by a massive explosion, the work of a *colon* counter-terrorist group, in a house in the crowded Moslem Casbah area that killed 70 Moslems, men, women and children. The Soummam Conference, at Abane's behest, directed Ben M'hidi to prepare an FLN offensive in the Algiers autonomous area.

For this Yacef, in the city itself, could field a force of more than 1,400 activists; these now included several attractive Moslem teenage girl students. Two of these, disguised as European girls, placed bombs in popular *colon* cafés on 30 September; the explosions caused deaths, maiming and disfigurement. A third similar attempt was a failure. To extend his activities Yacef adapted the Casbah to be an insurrectionary base by the preparation of secret cellar and roof-top passages and hides; it became in practice a 'no-go' area for French gendarmes and police. On 28 December the FLN further outraged the *colon* population with the assassination of Froger, a prominent *colon*. Froger was a war veteran, a Right-wing political leader and a landowner; his assassin was Yacef's lieutenant, Ali la Pointe, a street-wise product of the Casbah's underworld of crime and vice. Just before Froger's funeral a bomb exploded, fortunately prematurely, but the infuriated *colon* crowd turned on the Moslem population, killing four. This in turn was followed by further killing of *colons*, and the calling of a general strike by the FLN. Frustrated and trapped between the *colons* and the military demanding action, and political figures in Paris wanting to open negotiations, Lacoste summoned into Algiers City the elite, 8,000-strong 10th Parachute Division, a formation that above all represented the evolving professionalism of the French Army. The commander, General Massu, was a strong personality, prepared to use most means to serve the end. The division comprised four parachute regiments, two *Coloniale*, one *Légion* and one metropolitan *Chasseurs*, all among the most ruthlessly efficient units ever fielded by the French Army.

The last months of 1956 had seen several French military developments. Beaufre's *quadrillage* was beginning to yield results in the Constantine area; some of the SAS detachments there and elsewhere were gathering valuable intelligence. Helicopters, in particular the larger Sikorsky machines capable of lifting 10 men, were arriving. In a brisk and significant action in October 1956, Colonel Bigeard, at the head of the elite *3ᵉ Régiment de Parachutistes Coloniaux*, killed 126 insurgents in the first major helicopter-borne pursuit operation. Napalm was also used very effectively, although its use was never officially admitted.

In December 1956 General Salan arrived as Commander-in-Chief, bringing with him all his Indochina experience and personal vigour. He was, however, suspected by the *colons* of being *un bradeur d'Empire*, a man who would sell out, on account of his views on and service in Indochina. His arrival was marked by two events significant for the future. A subordinate general, Faure, in the Algiers area unwisely tried to inspan a senior civil servant in a plot to oust Lacoste and replace him by Salan. The civil servant reported Faure to the Prime Minister. Faure was recalled and imprisoned. More dramatic still was an attempt by *colon* extremists to assassinate Salan by means of a rocket attack on his office. The attack failed as Salan was out at the time, but one of his aides was killed. The plotters aimed to provoke a political crisis leading to a strong pro-*colon* regime in France, and it is possible, but not certain, that contacts had been made with certain Right-wing Paris politicians.[1]

Among the massive reinforcements sent from France were further elite *Coloniale* and *Légion* units with officers trained in the hard school of Indochina. Increasingly, Algeria was to be fought according to the precepts of the *guerre révolutionnaire* theorists. Their doctrine, almost Manichean, argued that revolutionary war was all-embracing, a good–evil conflict.[2] Indochina had been lost to the forces of evil, but the rest of the French Empire must on no account go the same way. Algeria was in any case still regarded as part of France and its defence part of that of the free world. It was argued in a doctrine that primarily represented gut-reaction to defeat that total revolutionary war, as the Marxists or the FLN envisaged, could only be met by total counter-revolutionary war. In this all means could be justified and order should precede law; military needs must override all legal and political factors, and in the last resort the military might have to dominate the political leadership. According to the doctrine, the Viet Minh success was due to the local-level mix of psychological action with insurrection, the insurgent leaders being not only expert guerrillas but also able political mentors, administrators and rural development agents, supported by a ruthless security system. Any counter-insurgency campaign had therefore to be fought with intelligence and psychological warfare agencies that could operate without restraint. At any local level communities could be deported or interned, individuals detained and subjected to severe interrogation, measures that in practice very

1 The event was hushed up and official documents were destroyed later. In his memoirs Salan named one or two personalities, who in turn denied the allegation.

2 For a useful summary of the *guerre révolutionnaire* doctrine, see G.A. Kelly, *Lost Soldiers* (Cambridge, MA, MIT Press, 1964), p.vii.

quickly turned to semi-legalized brutality. Intelligence and military priority targets were to be the insurgents' area command and logistic structures and key local insurgent personalities, either for assassination or capture for interrogation or for psychological re-education and use; the domination of areas to keep insurgents on the run; and remorseless local counter-terror in the case of ambushes or bomb attacks.

These drastic measures were justified in a theoretical philosophy of conflict set out in the writings of a group of elite force officers, many of whom were lower middle class in social origin, and almost all with outstanding combat or resistance experience during the Second World War as well as in Indochina. Indeed, as well as gut-reaction to defeat, two other psychological roots of this ruthless doctrine may well be identified as the fractured nature of the French Army after 1940 together with a French national liking for a philosophy neat, tidy, self-enclosed and logical.

At this wider philosophical level all colonial campaigns were seen as, if not actually Communist-driven, serving purely Communist interests with the nationalist leaders as dupes. Combating insurgents was therefore wholly justifiable, a moral, almost religious, imperative, requiring total effort. One theoretician, Colonel Lacheroy, analyzed a Communist challenge as developing in five phases: surprise; discreet demonstration; the opening of rebel action and the emergence of a distinction between political and military activity; a fourth transition phase of semi-regular units; and a final front and rear war involving regular and irregular forces. Vital to this strategy was control over particular areas so that it could be seen that legality and force were changing sides in favour of the insurgents.

As a counter, a theory of *parade* and *riposte* was postulated by the counter-revolutionary warfare theorists. *Parade* was argued by another theoretician, Captain Souyris, as ensuring that colonial territories were at all times governed by vigorous, progressive and humane administrations which in advance defused possible sources of grievance and actively propagated Western values in large-scale mass psychology campaigns. *Riposte* was set out by a third theoretician, Commandant Hogard, as being governed by 10 rules: first, no equal terms negotiation with insurgents; second, the isolation of rebel-held territory; third, early pre-emptive security force action; fourth, an infrastructure that linked all civil, military, political and social work in an effort to recapture mass support; fifth, the destruction of insurgent hierarchies; sixth, a psychological campaign to convince the population that the insurgents were false and that improved living standards would follow the restoration of law and order; seventh, recognition that the destruction of the insurgents was not enough in itself but was only a means to the end of recovering the loyalty of the civilian population; eighth, that insurgent groups should be stifled by deprivation of material and moral support; ninth, that the insurgents themselves should be harassed and tracked ceaselessly; and tenth, that the government's key installations should not be secured by static defence but by constant insecurity for any attacker. To these rules Captain Souyris emphasized the need for good intelligence, for an appropriate military infrastructure with direct military administration in the danger zones, and for civic indoctrination.

These theories clearly reveal the sense of alienation from the metropole, above all the profound distrust of Paris politicians, seen as ever-changing but almost all decadent, felt by these officers. Their distrust was reinforced by on-going wrangles with Paris over money and resources, and also by Suez. Many distrusted only slightly less the French Army's senior commanders; they began to insist that the reasons for operations and the value of forthcoming operations should be explained very fully to themselves and their soldiers. In 1957, in fact, orders had to be issued that officers must explain the political background to the campaign to all ranks.

The arrogance of the group was even from the outset viewed as excessive by both the more conservative French senior officers and also by those of a more liberal, often Gaullist, background. But in Algiers in 1957 they and their remarkable units were to have their day. When in command of their units, almost all *Coloniale* or *Légion*, officers commanded them in a very distinctive style – that of being tougher, bolder and more ruthless even than their men with whom they were very familiar; some colonels seemed to behave more as feudal barons than commanders in a disciplined structure. Their aggressiveness extended to their soldiers, for *Coloniale* empire in general and for the *Légion* Algeria in particular were the reasons for their very existence. The outward appearance of these awe-inspiring regiments with their special *léopard* parachute camouflage and distinctive headdress, well-behaved and controlled in the streets, carried an additional symbolism, that of a new force, formidable and unpredictable.

This, then, was the stage setting for the urban operations of early 1957. By far the most important of these was in Algiers, but others took place in Oran, Constantine and Philippeville. The general commanding the Algiers *Corps* was Allard, who had served under de Lattre in the Second World War and in Indochina. He and Massu were able to draw on past experience in their planning for the Algiers operations. As a result, Massu's parachute regiments took only two days to break the FLN's general strike, called from Radio Tunis to coincide with a UN session and show the world that France had lost control to the FLN in Algiers. Massu's success was achieved by visits to the homes of striking workers and school pupils, the latter lured back to school by means of sweets and military bands. On 1 February only 70 children attended school; by the fifteenth, 8,000 attended, and by 1 April, 37,500. They often arrived singing FLN songs, the only songs that they knew. Detainees were used to replace dockers, and shops that had been closed were forcibly blown open, leaving the owner little option but to do business. Light helicopters flew over the Casbah dropping leaflets telling people to return to work. Military personnel baked bread until the bakers returned to work; engineer specialists maintained other essential services. Almost simultaneous with the strike was a renewed FLN bombing campaign. Once again the targets were popular *colon* cafés and the agents young girls. The serious battle then began as the regiments moved on to attack the FLN structure in the city in a series of operations both systematic and ruthless.[3] An urban version of *quadrillage*, with street check points, known as the *îlot* system, was devised. Every member of every family or premise had to account for his or her movements to one appointed member, that person reporting to a street headman; all was controlled by a special *Détachement de Protection Urbaine* under another of the new school colonels, Trinquier. The Casbah area was cordoned off and every house carefully searched. Raids and arrests were carried out with surprise and speed, including helicopter landings on roofs. Constant foot patrols were maintained. Some 24,000 men, women and girls were subjected to ruthless interrogation and torture by a special *Détachement Opérationnel de Protection*. Some 3,000 died in prison – their corpses were either flown out by helicopter to be dropped, weighted, into the sea, immured in the walls of buildings, or buried secretly. The tortures, never officially admitted, included electric shock to nipples and genitals, crushing of limbs or other organs in vices, pumping air or liquids into bodies, or the Chinese style of endless blows on the head in the same place. The practitioners were mostly local *colons*, but a few parachute officers were also involved. In his defence it should be noted that Massu experimented with electric shock upon his own nipples. He argued the pain was not destructive – but he was in his office, not in a cell deprived of hope, food and sleep. In a remarkable circular the 10th Division's chaplain, Father Delarue, argued that pain-inflicting interrogation, without sadism, was

3 A very detailed account appears in François Porteu de la Morandière, *Soldats du Djebel* (Paris, Société de Production Littéraire, n.d.), p.i.

acceptable. Other less bestial tactics included double agents, stool pigeons and forged documents.

The interrogations enabled French intelligence, under Colonel Godard, another of the new-school colonels, to piece together the organization and members of the FLN and so preclude further loss of life of Frenchmen or loyalist Moslems in mass terror bomb attacks. The harsh measures were therefore seen as completely justifiable, and the conflict became, if possible, yet more brutal. To the French, bombs and mutilation justified torture and napalm; to the FLN, torture and napalm justified further bombings and mutilations.

By the end of February the French Army, in particular Bigeard's 3rd Colonial Parachute Regiment, had located the Casbah bomb factories, arrested a number of the manufacturers and transporters, known terrorists, and girl student agents, and most important of all had tracked down and caught Ben M'hidi. M'hidi was treated well by Bigeard personally, but later died in prison in circumstances never made fully clear.

To ease the pressure on its men in Algiers City the FLN ordered an intensification of operations in the hinterland of *Wilaya* 4. One force under Si Azedine, one of the new generation of trained and tough guerrilla leaders, ambushed a *Spahis* unit killing more than 70 at the beginning of May; they followed this success with an ambush of a *Tirailleurs* company, killing a further 10. The French retaliated by withdrawing three of the parachute regiments from Algiers. These, using intelligence supplied by the SAS personnel at work in the villages, quickly reasserted control. In an engagement described as the 'Battle of Agounennda', Bigeard's regiment inflicted a sharp reverse on Si Azedine, killing 96 ALN for the loss of only eight. The absence of the three regiments enabled the FLN to mount a renewed but short-lived wave of killings and counter-killings in Algiers. One section blew up the Casino crowded with dancers; in riposte the *colon* crowd staged a pogrom of Moslems. These events led to the recall of all Massu's units and the final destruction of the FLN organization the city. First, Yacef's two chief lieutenants were killed in late August; in September Yacef and another FLN leader were captured by the *1er Etranger de Parachutistes*; and in October Aly la Pointe was tracked down and killed. Other successes included the unearthing of FLN weapon-supply conduits, including some from Germany. Double agents played important roles in these operations. By the end of September the French Army could justifiably claim to have restored order in Algiers, and indeed the FLN were not to return there for over three years. Oumrane and the CCE had been forced to move to Tunis in February; it was in fact able later to operate more efficiently from there.

If the French won a military victory in the 'Battle of Algiers', as these events came to be called, they suffered a political defeat following massive criticism of their severity both in France and elsewhere. The severity reduced still further the small number of Moslem moderates, and fuelled the fires of hatred. French torture proved an effective FLN recruiting agent. A number of Frenchmen in Algeria, particularly those with first-hand experience of Nazi methods, were revolted. These included a general, de la Bollardière, who protested and was placed under house arrest, and a senior civil servant, Taitgen, who was with difficulty persuaded not to resign but later left Algeria.[4] Torture, connoting that ends justified means, served as a gangrene – a word much used at the time – further to corrode respect for law and order in certain elements of the French Army. In May, for example, as a reprisal for the killing of two parachute soldiers, a special forces unit massacred some 80 Moslems in a Turkish bath, an event for which no one was held to account.

There was massive intellectual, press and church protest in France, including books, notably J.J. Servan-Schreiber's *Lieutenant en Algérie* and H. Alleg's *La Question*; the latter, describing his own experience of torture, made a great impact.[5] The Prime Minister, Mollet, set up a safeguard Commission to try to prevent any recurrence. Although an economic crisis was the precipitating event, anxiety over Algeria was a major cause of the fall of the Mollet government a little later, on 21 May. Mollet was succeeded after a three-week interregnum by Bourgès-Maunoury, who included Mollet amongst his ministers, the support of at least some Socialists being as always almost essential.

The last months of 1956 and the year 1957 also saw a marked shift in the world of ideas. As early as 1954 the scholarly journalist Aron had noted, in the context of refuting Marxist argument about imperial exploitation, that the decolonization of the Netherlands Empire had not led to any fall in the prosperity of the Netherlands. In 1956 Cartier, another influential journalist, opened sharp and widely read criticism of the financial and military burden of empire, arguing that the costs were no longer effective or supportable, and that French resources should be concentrated on domestic modernization.

4 Significantly, Bollardière's outstanding war record had all been with de Gaulle's Free French forces, and Teitgen had survived Nazi torture and Dachau.

5 Alleg was the editor of a Communist newspaper in Algiers. He had been arrested and tortured in 1957. Servan-Schreiber's book was translated into English and published by Hutchinson of London in 1958 under the title of *Lieutenant in Algeria*.

Cartiérisme was endorsed by leading business interests who saw the future in terms of high technology rather than overseas colonies. These trends were evident in the results of another opinion poll, which showed that the percentage preferring some form of negotiation had increased to 57 per cent, with a further 34 per cent in favour of Algerian autonomy and 18 per cent in favour of complete Algerian independence.

In Britain several newspapers, notably the *Observer*, opened a campaign of severely critical articles, and Members of Parliament asked the Foreign Office to express British disapproval in strong terms. In the United States similar criticism was aroused. All served further to weaken diplomatic support for France in NATO and at the United Nations, with serious consequences later in the year. Within the NATO hierarchy the French Army was now losing important appointments, as France could no longer provide the manpower to justify any claim to them. These losses, in turn, increased French disenchantment with NATO.

FIGHTING IN FRONTIER AND RURAL AREAS

In the country areas, the FLN remained strong in several regions, notably Collo, Djidjelli and El Milea. In operations against them the French Army pursued the same mix of the development of professional skill and ruthlessness, as it had shown in Algiers and at Agounennda, throughout the year. Most significant was the cordoning off of Algeria by the development of the stop lines into two enormous frontier barrier systems on the Tunisian and Moroccan borders. The Tunisian system, 360 kilometres long from Bône to Bir el Ater, was the more complex, and largely the brain child of General Pedron. It was built by six engineer regiments. In the areas most favoured by insurgents for crossing, the Morice line, as it was named after Bourgès-Maunoury's Defence Minister, was 20 kilometres in depth, a distance not traversable in one night. In these particularly strengthened areas there would be up to four wire entanglements, of which two or three would be electrified to 5,000 volts, floodlighting, radar and minefields. Strong points were sited 2–3 kilometres apart, and behind the line ran a road for the quick movement of reinforcements. The Moroccan Pedron line was some 145 kilometres long, stretching inland from the coast at Sidi Aissa.[6]

6 Algeria's Saharan edge of operations was little used by the FLN and kept under a much simpler French surveillance by means of air reconnaissance, radar and motor or camel patrols.

The cost in money and manpower of these fortified lines was great; 40,000 men were needed for the Morice line alone. But, as systems, the lines were exceedingly effective, despite the fact that the ALN groups trying to enter from Tunisia often possessed better weaponry, including Bangalore torpedoes, high-tension cutters and tunnelling equipment, than the groups still operating within Algeria. On numerous occasions large bands of ALN insurgents were wiped out or gave themselves up at little cost to French manpower; the most spectacular example was to be one on the Morice line in 1958, when, out of a group of some 1,200, only two managed to cross the entire system. The FLN forces were, in practice, now split in two: effective organized units in Tunisia unable to join the fighting and beleaguered units, often on the run, in Algeria.

The pursuit groups of elite units pulled no punches. Villages or settlements would be burned down, sometimes with their inhabitants inside. On other occasions whole small communities would be gunned down with a clinical detachment, as though they were vermin, as a reprisal for soldiers killed. Equally horrific was a brutal FLN massacre of more than 300 men in May in south Kabylia; the community from which the men came was believed by the FLN to support Bellounis and the MNA. The FLN tried to pin the blame for the massacre upon the French, but it was without doubt the work of Amirouche. Once again Bellounis escaped, and by August was back in the field with another private army, subvented by the French. A little later an entire *katiba* in the newly formed southern *Wilaya* 6, led by Si Cherif, defected to the French cause. Si Cherif had been a *Spahis* NCO captured by the FLN who turned to them and then turned again back from them; he and his *katiba* were Arab, and they proceeded to kill a number of Kabyles before becoming for a time an effective *harkis* unit.

The pressures on the FLN led to further internal quarrelling and vendetta fights between rival groups, or for leadership within a group. Each *wilaya* now had a new leader: Mohamed Cherif in *Wilaya* 1 (Aurès), Ben Tobbal in *Wilaya* 2 (North Constantine), Mohamedi Said in *Wilaya* 3 (Kabyle); and a new, highly intelligent leader, Boussouf, a former teacher, in *Wilaya* 5 (Oran). After Oumrane, Ben Khedda and the CCE had been forced to flee from Algiers; the military leadership in the Algiers area, *Wilaya* 4, had passed to a remarkable team operating in the hinterland headed by Si Sadek with Si M'hmed as his political deputy. The team included three redoubtable field commanders: Si Lakhtar, Ali Khodja and Si Azedine. The group of new *Wilaya* leaders was referred to collectively as 'the colonels', but their methods differed from the conventionally hierarchic command structure of Boussouf's *Wilaya* 5 to a rankless organization with communal decisions in *Wilaya* 4. The old exterior leadership, including Ben Bella, who communicated by means of secret notes from his Paris prison, blamed Abane and the CCE for the failures, especially in Algiers; Abane, a sick man, reacted violently by blaming 'the colonels', in particular Boussouf. But these latter dominated a meeting of the CNRA held in Cairo; and a little later, in December, while in the company of Krim, Cherif and Boussouf in Morocco, Abane was murdered. It was at first given out that he had been killed in action. Later on, in a gesture of unity more showy than real, 'the colonels' accepted collective responsibility for his death. One reason for this was a point on which they could all agree: the 'internal' leaders, and not the 'external', were to control the FLN despite their own differences.

Violence in the form of vendetta fighting spread also to metropolitan France, where clashes between the FLN and other nationalist groups were to lead to 779 deaths in 1957, a number to increase to 900 in 1958, with scores more injured in both years.

The extension of the SAS military administration continued throughout 1957. The detachment teams could now include one or two officers, one or two NCOs, a doctor if available, an interpreter, a wireless operator and a section of irregulars, usually *harkis*, for protection. By 1958, more than 58,000 pupils were studying in 750 schools staffed by Army teachers. The work of the SAS was supplemented, with less successful results, by the work of the special psychological warfare units, the Ve *Bureaux*. These, largely the brain child of yet another of the new school colonels, Lacheroy, had two tasks. The first was to explain and justify the campaign to France's conscript soldiers. Films and lectures were used, and a weekly magazine, *Le Bled* (The Desert) was produced. The line taken was that the Army's role was one of a higher, purer morality, that of a sound *pays réel*, above the criticism emanating from a sick society with a corrupt legality. A special training centre was opened at Arzew which from 1956 provided 12 day courses for conscript officers in batches of 250. These courses set out reasons and justifications for all aspects of French policy in Algeria, including interrogations. The officers were then tasked to pass this material on to their soldiers. The second role was that which in British counter-insurgency was called 'hearts and minds', targeted upon the Moslem population. Here the material was often simplistic anti-Marxism, Indochina war themes not adapted to Algerian circumstances, or approaches even more crude, almost Pavlovian, that loyalty could be restored by a process of thought-cleansing followed by re-education programmes, with material rewards for those who completed the programmes successfully. Centres for re-indoctrination were opened and FLN deserters or prisoners who agreed to 'turn' were used. Other methods included loudspeakers and tracts. Overall the *Bureaux* proposed an integrationist aim, in part a reflection of military dislike of the *colons*. The *Bureaux*, however, generally confused acquiescence with acceptance and in both roles tended to fall victim of their own propaganda.

One area in which both the SAS and the *Bureaux* failed was that of the forced mass evictions necessary for the *zones interdits* or other movement control. Here an increasing number, now nearly a million wretched Moslems, men, women and children, were crowded in squalid camps, existing on little more than semolina, with little or no prospect of freedom or return home. Many thousands escaped to join the FLN; the degradation and shared suffering created an anti-French solidarity.

In accordance with the teachings of the new school other special and intelligence-gathering units appeared. One became revealed as a disastrous failure when the French discovered that a force of 1,000 Kabyles which they had formed for special operations was in fact deceiving them and had been quietly collecting weapons and intelligence for the FLN. More successful was the achievement of a small group of double agents under a French officer which penetrated and then destroyed the ALN command in the western zone of *Wilaya* 3, securing a rich haul of prisoners and documents. Other French counter-gangs masquerading as ALN also scored a number of local successes.

The year 1957, the final full year of the Fourth Republic, saw the completion of the build-up of the French Army in Algeria. The scale was remarkable, and before turning to the new situation that followed the collapse of the Fourth Republic, merits being set out.[7] The former division-level headquarters at Oran, Algiers and Constantine were now *Corps* headquarters; these in total controlled some 300 units.[8] The Oran *Corps* included an armoured division, a motorized infantry division and three infantry divisions; the Algiers *Corps* comprised two infantry and one alpine infantry divisions; and the Constantine *Corps* three infantry divisions and one motorized infantry division. Most of the units in these divisions were composed of conscripts or recalled reservists. In addition, there was the general reserve of two parachute, one rapid motorized and one large infantry division; in these general reserve divisions were a number of the elite *Coloniale* and *Légion*

7 The French Army Order of Battle is set out in detail in Morandière, *Soldats du Djebel*, pp.361–73.

8 The land Army comprised 240 battalion or equivalent units, 35 cavalry regiments and 5,000 naval marines. The French Air Force strength totalled some 12,000.

units. Their deployments varied according to operational needs except in the case of the infantry division whose role was securing the Morice line. Finally there were, outside these structures, a number of specialized units and units detached for particular purposes.

Serving in this force were 20,000 Moslem regular soldiers of whom some were Moroccan or Tunisian, and 20,000 purely Algerian Moslem conscripts; a further 20,000 Moslem soldiers served in French units in France or Germany.[9] One *Tirailleurs Sénégalais* regiment, one or two additional battalions, a number of Black African and Malgache artillery units and a few Black African logistic units were also in Algeria, though from 1958 the structures changed with almost all the Black African troops being included in *mixtes* regiments in which black and white personnel served alongside each other.[10] By 1957–58 also the irregulars totals had reached 60,000 *harkis*, together with 35,000 other full- or part-time levies of different types. A number of disillusioned insurgents joined the *harkis*.

The difficulties of the campaign and of recruitment meant that often *ad hoc* units had to be put together from small detachments or from individuals of very varying military origin. These lacked cohesion, and local morale could suffer slightly in consequence. However, dependability of the locally recruited Moslem units improved considerably in 1957. The previous two years had seen a concerted FLN effort to suborn the loyalty of the Moslem *Tirailleurs* and *Spahis* serving in the French Army. Initially a trickle of men deserted with weapons. Numbers increased when a unit had been successfully attacked and ambushed, companies led by NCOs murdering their officers and loyal soldiers. Three notable incidents of this type occurred, one at Guentis in May 1955 and two in the Tlemcen area in February 1956. By 1957, however, the issues of loyalty or otherwise had been decided – a process assisted by the dilution of *Tirailleurs* units by the addition of Frenchmen, Tunisian *colons*, Caribbeans and others, and there were no further difficulties until the end of the campaign. Some *Tirailleurs* and *Spahis* officers defected to the FLN and many found their loyalty to France stretched most painfully. A group of 52 officers petitioned President Coty, to no avail.[11] There appears also to have been a

9 Although Morocco and Tunisia had attained independence, long-service volunteer regular *Tirailleurs* remained in French Army units until the mid-1960s.

10 A full breakdown of this complex system appears in Anthony Clayton, *France, Soldiers and Africa* (London, Brasseys, 1988), pp. 327–28.

11 The group was headed by Lieutenant Abdelkader Rahmani, a Saint-Cyr graduate and holder of the Legion of Honour. He, and others, were later arrested. Rahmani describes these events, and notes the demonstration in Germany in his *L'Affaire des Officiers Algériens* (Paris, Seuil, 1957).

nationalist demonstration in an Algerian *Tirailleurs* regiment stationed in Germany.

The nature of the elite units, too, changed in an important respect. In early 1957 these had been unsympathetic to the *colons*, viewing them in class terms as large estate and property owners. However, during the operations in Algiers the parachute troops found that the vast majority of the *colons* were like themselves, of working or artisan class; this identification of interests was strengthened by the option of many young *colons* to join these units for their period of national service.[12] This dilution in turn widened the gap between the elite and conscript units, a gap already sharpened by the revulsion of many conscripts – and their families in France – against the excesses in Algiers. Fewer and fewer metropolitan conscripts were prepared to risk their lives in any unnecessary adventure. Many wondered what they were doing at all in Algeria and some, shocked by excesses they had witnessed, began to question not only their political leadership but also their own identity as Frenchmen.

This difference in attitude and morale between the members of the conscript units primarily concerned with a safe return home and the increasingly uncompromising views held in the elite units sharpened in 1957. The elite unit commanders also now began to take the theories of the counter-revolutionary warfare schools to extremes, arguing that the government of the Republic itself must be subordinated to the needs of the campaign and under their control. The indications that some in Paris might want to negotiate and the continuing evidence of compromises and weaknesses in the political direction to these commanders seemed to deny the Fourth Republic any legitimacy. To them, as soldiers of outstanding battlefield ability and originality, the Army, or more accurately those in it holding their views, represented the true national will and legitimacy – and the basis for a sound discipline and behaviour. Their effort, hardship and suffering could not be in vain; to them victory was in sight and must not be thrown away. Further, if defeat was conceded, the French Army would go down in history as the Army of brutality and torture; with victory all would be forgotten. Soldiers, especially conscripts, could not be told to risk their lives without a full explanation of the reasons, the policy. If Paris could offer only either evasive answers or none at all it seemed imperative that commanders on the spot devise their own strategies and impose them. Their views were not necessarily reactionary in purely

12 The young *colons* who so joined did not receive a proper professional basic training. They were trained in a training company of the regiment they joined. If they served well they received a brief parachute course as a reward.

local political terms; on the ground they were in day-to-day contact with the inequalities of Algerian society, a contact reinforcing their beliefs that they knew better than comfortably ensconced politicians in Paris. But this extremism represented the counter-revolutionary warfare school turning in on itself. The consequences were shortly to become evident, for all to see.

In claiming that they were winning the fighting on the ground the elite force commanders were already confusing local military success and an overall military re-assertion over most of Algeria with suppression of the rebellion, a confusion to worsen in the next year. The FLN realized that both in towns, in the bled and on the frontiers, the French Army was going to win in any purely military encounter. Signs of war-weariness, in particular individual desertions and communal rallying to the French, were appearing, too, in the mass of the Moslem population; the FLN's failures cost it prestige, and many doubted whether the FLN could ever win. The FLN itself now saw eventual victory as attainable only by a greater political and international action in support of such operations as they could mount.

POLITICAL AND INTERNATIONAL CONSEQUENCES

If the Army's re-assertion could provide no political answers, neither could that of the Fourth Republic whose structural inability to move towards any political solution became ever more clear after the fall of Mollet. An additional factor to complicate the internal French political scene was the prospect of Saharan oil, due to begin to flow in January 1958. The prospect was in fact later to prove an over-estimate, but at the time it appeared a great opportunity to strengthen the French economy and end the worsening imbalance of payments caused largely by fuel imports. Retention of Algeria seemed ever more important. The Bourgès-Maunoury government accordingly prepared a framework law, *loi cadre*, developing Lacoste's ideas of a new cantonal structure for Algeria, a 'divide-and-rule' policy in which each canton the majority race, under a French official, would control administration. Later, on the return of peace, it was proposed that an all-Algerian assembly should be elected on a common franchise. The whole was to remain linked to France, presided over by a French official, with France retaining direct control over defence, foreign affairs, justice, education and major economic subjects.

The FLN inevitably rejected these proposals as did the Algerian *colons*, who tried to stage a general strike – of *colons* – a move thwarted by Massu's parachute troops. Fatal to the proposed *loi cadre*, however, was its defeat in the Paris *Chambre*, where *colon* links and, significantly, Soustelle, ensured Right-wing support for rejection on 30 September. Bourgès-Maunoury resigned, and a second interregnum, this time over a month, followed during which several political leaders tried in vain to form an administration. Eventually, on 5 November Gaillard succeeded in forming a new government. In this administration the Centre-Right MRP returned to reinforce the old non-Poujadist, non-Gaullist Right. As a whole the government marked a limited swing to the Right, although it still perforce included Socialists. Overall in domestic political terms the year 1957, with its criticism of the conduct of operations, the moral issues, and the absence of any clear political direction fatally undermined what was left of the credibility of the Fourth Republic. The mood in Paris was uneasy and irritable.

The irritability expressed itself in xenophobic reaction to the mounting foreign, especially British and American, criticism of French actions in Algeria. It was alleged that Britain had supplied rifles to the FLN, but the weapons were in fact ones seized by the Egyptians in the former British Suez Canal bases. A small supply of British rifles and American helicopters sent to Tunisia – to avert a Soviet offer – was similarly denounced. American designs on Algeria's oil were suspected, not without some justification. In America herself two very articulate FLN spokesmen, Abdelkader Chanderli and Mohammed Yazid, toured college campuses and lobbied political figures and journalists with notable effect. Early in 1957 the United States, trying to retain French support for the Western military and diplomatic stance in the Cold War, had blocked a hostile Afro-Asian UN resolution demanding a General Assembly discussion on Algeria. But this American attitude was to be modified as the year progressed and the administration came under criticism, as a result of the work of Chanderli and Yazid. Their most successful convert was Senator J.F. Kennedy, who in a major speech called for self-determination; his criticism did more than anything else to secure the shift in American policy away from supporting France to a policy of abstaining. Elsewhere the FLN enjoyed easier propaganda success; at a Cairo Afro-Asian conference the FLN were fully recognized, and contacts with other Moslem countries, the Soviet Union and China were all developed.

By the end of 1957, then, France was blocked in every direction. Military severity had destroyed any chance that might have remained of a dialogue with moderate Moslems. The constitution and politics of the Fourth Republic aborted any liberal political initiative.

Internationally France was now deserted, even by her major NATO allies. As in other crises in her history, France was to turn next to a strong man.

8 ALGERIA, 1958

The opening months of 1958 saw events that were to prove the catalysts for the dramas in the month of May; as will have been seen earlier, implosion had become inevitable.

THE FALL OF THE FOURTH REPUBLIC

On the political stage the Gaillard government secured the approval of the *Chambre* for a version of Bourgès-Maunoury's *loi cadre*; the version was, however, mutilated to appease the *colons* and was therefore valueless in practical terms. Increasingly, both in France and Algeria, thoughts were turning to Charles de Gaulle, seen as the one strong man who could resolve the Algerian problem – though there were even at this stage differing ideas as to how he might actually do this.

De Gaulle had, of course, the enormous prestige of his achievements in the war years as his major asset; no other military or political figure in France, not even Marshal Juin, could approach this. He had from 1946 distanced himself from the politics of the Fourth Republic, repeatedly making the point that it was the system, the *régime d'Assemblée*, that was at fault and responsible for all of France's misfortunes, including Algeria. This criticism remained consistently misunderstood, generally represented by de Gaulle's opponents as thirst for personal power and an authoritarian regime. But such a regime was never de Gaulle's aim. He continued simply to argue for an executive strong enough to determine and carry out policies, with both the executive and the policies chosen by the electorate in free elections. He flatly refused to consider any return to power unless invited and with evidence of general popular support. He was now sixty-seven, no longer the slim figure of 1940 and with short sight as a result of cataract.

De Gaulle was a northern Frenchman, his gaze looked north and east to Europe rather than to the Mediterranean and Africa. Unusually for a French officer, he had also never served in either North or Black Africa. After the First World War, in which he had spent many years in a German prisoner-of-war camp, de Gaulle had opted to go to Poland with the French military mission to fight the Bolsheviks, rather than to Morocco where de Lattre, Juin and later Leclerc all participated in one or other of the pacification campaigns. The Second World War years had left de Gaulle both with a profound distrust of the Algerian *colons* and an ability before long to recognize a freedom fighter when he saw one. In sum, de Gaulle had no personal emotional ties with Africa or Empire to skew him from realistic thinking.

For de Gaulle, what mattered was the international standing and influence of France, with a recognized great power status equal to either Britain or the United States at the United Nations and in world international relations, and a Napoleonic leadership role in a *Europe des Patries*. If Empire served to reinforce this great power assertion, then Empire should be preserved. But if imperial wars weakened France, as a last resort, losses might have to be cut, though offers of autonomy or other status within the Union should first be attempted. Manpower and resources needed to be committed to technologically based industries in order to modernize France, not to support collapsing colonial structures. Some prescient military officers thought in similar terms; nuclear weaponry was now more important than Maghreb *Tirailleurs*. In his pre-1958 utterances on North African questions de Gaulle had remained delphic. At the height of the Moroccan crisis he had recalled that the Sultan held the Order of the Liberation, he had been critical of the deposition and he had commended Mendès-France's Declaration of Carthage. In respect of Algeria he had openly commended General de la Bollardière for his criticisms of the excesses in Algeria. More significant, certain informal remarks made by de Gaulle in the years 1955 to 1958 suggest that he envisaged at least emancipation, if not independence, for Algeria.[1] He very carefully never committed himself to any policy for Algeria in any public statement.

The first of the catalytic events of 1958 was a French air raid on a town in Tunisia, just across the border from Algeria. Under the independence arrangements France still maintained troops in Tunisia, and President Bourguiba, despite all the stresses of the Algerian campaign and the denunciations of Nasser from Cairo, retained his basically francophile policy – no easy achievement when armed ALN troops in

---

1 A selection of these appear in Frank Giles, *The Locust Years, the Story of the Fourth French Republic* (London, Secker & Warburg, 1991), p.291. Examples include 'Algeria is not France' and 'Tunisia and Morocco will soon have their independence, and so will Algeria'.

his country outnumbered his own Army and the CCE was in exile in his own capital. He and King Mohammed V of Morocco had twice offered to act as mediators between France and the Algerian nationalists; on both occasions France had turned down the offer, Gaillard in October 1957 flatly rejecting any idea of Algerian independence.

In January 1958 in three incidents near the border, the French Army took casualties from ALN units clearly based in Tunisia; in riposte on 8 February the French Air Force destroyed the small town of Sakiet, hospital, school, market and homes, killing more than 80 Tunisians, including women and children. Gaillard and Lacoste both denied responsibility, others openly blamed an out-of-control military command. This charge was widely resented amongst Army officers, especially as it coincided with some limited reduction in the number of troops deployed as an economy measure, but in Tunisia, General Gambiez, the French commander, behaved as if Tunisia was still French, arresting Tunisian officials whom he regarded as obstructive. A wider range of Army officers than just the new school colonels now felt let down by the political establishment.

Sakiet received the widest publicity, photographs of dead women and limbless children appearing in the world's press. Bourguiba ordered the departure of the remaining small bodies of French troops in the border area of Tunisia, and virtually sealed off the French garrison at Bizerta; he also protested against French aggression to the UN Security Council. Britain and America tried to defuse the crisis, offering a 'good offices' mission of two diplomats, one from each country, to restore Franco-Tunisian relations. The Gaillard government reluctantly accepted this offer, but the mission achieved little real success. It was also widely believed in France that the United States hoped the good offices mission would provide the Americans with an opportunity to intervene and mediate very much further in the Algerian conflict. From different positions, senior officers and Moslem Algerians wondered whether the good offices mission was not the prelude to negotiation and withdrawal.

A press campaign against the mission, presented as 'foreign interference' was opened, as a consequence of which the campaign moved to the legislature. There the Communists, Poujadists and the Right all voted to force the resignation of the Gaillard government on 15 April. There followed yet another interregnum. The reasons for this were that the Socialists were still pivotal but unwilling to join any new coalition unless policies for Algeria were liberalized, and the holding of cantonal elections for which the nomination of a Right-wing prime minister could be seen as strengthening the Right in the elections.

Attempts to form a government by two Right-of-Centre figures, Bidault and Pleven, both failed for this latter reason, as they led to combined Socialist and Communist opposition.

Eventually Pflimlin, an MRP member of Leftward inclination, was invited by President Coty on 8 May to form a government. He finally cobbled together the tottering Fourth Republic's last government on 13 May, all in the relative cool of Paris. By this time, however, events in Algeria reflecting the emotive, fevered temperament of the *colons* and the disillusion of the officers, all now heightened by hot winds blowing in from the desert, were fast overtaking any such government.

In Algiers, restlessness, and at least a dozen very varied conspiracies, were fuelled to flashpoint by the hiatus in Paris. Many thought a return to power of de Gaulle would give the new-school colonels the powers they sought, but others thought the military should have these powers without de Gaulle. These included the populist bar-owner Ortiz, who had been active on the streets in 1956, the twenty-seven-year-old student leader Lagaillarde, fresh from his period of conscription with the parachute troops, and the influential de Sérigny, the Pétainist editor of Algeria's leading newspaper. As notably vocal supporters of de Gaulle, Debré and Chaban-Delmas were prominent in Paris, with in Algiers the leader of the Ex-servicemen's Association, Sanguinetti, and a prominent *colon* lawyer of Corsican origin and passion, Biaggi; these latter had contacts with one or other of the conspiracies. In both metropolitan France and Algeria ex-servicemen's associations were particularly active in the cause of keeping Algeria French.[2] In Algiers a mass demonstration of *colons* calling for a government of public safety took place on 26 April.[3] Pflimlin very unwisely let Salan know that he proposed to ask Morocco and Tunisia to mediate, and he was widely believed by the *colons* to want to negotiate with the FLN. The prospect of Pflimlin as Prime Minister secured an important conversion to the de Gaulle cause, de Sérigny and his newspaper. In addition, as an immediate local drama, on 9 May the FLN executed three French soldiers whom they had captured; this event led Salan to send a signal to the Army Chief of Staff General Ely, demanding of the French President, in the name of the Army, a government that would never surrender Algeria. Lacoste, in despair, departed for Paris to see President Coty. Then on 13 May a frenzied *colon* mob led by Lagaillarde seized the main government

2 Detailed accounts, with descriptions of the supporting casts of the various groupings, appear in Giles, *Locust Years*, chapters x and xi; and Alistair Horne, *A Savage War of Peace: Algeria 1954–1962* (London, Macmillan, 1987), chapter xii.

3 The original inspiration for the march of the mob came from a group of Gaullist conspirators; it was, however, taken over by Lagaillarde and his followers.

buildings in Algiers, having sacked the American Cultural Centre on the way. Men from the parachute regiments stood by watching, taking no action. *Colon* cars in the city streets beat out 'Algérie Française' – three short and two long blasts – on their horns. Salan was booed and Massu cheered, to his fury as he was above all a disciplined, professional soldier.

With the tacit acquiescence of Salan, Massu then drew up a list of a 'Committee of Public Safety', himself, three parachute colonels, Lagaillarde and other front men from the mob; these were announced to the rapturous crowd.[4] Other local public safety committees appeared elsewhere, but not everywhere, in Algeria. Massu next despatched an open signal to Paris where Pflimlin was barely installed, demanding a government of public safety in Paris also, to safeguard Algeria. Later that day, Salan sent a message to Paris urging the appointment of a 'high arbitrator', an oblique reference to de Gaulle. Pflimlin dithered, on the one hand giving Salan supreme power to maintain order in Algeria and on the other arresting one or two officers in Paris and placing Soustelle under surveillance. On the next day Pflimlin made plans to cut off supplies from Algeria, a move which was followed by Salan discarding his ambiguity and, at a large public gathering on the fifteenth, openly calling for de Gaulle.[5] In Paris a senior general, Challe, moved much of the air transport service to Algeria and also declared for de Gaulle, for which he was arrested. At this point, de Gaulle announced publicly that he was prepared to assume power if invited; his offer represented his fear that otherwise the country would slide into anarchy or military dictatorship.

On the sixteenth huge, excited crowds again thronged the centre of Algiers; among them were very large numbers of Moslems openly fraternizing with the *colons*. Their presence was in part the result of encouragement by the Vᵉ *Bureaux* staff but was also a reflection of the general euphoria of all, that at last the horrors of recent months might be coming to an end. On the next day, the seventeenth, Soustelle arrived after a dramatic escape from his surveillance, to fuel still further the hysteria and excitement. Soustelle's return and enormous popularity with the *colons* closed one option that Salan had still been considering, returning to token obedience to Pflimlin and arresting the Committee of Public Safety. To add to Pflimlin's difficulties, General Ely, a Gaullist, resigned from his post as Chief of Staff of the Army in protest against

4 The committee was later expanded to a total of 74 as more members, some very strange, of various other conspiracies decided that this was to be the successful one.

5 Salan, unlike Massu, was not a Gaullist. Some evidence suggests that at the start of his speech he had not intended to mention de Gaulle by name, but was prompted to do so.

the arrest of Challe, and a Left-wing strike designed to demonstrate opposition to de Gaulle failed. Pflimlin's Right-wing ministers began to talk of resignation.

Salan next warned Paris that he might not be able to prevent military units from Algeria arriving in France; this point was emphasized when, on his orders, detachments from parachute regiments began to arrive in Corsica.[6] In Toulouse General Miquel, whose hard-line views had been evident in Morocco in 1955, was also assembling a force of parachute troops. Salan was now openly in revolt. Paris, it appeared, would be the next stop, the combined force assembling at an airfield near the capital. Salan, addressing another vast crowd, talked of marching up the Champs Elysées covered with flowers. On the twenty-third he also reorganized the Committee of Public Safety to include Soustelle together with a few token Moslems. Tension rose during the Whitsun holiday weekend of 25–26 May. Parachute regiments officers were seen in Paris. Pflimlin toyed with a plan to recapture Corsica but was advised that troops might refuse to act. Mollet spoke to the British ambassador of the dangers of a 'French Franco'. He attempted to mediate between Pflimlin and de Gaulle; the latter still insisted on a formal constitutional and not military invitation to accept power, though he noticeably refused to disavow the take-over of Corsica or to restrain the military. Both Salan in Algiers and de Gaulle in Paris were throughout much concerned that there should be no split within the Army.

At this point, in despair and exhaustion, Pflimlin resigned. Despite a several hundred-thousand-strong anti-military demonstration in which Mendès-France and Mitterrand both figured, President Coty decided that it was not unconstitutional to appoint a prime minister from outside the legislature. His thoughts were concentrated for him by an ultimatum from Algiers to the effect that if de Gaulle were not appointed, the parachute troops would act. Accordingly, on the twenty-ninth Coty formally invited de Gaulle to accept the prime ministership, and added that if the Assembly refused to approve de Gaulle, he would resign his own presidency. On 1 June, the Communists vociferously protesting, de Gaulle was voted into power by a majority of 329 to 224 votes.[7] Legitimacy was thus secured; de Gaulle was not beholden to the Army.

6 Corsica possessed an especial symbolic significance. It had been the first region of France to be liberated in September 1943. This seizure was accordingly portrayed as a second 'liberation'.

7 Some cautious wooing of the Socialists by de Gaulle in the previous week ensured that just under half of the Socialist deputies voted for him. These included Mollet. Mitterrand was one of those who opposed de Gaulle, Mendès-France another.

With hindsight, the Algerian crisis need not have destroyed the Fourth Republic so easily; the passions that were to bring France close to civil war were not yet fully inflamed. People still believed some form of acceptable settlement could be reached and Algeria would not have to be totally abandoned. De Gaulle certainly used the military threat to his advantage, but there is no substantial evidence to support allegations that he would have backed any coup.[8] The reality of the military threat, Operation *Résurrection*, was much less strong than it appeared. The plotters certainly hoped that the drama of the threat would be adequate, without the necessity of action that might have led to bloodshed. Even if the generals had been willing to translate show into action the conscript soldiers in France and Algeria might well have refused to participate, as was to be the case in 1961. The two most noteworthy conclusions from the whole affair remain that of the events' illustration of the structural weakness of the Fourth Republic, and the extraordinary naivety, soon to be dispelled, of the generals' and colonels' beliefs, both that de Gaulle would act as they wished and that conscript soldiers would obey illegal commands.

Within the French Army as a whole, the attitude was generally one of 'wait and see'. Those who admired de Gaulle's activities in the war years were cautiously optimistic that he would find a solution to Algeria's problems. Those who were critical of de Gaulle in the war were, from the start, guarded and suspicious. Personnel from elite forces who had had a hard war in Indochina looked at de Gaulle's portly figure and commented sceptically that it was easy to see that he had not 'done Indochina'.

DE GAULLE'S INITIAL MOVES

De Gaulle had demanded certain conditions for his assumption of power – full powers for six months in which he could rule by decree and full powers in respect of Algeria; that the legislature take a four months break; and that he could present a new constitution to the country, ending the *régime d'Assemblée*. His first cabinet included Mollet, Pflimlin and Pinay, but significantly neither Soustelle nor any of the other *Algérie Française* vocalists. His early policy statements did not give any indication of his thought on Algeria and certainly no support for the new-school colonels.

8 Some years after these events a general, Jouhaud, alleged that de Gaulle was initially in favour of the military coup. Jouhaud was, however, one of those involved in the 1961 anti-de Gaulle conspiracy and this allegation needs to be treated with great caution.

Different opinions exist as to the precise views of de Gaulle on the Algerian question at this point. His character was complex, his views almost certainly equally so. He certainly believed that his own personal prestige would carry more lasting weight with Moslem opinion than just the euphoria of the crowd on 16 May. It seems likely that he still hoped that time, military success, and constructive economic and social reform could retain an emancipated Algeria in some 'association' linkage with France, though he was also aware that at his age he might have at some stage to act quickly. For this, at the political level it would be best at first to listen and remain uncommitted, and at the local and military level appoint officials in accord with his views, while initially firmly re-asserting authority and discipline. Several hundred officers, including some from the parachute regiments, were posted out of Algiers, many out of Algeria. An exception was Massu, a trusted follower of de Gaulle from the summer of 1940. In Paris General Ely was reinstated.

This interpretation seems justified by de Gaulle's initial actions in 1958. Almost immediately, on 4 June, he visited Algeria. He received a tumultuous reception from the Algiers crowd; his reply was totally non-committal. With arms outstretched in a V-sign he opened by saying, 'Je vous ai compris', on this occasion perhaps best translated by the Americanism 'I hear you', and then talked briefly on the theme of reconciliation, with a guarded reference to equal rights for all 'Frenchmen in the full sense'. Only at his final stop, Mostaganem, and there perhaps only inadvertently, did he utter the words *Algérie Française*, words that he never repeated. Predictably, each interest in Algeria chose to believe he supported them. No immediate replacement for Lacoste was announced, Salan assuming an acting civilian authority as well as his military command. The local committees of public safety were dissolved, though not that in Algiers for the territory as a whole.

Policy was slow to unfold despite several further visits by de Gaulle to Algeria; the FLN were able to allege that nothing really had changed. In the late summer de Gaulle unveiled his proposed package for France and the French Union. For France a new constitution was to redress the balance in favour of the executive against the legislature.[9]

---

9 The new constitution institutionalized the control of all external affairs, de Gaulle's main interest, by the President while giving greater powers in domestic matters to the Prime Minister, who was to be appointed by the President. Ministers were no longer members of the Assembly. The President was to be chosen by a very large electoral college of members of local government bodies; the college was weighted in favour of the rural areas.

For the black African colonies 'Association' was openly proposed, to provide internal autonomy, including locally raised gendarmerie forces for internal security, but with France responsible for defence and external affairs.[10] Behind this proposal, as in fact he was later to admit as the main reason for it, was de Gaulle's hope that 'Association' might also solve the Algerian dilemma. Algeria was invited to vote on the constitution, all adults, men and women voting in a single college in what was in effect a vote of confidence in de Gaulle. Despite all the propaganda efforts of the FLN, de Gaulle received this in a very free election – 76.4 per cent of the total electorate, 96.6 per cent of those who voted. De Gaulle also secured a similar large majority in France herself.

The next step was de Gaulle's announcement in early October of a massive five-year programme, the Constantine plan, for economic and social development; 400,000 jobs to be created in light industry, 200,000 houses to be built; 250,000 hectares of land made available to Moslems; salaries and wages to be raised to French levels; an ambitious education scheme to cover two-thirds of the Moslem children. Although the plan met with some hitches, the standard of living of Moslems in cities increased dramatically, and many more Moslems served in the administration or in local government. *Colon* disquiet was evident, especially after de Gaulle's observation that he expected two-thirds of the deputies from Algeria in his new Assembly to be Moslems.

The Constantine plan was followed by a first amnesty for detained rebels, further releases were promised and all death sentences were commuted. On 23 October de Gaulle offered a *paix des braves* amnesty for insurgents who gave themselves up, an offer that was promptly rejected by the FLN, and further enraged the *colons*. The failure of the offer caused de Gaulle much distress; it was, however, for him a step towards realizing the full determination of his opponents.

The last formal political step of 1958, also unsuccessful, was the November elections under the new Fifth Republic Constitution. Of the 71 Algerian deputies elected to the Assembly, 48 were avowed supporters of the French link; they had been 'elected by the Army'. These neither convinced a sceptical de Gaulle that they truly represented Moslem support for *Algérie Française*, nor were they drawn from the rapidly diminishing number of men brave enough to declare themselves moderate nationalists with whom the French could negotiate. Further,

10 All accepted this offer except Guinea; in the event, nationalist pressures were such that flag independence with treaties of co-operation followed two years later.

they aroused apprehensions among metropolitan Frenchmen at the influence they might wield in a balance-of-power situation. Their presence simply obscured the issues. Delouvrier, an able and honest metropolitan administrator appointed in October to succeed Lacoste with the new title of Delegate-General, was not deluded. When asked by de Gaulle, after an acquaintance visit to Algeria, what he thought for the future, he replied that Algeria would be independent. De Gaulle needed all his powers of persuasion to ensure that Delouvrier would accept the post.

Finally, and in the conditions of the greatest secrecy, de Gaulle attempted to make contact with the FLN leadership through an intermediary, the former president of the Algerian Assembly, a Moslem. These attempts, although pursued into the autumn, proved abortive ostensibly because de Gaulle sought discussions in Paris but in reality because the FLN adhered rigidly to the Soummam Valley war aims.[11] They were little impressed by de Gaulle's ill-defined policies, but were very concerned at his prestige and apparent impact upon the Moslem population. De Gaulle's accession to power coincided also with a serious loss of ALN morale. The heavy casualties taken by the ALN on the Morice Line and the inability of the external FLN to supply arms across the Line, the effect of leadership quarrels and the murder of Abane on the rank and file, and general war-weariness were all taking a toll.

To counter this attrition, a Provisional Government of the Algerian Republic (GPRA), headed by the veteran nationalist leader Ferhat Abbas, was set up in Tunis on 19 September, and it was as head of this government that Ferhat rejected de Gaulle's attempts to make contact and, later, the *paix des braves*. The GPRA went on to denounce the November polls as a 'colonialist election' and the Constantine plan as a new form of colonialism. Within the GPRA real power lay in the hands of the War Minister, Krim, together with Tobbal and Boussouf, though Ben Bella (still in prison) was made a Vice-President; Ferhat Abbas was used as a 'front man' to appeal to moderates and the French Left. The newly formed GPRA sent a delegation to Peking and Moscow in December.

The second course of action taken to revive flagging morale and enthusiasm, a campaign of bombings and assassinations in France herself, proved a tactical mistake. The targets were primarily Algerians who supported the French or the MNA, or armed services or police personnel. A number of fuel storage tanks were set ablaze and there

11 Horne, *Savage War*, p.319, notes these contacts.

was some railway sabotage; an attempt to place limpet bombs under a battleship in Toulon failed, as did an attempt to assassinate Soustelle in the heart of Paris. More than 80 people were killed between 24 August and 28 September, when the campaign was called off. It was proving counter-productive, alienating French sympathizers and attracting efficient police attention not only to the terrorists themselves but to the vital clandestine fund-raising organization.

MILITARY OPERATIONS

In the meantime, in the rough *bled* of the rural and mountain areas of Algeria, the war continued, the French pressure on the ALN intensifying. An ALN attempt to take advantage of French disarray in mid-May led to sharp clashes in which the French lost 300 killed, including Colonel Jeanpierre of the *Légion*, the captor of Yacef; the ALN, however, lost at least twice that number.

The French Army's aim was now increasingly to root out the OPA cell structure of the FLN in order to prevent recrudescence rather than simply to kill insurgents. More systematic training for Algerian conditions at all levels from Staff College to recruit training had vastly improved efficiency and raised morale. Of the Army, only 18 months previous, one officer had written, 'eighty percent of the units are dirty, slack and ill-disciplined. Their attitude to the civilian population oscillated between supine weakness and the most reprehensible violence, pillage and collective torture.'[12] Control was now exercised. Officers culpable of atrocities were punished, and slack officers who believed that they had pacified areas that were in fact left alone by the ALN for use as recuperation zones removed. Regiments which saw their role as simply sitting inside a fortified camp were bestirred. *Quadrillage* developed from simple protection to engagement and control. Units were moved less often, and so learnt more of their area and its personalities for intelligence purpose. Areas cleared were not allowed to become complacent, and an enormous effort was made in road building to surmount the logistic problems that Algeria's mountainous terrain presented.

Training – including emphasis on long mountain marches in extremes of heat and cold, and ambush and cordon-and-search operations by night without artillery support – paid off. Practice increased skill in unearthing ALN refuges in underground hides, caves and

12 François Porteu de la Morandière, *Soldats du Djebel* (Paris, Société de Production Littéraire, n.d.), p.168, quoting Colonel Argoud.

grottoes.[13] When insurgents were caught, they – or, if dead, their corpses – would be displayed in their home areas as a warning. The intelligence war, too, became more coolly professional, the French use of turned ALN members as double agents continuing to yield good results, and with the use by both sides of signals intelligence. The ALN set up intercept units on the Moroccan and Tunisian frontiers to monitor signals traffic; the French became aware of this and on occasions used developed disinformation tactics. The French also continued 'hot pursuit' operations on occasions into Tunisia. In May, after the events in Algiers, they occupied a post in southern Tunisia. Bourguiba again demanded a complete French military withdrawal, which de Gaulle conceded except in respect of Bizerta.

Occasional FLN bombing still occurred; one isolated example in Algiers occurred in June, when 19 people, mostly Moslems, were killed. In July the ALN were freed from one threat, Bellounis's men, now grandiloquently styling themselves as the Algerian National Popular Army. After some successes against the ALN in *Wilaya* 6, power appears to have turned the balance of Bellounis's mind. He and his men embarked on mass killings which the French could not control and had the effect of pushing people back into the FLN camp. It was decided to disarm him and his men, and in July this was achieved. Bellounis himself and some of his followers resisted; in the course of the fighting Bellounis was killed. In late August and September the ALN embarked upon a fresh campaign of attacks, averaging 50 to 60 per week against Moslem notables in an attempt to deter Moslems from voting; in this overall aim they were unsuccessful. On 1 November, to mark the anniversary of the outbreak of the uprising, a large force attempted to break through the Morice line; the force was massacred by the powerful French defences. Later in the month the commander of *Wilaya* 4, Si Azedine, was caught.

The frustrations and strain caused by these successive failures, at a time of apparent numerical strength, further eroded ALN morale.[14] Defections to the French increased in number, unit sizes had to reduce, a *katiba* might now only number 40 or fewer. There was a growing shortage of weapons following French successes in recovery. Vendettas

13 One odd example of the skills needed arose from the habit of ALN insurgents who had hidden in a hide for long periods of time to conceal the tell-tale odour with patchouli.

14 The precise strength of the ALN is impossible to assess accurately. The French estimated that there were some 30,000 full-time insurgents in the field in early 1958. Of this total some 15,000 were active at any one time. There were in addition, the French calculated, a further 30,000 auxiliaries. The GPRA claimed a total of 100,000 under arms.

broke out among ALN commanders, with angry quarrels over tactics, strategy, political direction and personalities. The Morice line disaster led to a conspiracy of four colonels who plotted to take out the GPRA. Their plans became known and the four were given a brief field trial and then executed in Tunisia.[15] The vendettas were occasionally stimulated by the French, whose intelligence staffs would fake letters apparently compromising ALN field commanders and arrange for these to be captured by other commanders. The only real encouragement that existed for the ALN was the developing strength and efficiency of its units across the border in Tunisia. There, with the units waiting for the opportunity of profit from a French collapse and ensure that victory would reward the external FLN, military leadership had passed to the ALN's new Chief of Staff, Houari Boumedienne, a single minded and highly intelligent guerrilla leader. Boumedienne had won his spurs first as adjutant to Boussouf in *Wilaya 5*, and then as that *Wilaya*'s commander.

In military terms the ALN appeared near total defeat at the end of 1958. In political and international terms, however, the FLN remained unbeaten. The mix of effective propaganda, the establishment of the GPRA and the on-going fighting in Algeria, combining in the new strategy in which political activity might outweigh military action, kept the FLN and Algeria on the forefront of the international stage. The political activity was doubly needed. First, the war-weariness of the ALN was beginning to be reflected in a war-weariness among the external suppliers of aid and weaponry. Second, in propaganda work for the GPRA, a major handicap had been the large number of Moslem voters in the September referendum. In the United States Yazid and Chanderli had a difficult, but in the circumstances relatively successful, year.

A measure of the success achieved was that the UN General Assembly only narrowly voted down a resolution recognizing the right of the Algerian people to independence. The Arab countries and China had recognized and supported the GPRA. Britain and the United States attempted a policy of balance by neither recognizing the GPRA nor supporting the French at the United Nations. This policy fuelled de Gaulle's opposition to the Anglo-American hegemony in NATO within which only Adenauer, a fellow Catholic, was sympathetic to de Gaulle. On the lowest level of self-interest was the policy of Khrushchev's Soviet Union, which deliberately declined to recognize the GPRA for

15 Horne, *Savage War*, p.326, believes this group of four colonels were supported by Nasser in Egypt; Nasser was not in agreement with the GPRA.

fear of irritating either de Gaulle, whom Khrushchev hoped to decouple from NATO, or the French Communist Party.[16]

In October Massu and all Army officers were directed to leave the Committee of Public Safety, the committee itself being wound up a little later. In December, somewhat abruptly, Salan was recalled to a metropolitan command that he resented as inferior. The reason for his recall appears to have been de Gaulle's irritation over the Moslem deputies 'elected by the Army'. Allard was also recalled, but to stifle hard-line criticism de Gaulle promoted Massu to command the Algiers Corps. A new Commander-in-Chief, Challe, was appointed in his place. Challe arrived in Algiers with Delouvrier, carefully walking behind him to make it clear to all that civilian authority predominated. But under Challe the field war was to enter a new phase.

16 Ho Chi Minh had, of course, received the same treatment from Stalin; see Chapter 3, footnote 9, *supra*.

9 ALGERIA, 1959–62

The last three years of French rule in Algeria are ones of paradox and dramatic reversal of fortune. At the end of 1958 the ALN were approaching military defeat; by mid-1959 that defeat was almost total. Yet by July 1962 Algeria was independent, the FLN in control and French troops and *colons* in hurried evacuation to France.

Five themes lie behind the events that follow. The first was the illusory nature of the French military success; although the Army's spectacular 1959 operations squeezed the ALN into virtual extinction, the success solved none of the political problems. Second, the FLN's political offensive both in Algeria and on the international stage, helped by French errors, slowly turned the tables; the FLN saw more clearly than the French that the war was no longer – if it ever had been – primarily about killing people, but about public opinion, particularly in the metropole. Third, certain French officers, those of the new counter-revolutionary warfare school who did see the war in political terms, returned to their May 1958 conclusion that they must have full political control in order to fight the campaign successfully. The Army's apparent military success added edge to this view; these officers believed they had already won, and at all costs that victory must be made secure, or the Communists would be the winners. Fourth, as the possibility of total withdrawal, abandonment, of Algeria seemed to become more real, passions rose and divided French society almost to the point of civil war. Lastly, the formidable personality of de Gaulle, now with the added legitimacy of being an elected President, saw behind the military success; he came to see that the divisions in the French nation were assuming the proportions of the Dreyfus case or of 1940; he recognized the enormous cost in money and the (albeit reduced) cost in men killed; acutely conscious of French prestige he could not accept the harm done to the international standing of France, a price he judged that the wider interests of France should not support for any length of time.[1] War-weariness was becoming increasingly evident in the metropole.

[1] An additional complicating factor was demographic. As a result of the Second World War years, far fewer men were available for conscription.

CHALLE'S MILITARY RE-ASSERTION

It seems that, in appointing Challe and authorizing new offensive operations, de Gaulle sought a final round of visible military success, and that success was to be under his regime, to strengthen his position in any negotiations with the FLN. He may also have had the desirability of keeping the Army occupied in his mind, and perhaps even the prestige factor of letting the Army achieve victory as a sugar coating to the pill of inevitable political negotiations.

Challe himself was an Air Force general with an outstanding war record; in contrast to the wily Salan, his personality was open and frank. He approached the military problem of Algeria with a fresh mind. His plan, received at first with scepticism by the soldiers, provided for a reduction in the number of units employed in *quadrillage*, the personnel being replaced by an increased number of *harkis*, an extension of the free-fire zones, and even more aggressive pursuit group operations. These were first to be mounted as before by elite units from the general reserve, now commanded by General Gracieux. The reserve could be more flexible and arrive in strength much more quickly using the big new Boeing Vertol H21 helicopters, *les bananes*, as they were called from their banana shape, which began to enter service in 1958 and were now available in quantity. The general reserve regiments, after they had destroyed or split up large groups of insurgents, were to be followed and replaced on the ground by *commandos de chasse*.[2] These commandos were tasked to pursue small parties of five or six insurgent survivors relentlessly, by day and night; they were guided by *harkis* with local knowledge. They were meant to live like the insurgents and learn their preferred itineraries and refuges. They proved exceedingly effective; ALN members on the run could not cook hot food – despite the cold of Algeria's mountains; often they could not speak above a whisper for days or even weeks. Crude medical facilities were occasionally to be found in remote areas; more often no medical help for the ALN injured and sick was available at all. Those insurgents not destroyed in these two phases were also to be harried by day and night air-to-ground fire, guns, bombs and rockets from any aircraft available. In particular, Challe used Second World War American Harvard trainers, which type the British had used in a similar role with success in Kenya. The lift capacity of the big helicopters also enabled artillery to be lifted

---

2 These reflected Indochina experience, the sorties of *commandos d'intervalle*. A special training course for *commando* commanders was instituted and over 80 *commandos* formed.

in to support the general reserve elite units. From a field headquarters, with advanced field signal communications and intelligence-gathering equipment and special staffs, Challe exercised personal command and control.

These tactics were applied in a series of operations across Algeria from west to east, in order to squeeze the ALN against the Morice line. Opening with *Couronne* in the Oran hinterland area in February 1959, in which 1,600 ALN were killed and 460 captured, Challe moved east to the Algiers hinterland with *Courvoie* in April to June. For July he organized the double-pronged *Jumelles* for the Kabyles, but with remarkable flexibility switched units to the Hodna in an operation called *Etincelles* following intelligence reports. Controlling this area secured his flank for his return to the Kabyles, cleared by October with 3,746 ALN killed; finally followed *Pierres Précieuses*, a series of operations in the North Constantine beginning in November. There were also numerous smaller local sweeps, all serving to break up not only the insurgent units but also the OPA cells as well, by the extensive use of double agents.

The manpower deployed in Challe's major operations was massive. For *Jumelles*, for example, 25,000 troops were committed in addition to those already in the area and a few *fusiliers-marins* units used for amphibious operations. Only two or three major British operations in Malaya engaged 12,000 men, at the most; in Kenya, the largest sweeps only engaged two brigades, 5,000 men. For even the smaller sweeps Challe would commit 10 or more battalions, often for two weeks at a time.

A successful signals interception led to the capture of a *Wilaya 5* leader; the French then ran a fake substitute, thereby capturing arms, ammunition and money for several months until the deception was recognized. By mid-1959 the ALN was shattered, able only to mount occasional attacks on individual *colons* or Moslem loyalists, or occasional acts of sabotage, so giving the French the lowest incident rate of the war. The French Army casualties in the fighting, too, were small, an average of one-tenth of those of the ALN. In sum, Challe's 1959 operations will always remain one of classic counter-insurgency field campaigning.

Once Challe's formidable war machine had cleared an area, SAS detachments arrived for administration and welfare work, roads were built and attempts made to restore shattered rural economies. But these efforts could not compensate for one of the few weaknesses of the Challe plan; several hundred thousand more people had to be moved against their will for the expansion of the free-fire zones, bringing the total moved to 1½ million. The initial arrangements were appalling, with once again, overcrowded and insanitary camps, malnutrition and disease. Only towards the end of the year and following press criticism in France did conditions improve. By this time the French had in any case secured such control of ground with the increased use of *harkis* that Challe was able to suppress free-fire zones entirely.

The French success resulted in further bickering and recrimination among the *Wilaya* leaders. At the end of 1958 the outstanding leader was perhaps Amirouche in *Wilaya* 3. But Amirouche's ferocity extended to any he suspected of disloyalty, both in his zone of operations and elsewhere. Several hundred were killed for this reason, a sizeable percentage no doubt as a result of French double agents laying false information. In March 1959 Amirouche was tracked down; he narrowly escaped death in an engagement in which 73 of his followers were killed. A week later he was located as a result of a tip-off, probably from someone disgusted by his excesses, in a small Saharan trading centre. The French Army despatched a force of eight-wheeled EBR armoured cars and half-track troop carriers; Amirouche and another insurgent *Wilaya* leader were killed. Six weeks later the leader of *Wilaya* 4, Si M'hamed, disappeared; he too had been excessively ruthless, and it is also uncertain whether he was killed in battle or by disgusted followers. One leader who disinformed the French, however, was Si Azedine, who from captivity was allowed, at his request, to open negotiations with the leaders of *Wilaya* 4. To these leaders he gave intelligence, returning to the French with false information, until he chose to escape completely and rejoin the ALN.

'SELF-DETERMINATION' AND BARRICADES WEEK

But even at the height of his success Challe was made aware of its limits. In late April de Gaulle's Prime Minister, Debré, directed him to effect economies in both logistics and manpower, and on a visit to Challe's field headquarters on 30 August de Gaulle commented that military success had not solved the underlying problems. Nor, despite much hard work and much expenditure that were already bringing visible material benefits to thousands of Moslems, was the Constantine Plan any more successful.[3] In his first overt high-policy move towards

3 The plan was most advanced in education expansion, and job creation following light industrial development. It was moving more slowly in terms of land re-allocation; it had made little progress in introducing Moslems into the administration and virtually no progress at all in respect of the administration's senior appointments.

a solution of the Algerian problem, a major speech in September 1959, de Gaulle disclosed his project of the previous year by openly offering Algeria 'self-determination'. He stated that he saw this as a choice between total secession, 'integration' or 'association', making clear that he thought the first disastrous and the second impracticable; 'Association' was described somewhat vaguely as a federal or cantonal Algeria linked to France for economic, military and foreign affairs. At the same time the *paix des braves* offer was repeated – over a period of time achieving some limited success. The self-determination proposal was generally warmly welcomed in France herself, but in Algeria and among a number of senior officers self-determination was seen as confirmation of their growing doubts and misgivings about de Gaulle. Self-determination obviously predicated power to the Moslem majority. Was victory then to be thrown away, and were soldiers to be asked to fight and die for an Algeria that might not remain French? To the FLN the self-determination proposal was welcome evidence that they were winning the political war. Encouraged, the FLN managed to mount a limited offensive of bombing and killing in the Algiers area over the Christmas and New Year period, and a renewed assassination campaign in France itself in 1960 which, in the Paris area, the French met by organizing *harkis* to track down the assassins, sometimes in spectacular shoot-outs.

Colon fear and frustration increased, finding two new political leaders to reinforce Ortiz; these were Perez, a doctor with a record of counter-terrorist vigilante activity including bombing, and Susini, a fiery orator. They formed the *Front National Français* (FNF), encapsulating almost all of the various *colon* groupings with the exception of that following Lagaillarde, and a special 1,000-strong Home Guard force, the *Unités Territoriales de Choc*.[4] Three of the new-warfare-school colonels, Argoud, chief of staff to Massu, Godard, chief of security, and Gardes, of the Ve *Bureaux*, were in contact and sympathy with the FNF, assuring the latter that the parachute troops in Algiers would not open fire in the case of a *coup*. In Paris, Juin attacked de Gaulle's policy in the press.

The crisis broke in January 1960 when Massu gave an interview, full of unguarded criticism of de Gaulle and saying that he would not in all circumstances obey him, to a German journalist. His comments appeared on front pages in Paris.[5] Massu was immediately transferred

4 The style of the FNF was neo-fascist, with a Celtic cross armband; the black-bereted UT *de Choc* were even more sinister.

5 Massu was particularly concerned at the commutation of death sentences on convicted insurgents, and the release of 7,000 detainees, many rejoining the ALN.

out of Algeria by a furious de Gaulle; he was retired for a year before being given another appointment – in France. The occasion gave Ortiz the pretext he needed to try and repeat the street successes of May 1958, and present de Gaulle with a united Army-*Colon* front in control of Algiers. A general strike was called for 24 January, on which occasion Ortiz decided to move; he later claimed that Challe had given him freedom to demonstrate so long as the government headquarters were undisturbed.[6] Large crowds, of *colons* only, appeared in the streets; this time there were no Moslems. Challe's intention was to corral and control these with gendarmes, the parachute regiments not yet having arrived from the hinterland.

In the fevered, hysterical atmosphere violence soon erupted, probably initiated by Ortiz's men, a number of both demonstrators and gendarmes being killed, others wounded. The FNF and the followers of Lagaillarde, confident of success, then set up barricaded 'no-go' areas, soldiers, a number now local by origin, from the parachute regiments fraternizing with them on their arrival. 'Barricades Week' had begun; it was clear that any move against the barricades would result at least in many more deaths and very probably Army unit fighting Army unit. Delouvrier and Challe were pessimistic, and secretly left the city for a nearby air base to the alarm of the *colon* leaders, who saw in their departure plans to rally French regiments for a forcible suppression. In Paris, Juin implored de Gaulle to give way and Debré attempted in vain to resign. De Gaulle remained steady and adamant; he correctly assessed that in France herself both the Army and the general public were behind him. The revolt began to crumble, the *colons'* morale was further undermined by heavy, wintry rain. The process was completed by an immensely powerful speech – de Gaulle's oratory at its best – calling all Frenchmen, civilians and soldiers, to their duties. Pardon was given to rank and file who had supported the insurrection. After final recriminations Ortiz left Algeria for good and Lagaillarde, Susini and others were arrested.[7] The *colons* blamed the military for letting them down.

There followed purges. Three generals, including Faure who, despite his earlier plotting to oust Salan, had been given another command in Algeria, and Gracieux of 10th Parachute Division together with a number of other officers, were posted away. The Parachute Division was withdrawn from the city and much *Vᵉ Bureaux* work stopped.

6 A contributory factor was the fact that Lagaillarde was also preparing a move and had to be pre-empted.

7 They were later tried and given light sentences, except Ortiz, tried *in absentia*, who was sentenced to death.

A protesting Challe was recalled in April for a promotion that he did not want; the recall was almost certainly a mark of de Gaulle's disapproval of Challe's failure to prevent the events. His successor, Crépin, a devotedly loyal Gaullist, was not authorized to carry out the last grand operation in the Aurès that Challe had planned. At the same time a number of detainees were released. De Gaulle, in between cutting an increasingly prestigious figure on the world stage with the explosion of the first French nuclear bomb, a state visit to Britain, and plans for the hosting of a Summit conference, secured himself special powers for a year in respect of Algeria.

POLICY REAPPRAISED

It would seem that, during this first half of 1960, de Gaulle came to the conclusion that the running sore of Algeria had now continued for too long and was delaying the whole process of modernizing France and her Army, and also that if the war were to continue, nation and Army were both in danger of destruction. The passions aroused by the Algerian conflict were bringing the hysteria of the streets of Algiers to the heart of the metropole. For thousands, any independence for Algeria would be abandoning part of the patrimony of France; equally, for other thousands it was the only morally justifiable solution. Except the Communists, every political party, Radicals, MRP, Socialists and the smaller groups were split; the trade-union movement was split, some of its members seeing the hand of Communism in Algeria or fearing for the future of Marseille; the student organizations were as sharply divided; some Catholic leaders saw a Moslem victory in Algeria as a danger equivalent to the Arab conquest of Spain in the seventh and eighth centuries, others saw the violence of the French campaign as a betrayal of Christian standards. Some intellectuals spoke of decadence and the honour of the Army, others argued that the identity of France meant nothing if it did not mean political liberty. Passions were very much nearer to the point of widespread civil conflict, perhaps full civil war, than in 1958, when events had contained an element of posturing. Barricades Week had been a close shave and had exposed cancerous divisions within the army. De Gaulle, if not his generals, could now not fail any longer to see that the war was not one against a rebel leader and army that could be destroyed, but was a never-ending conflict with a movement which if suppressed in one area reappeared elsewhere, and had every appearance of being a genuine movement of national resistance, something de Gaulle could well recognize. So, if negotiations with the FLN could produce a deal, so much the better;

if not, then to avert civil war in France, Algeria would have to go.[8] This was not a line of thinking, however, that in the highly charged political climate could be declared openly. In his tours of the Army in Algeria and elsewhere, and in occasional statements at home and abroad, de Gaulle's choice of words remained ambiguous, even contradictory, sometimes portraying the FLN as a minority group to be fought to the end, which he must have known to be impracticable, sometimes even offering assurance, tailored to his restless military, that he would never negotiate with the GPRA. He also hinted at a retention of French enclaves in Algeria and Oran. All these served their purpose at the time, but later such assurances were to form the basis of accusations of betrayal. Finally for de Gaulle was the personal issue; he was concerned about his age and staying power, the absence of any successor whom he could trust and the successive rumours of palace plots to remove him. His vision of France and all that he had stood for since 1940 were at stake in Algeria; a solution had to be found – quickly.

The FLN, too, were divided. De Gaulle's prestige and the offer of self-determination had in some measure restored France's international reputation. Challe's successes had sharpened divisions between the 'internal' and 'external' leaders. At a secret meeting in December 1959 in Tripoli of the Third National Council of the Algerian Revolution, the GPRA was restructured. Krim, blamed for the military reverses, lost power, becoming Minister for Foreign Affairs. The extreme hard-liner Boumedienne emerged as the most powerful figure as Chief of Staff, in effect Commander in Chief, of forces both internal and external. Krim was, however, partially to redeem himself by a successful funds- and arms-raising visit to Peking, Hanoi and Pyongyang in April 1960. In these capitals the fact that the FLN was not Marxist was overlooked.[9]

The success of the hard-liners in safety outside Algeria was not shared by all who carried the burden of fighting in the territory. Particularly affected by war-weariness following the excesses of Amirouche and the successes of Challe was the leadership of *Wilaya* 4. A trio of these leaders, headed by Si Salah and Si Lakhtar, made contact with the French, indicating a wish to negotiate. Talks in conditions of the utmost secrecy opened in March 1960, the French side being personally chosen emissaries of de Gaulle. Discussions in

---

8 De Gaulle's memoirs, published later in the decade after Algerian independence, advance claims of foresight that need to be treated with reserve.

9 Krim, together with Boussouf, also visited Moscow, where once again the atmosphere was not as enthusiastic.

remote country areas continued; on 9 June the three were taken to Paris to meet de Gaulle face to face. It seemed, briefly, that the long-cherished French hope of an FLN split was happening; but events overtook Operation *Tilsitt*, as the French named the secret talks.[10]

Alarmed by Krim's success in the Communist capitals, de Gaulle launched another major political initiative on 14 June, openly appealing to the GPRA to join in talks to end the fighting. This appeal disillusioned the *Wilaya* 4 leaders, one of whom returned to the FLN fold, probably under duress.[11] Three, including Lakhtar, were immediately killed by the FLN; Si Salah was executed after a year in custody.

De Gaulle's appeal was a total failure. The GPRA accepted the invitation, sending two negotiations to Melun in France, but the positions of the two sides appeared irreconcilable. The French demanded a cease-fire as a preliminary, the GPRA sought direct negotiations with de Gaulle personally and a freed Ben Bella; neither side moving an inch, the negotiations collapsed. This whole series of events was a disaster for de Gaulle. The failure of *Tilsitt*, whether it was his fault or not, aborted all attempts to split the FLN, and left de Gaulle with no one to deal with other than the GPRA. The Melun invitation seemed a recognition of this, and was certainly proclaimed as such by the GPRA. Watching increasingly moodily, the French military saw betrayal, a double betrayal in the eyes of the few who knew of *Tilsitt*.

The year 1960, which had started apparently so promisingly for the French, drew to a close with their difficulties mounting. In Tunisia, Boumedienne was carrying out a reorganization and retraining of the ALN, making it a much more professional force. Due to political hesitations in Paris, a huge consignment of weaponry from Bulgaria had arrived in Tunis for the FLN without interception. With this new equipment, including mortars and light artillery, it was now able to harass the French troops on the Morice line. In conditions of great secrecy, and based on one man to one man only connections, an ALN organization was being rebuilt in Algiers. The failure of Melun had increased the war-weariness in France where appeared in September the Manifesto of the 121, a declaration signed by 121 notable figures of the non-Communist soft left calling on conscripts drafted for Algeria to desert. A group of FLN sympathizers and fund-raisers, some French,

10 Tilsitt was the venue of the meeting of Emperors Napoleon and Alexander I of Russia in 1807.

11 General Jacquin, one of the French emissaries selected by de Gaulle, claims that de Gaulle himself let the GPRA know of the *Wilaya* 4 leaders' initiative, in order to compel the GPRA itself to negotiate and not be marginalized: Alistair Horne, *A Savage War of Peace: Algeria 1954–1962* (London, Macmillan, 1987), pp.393–4.

some Algerian, used the trial of the Manifesto's signatories as a political platform. Opposed to them were new, vocal, Right-wing *Algérie Française* groups including such figures as Juin, Bidault and Soustelle; the most significant of these, as it had a massive membership in Algeria, was the *Front d'Algérie Française* (FAF). To complicate the issues further, Salan on his retirement attempted to settle in Algeria, clearly with political activity in mind. He was ordered back to Paris where he openly and sharply attacked de Gaulle. He was placed under surveillance, but in October he slipped his watchers to appear in Spain. Another general of *colon* origin, Jouhaud, who had been retired at the same time as Salan was recalled, also returned to Algiers and immediately opened contacts with the FAF.

Abroad, the new US President, Kennedy, had been talking freely about the need for France to withdraw from Algeria during his election campaign and was planning drastic cuts in military aid to France. Ferhat Abbas, still the 'front man' head of the GPRA, had received a very cordial welcome on a visit to both Moscow and Peking in September, Khrushchev now moving to fuller support. The fruits of all the external FLN's political hard work were later to be seen on 20 December, when the United Nations, now with many new African members, recognized Algeria's right to self-determination.

De Gaulle's reactions were a clear case of politics being the art of the possible. 'Association' was now discarded and on 4 November, in a major speech, he talked of an 'Algerian Algeria', with its own laws and government, concluding perhaps inadvertently with the words an 'Algerian Republic'. To endorse this, on 16 November, he proposed a national referendum on self-determination for Algeria in France and Algeria. Delouvrier and others resigned in chagrin. Three loyal Gaullists were appointed for Algeria; Joxe, a minister to live in Paris; Morin, an administrator, as Delegate in Algiers; and General Gambiez to replace Crépin. Gambiez was tasked with a purely defensive strategy, justified on the grounds that victory had been won, but clearly with other political considerations in mind. Any violent campaigning would be unpropitious. French officers drew their own conclusions, as did the *harkis*, desertion now beginning. For some, de Gaulle appeared to be bringing defeat, abandonment of loyalists and humiliation – all at a time when victory had been won. Some, uneasy over recent events, felt that while a victory might justify these events, defeat would lead to bitterness, recrimination, enquiry, perhaps even prosecution. But others, particularly metropolitan conscripts, resented the demands of the Algerian war, and from points of view ranging from Catholic conservative to radical, hated the elite parachute units. The *harkis*, too, drew further conclusions, desertions increasing.

In December de Gaulle, unwisely, visited Algeria to campaign for his package in the referendum, timed for early January, and to try to limit damage he anticipated in the forthcoming UN debate. The FLN, too, was aware of the UN debate and had launched a limited attention-seeking bombing campaign; tension was at its highest.

The visit was a disaster, and de Gaulle was lucky on four occasions to escape assassination at the hands of extremists in Algeria, and on a fifth on his return to Paris. He did not immediately go to Algiers, but the pattern of cheering Moslems and hate-loaded, booing *colons* was set from the moment of his arrival in Algeria. Jouhaud had planned a *coup* in which the FAF's private underground military units, together with three parachute regiments, would seize de Gaulle in Algiers and take power. Huge *colon* crowds filled the streets, rioting against the gendarmes and destroying buses, the synagogue and Jewish property. An incident in one suburb sparked off violence which led the FAF units to turn their hysteria and violence on to Moslems. This was too much for the parachute regiments, who refused to move in support of the FAF, and Jouhaud abandoned his *coup* plans. To enhance this enormous propaganda success – and to incite still further the *colons* – the new FLN underground in Algiers had the city decorated with green and white nationalist flags, photographed by the world's press. In the riots 120, almost all Moslems, were killed. De Gaulle cut short his visit. The referendum results were one of clear success for de Gaulle in the metropole, and one that was controversial in Algeria. There, despite the massive 'no' of the *colons* and despite the boycotting of the elections by the Moslems at the command of the GPRA, there was a 69.09 per cent 'yes' vote.

THE GENERALS' *COUP* AND THE OAS

Two clear warning signals followed in January 1961; the resignation from the Army, in protest, of Challe; and the emergence in Algiers of a new underground *Organisation Armée Secrète* (OAS), dedicated to the 'elimination' of de Gaulle and any others who would abandon Algeria, with further attempts on the lives of de Gaulle and Mitterrand. As catalysts for the drama to follow were an announcement that bilateral peace talks with the FLN were to open and that Gambiez was to order a 'unilateral truce', ending operations.

In April came the final crisis, an ill-conceived and hurriedly pre-pared attempt to seize power by means of a *putsch* in Algiers. The conspiracy was headed by four generals; Salan; Jouhaud; Zeller, an old *Armée d'Afrique* veteran; and a late recruit to the conspiracy, Challe.[12] Also involved in Algeria, in France, or elsewhere were Generals Gardy and Faure, Colonels Godard and Argoud and some other officers, notably the commander of the *1er Etranger de Parachutistes*, 1er REP, the new warfare school's most forceful unit, many of whose soldiers were Germans, and Susini. Challe's motives were different from those of the others; he felt himself pledged to the *harkis* he had recruited and used, and who in his view must not be abandoned to a terrible fate, as had befallen the allies and supporters of France in Indochina. He only envisaged changing policy, not destroying the Republic.

On the twentieth Challe and Zeller arrived secretly in Algeria and amid much confusion the *coup* was launched; Salan arrived later. The *coup* leaders' first broadcasts were received ecstatically by the *colon* population. The conspirators, not agreed amongst themselves, had only a hazy plan that if they were disavowed by Paris, they would create a French form of Israel after a three-month pacification of the rural areas. They forecast that eventually France and the world would recognize this state and restore it to the fold. They also believed that there might be some American support, Challe being popular with the senior American military while de Gaulle was detested, a belief both naïve and incorrect. They fully expected that the Army in Algeria would follow them. In this they miscalculated totally, only the 1er REP actively participating, though one or two other units were clearly sympathetic. To the grief of Challe and Jouhaud, the air force refused to join in. The 1er REP successfully arrested Gambiez, but killed one soldier trying to defend Algiers radio station. Challe refused to authorize any Frenchman to fire upon another. A number of generals, in particular those who as junior officers had served with de Gaulle after 1940 amongst whom was the Air Force commander, General Fourquet, a key figure, believed loyalty to de Gaulle must be unquestioning whatever their own anxieties. Others saw the *coup* attempt as disastrously divisive for the Army. Outside the Algiers area, the plotters could find little support.

Three days of tense crisis followed. In Paris and other cities troops and tanks were deployed on the streets, alerted for an assault either by road or from the air. But the arrest of General Faure aborted an ill-conceived project to march a force of metropolitan parachute troops and tanks on the capital. De Gaulle appeared on radio and television

12 One figure not involved was Massu, whom everyone knew would never act against de Gaulle.

to give perhaps the most moving of his great classic broadcasts. He declared that disobedience was personal and national dishonour, concluding emotionally, 'Françaises, Français, aidez-moi'. This appeal went directly over the heads of the officers to the mass of conscript soldiery, listening in sections and platoons grouped around their transistor radios.

The conscripts followed their President, as did the majority of the Army's officers with careers at stake.[13] They disobeyed orders from the conspirators, on some occasions arresting officers known to be sympathetic to the *coup* or sabotaging key equipment. The *coup* collapsed on the twenty-sixth, Challe with great dignity gave himself up, Zeller following a little later. Salan and Jouhaud went underground to become leaders of the OAS. The 1er REP was disbanded. As a final gesture it blew up its own barracks and its officers hung their medals on their cell doors; two other parachute regiments were also disbanded. Many of their soldiers deserted to join the OAS.

The events shook the world, in particular Britain, where it was thought that, if successful, Challe and Salan would enter Tunisia to destroy the GPRA, an invasion that might spread the war across all North Africa and perhaps tempt the Soviet Union to offer to protect Tunisia. Staff planning to move British troops to Tunisia from various bases in the Mediterranean was put in hand, but no actual moves were made.[14]

Despite the fact that, at the height of the drama, France exploded her first atom bomb, de Gaulle's difficulties increased as a result of the *coup* attempt. His Army was divided, which seriously weakened his negotiating position; *colon* and OAS reaction was quickly to prove horrific. This reaction in turn compelled – in its perception – the FLN to its 'ethnic cleansing', coffin or suitcase, solution for the *colons*.

But if his difficulties increased so also did de Gaulle's resolution to dispose of Algeria in the wider interests of France. In May he followed his unilateral armistice with troop reductions, including the evacuation of certain garrisons. ALN activity, however, increased and *harkis* began to desert in scores.

Following secret contacts, negotiations with the GPRA had been resumed at Evian in March. They very soon highlighted the extent to which France had lost the political war. De Gaulle's negotiators, headed by Joxe, were obliged to accept the FLN, headed by Krim, and drop

13 Horne, *Savage War*, p.462, provides figures of 14,000 personnel implicated, in the coup attempt, with 200 arrests.

14 The British government also authorized extradition back to France of any of the four generals who might try to escape via Gibraltar.

the previous French insistence on an ALN cease-fire.[15] The FLN, further, progressively rejected all French demands for any safeguards for the *colons* unless negotiated with the GPRA, which de Gaulle refused to recognize; they also repudiated French claims to the retention of the Sahara and its oil. The talks had twice to be adjourned and resumed; de Gaulle in impatience threatened to partition Algeria, a threat that led to an FLN riposte of riots and killings in July.

Worse was to follow when, following disputes in the FLN leadership in July and August, the extreme hard-liners gained control after a reshuffle in the GPRA, a reshuffle reflecting the power of Boumedienne. Ferhat Abbas was removed from the Presidency and replaced by Ben Khedda, and Krim was replaced by Saad Dahlab, another militant; Krim was, however, to return later.

The other main consequence of the failure of the generals' *putsch* was that many of those in sympathy with it joined the OAS, some of them embittered and despairing *colons*, and other deserting soldiers who contributed weapons and equipment. In addition to Salan and Jouhaud, Susini, Perez, General Gardy and several of the hard-line colonels all joined, though its most effective leader soon proved to be a *Légion* lieutenant, Degueldre. The OAS was directed by a Command and Staff structure, below which separate sections concerned themselves with organization of the masses, intelligence and operations, and political work. Funded initially on purloined government money it soon turned to extortion and bank and other robberies; for concealment its members could draw on the help of the vast majority of the *colon* population who saw the OAS as their last hope. Its views on Algeria were fully supported by both Bidault and Soustelle, though neither were members; both had to leave France knowing that warrants for their arrests on grounds of subversion and conspiracy were to be issued.

The OAS's initial post-*putsch* strategy was one of a savage campaign against the Moslem population, designed to provoke a Moslem reaction that it was hoped would oblige the French Army to reassert authority. Over 3,000 attacks per month were launched by OAS 'Delta Commandos' in the second half of 1961, in addition to the hundreds of Moslems killed at random; other specific OAS targets included French officials and officers loyal to de Gaulle, among them the general commanding the Oran Army Corps, and any French *colons* who were known to favour partition or enclaves. The OAS offensive was matched

15 The FLN were aware that once a full cease-fire was called, a re-mobilization of the ALN, in the event of failure in the negotiations, would prove exceedingly difficult.

by a renewed FLN campaign of particularly brutal killings. OAS political activity was spectacular, including the display of their black and white flag everywhere in Algiers, and a pirate radio broadcast coinciding with a visit by Joxe. But in October the OAS suffered its first important check with the smashing of two networks, one in France and one in Algeria.

One other extraordinary military event occurred in July 1961. Following a further series of frontier clashes President Bourguiba led a national campaign demanding a final French withdrawal from Bizerta. 'Volunteers' demonstrated, and the small French garrison was harassed by light artillery fire. As much to improve their bargaining position against the FLN as to chastise Tunisia, the French rushed reinforcements in, some by parachute, and re-asserted full control of their area at a cost of 26 killed with others wounded; the Tunisians lost at least 350. Once again, at the United Nations and elsewhere, France incurred sharp criticism, now including NATO member countries, and withdrew from Bizerta a little later. But there could now be no hope of further Tunisian help in negotiations with the FLN over the Sahara.

During the autumn and winter of 1961–62 the three-sided fight – OAS, FLN and the French government – spread to France with killings and a campaign of bombings. The OAS attacked French liberals, Left-wing figures and Moslems, the police retaliating against them and the Moslems with equal brutality. One splinter group almost succeeded in assassinating de Gaulle in a bomb attack in September. In February Left-wing resentment against the bombings culminated in a massive anti-OAS demonstration in Paris in which the police panicked, killing eight, including a woman.

In March the OAS, now crazed to dementia, adopted a new strategy, the destruction of the infrastructure of Algeria, professional men, economically important buildings and education centres.[16] Algiers resembled a battlefield and became ungovernable. In reply to the OAS killings the FLN seized *colons* and tortured them to death. The French Army, sometimes with loyalties divided and uncertain, found itself increasingly committed in operations against the OAS; also deployed were a hurriedly recruited and somewhat amateurish task force and a small number of metropolitan police officers; these were all collectively known as *les barbouzes*. Degueldre's men finished off those locally recruited with little difficulty but the metropolitan police officers were more effective.

16 Colonels Argoud and Gardes, both OAS chiefs, went so far as to attempt to turn the *harkis* against the French Army.

NEGOTIATIONS AND WITHDRAWAL

These mounting horrors in France and Algeria strengthened both de Gaulle's resolve finally to dispose of Algeria, and public support for such a policy. Despite the July 1961 impasse, low-key negotiations continued near the French–Swiss border. Ben Khedda, Krim and most of the GPRA, faced with the challenge of the OAS, were also anxious to talk. Boumedienne remained hard-line but was won over to grudging acquiescence by the undertaking that negotiations must now include Ben Bella, a condition which the French conceded.[17] On 17 February 1962 de Gaulle indicated he was prepared to make major concessions on the main contentious issues – the use of the Mers-el-Kébir naval base, safeguards for the *colons* and the post-independence stay of French troops, and the Sahara rocket-testing sites. At 5 a.m. on the eighteenth Krim and Joxe shook hands, having reached the basis of agreement. The details were to be drafted in March after a special session of the CNRA in Tripoli, at which Boumedienne forced Krim to take a harder stance over the *colons*.

Recording the details of the agreement is only meaningful if with each major point one looks ahead at what actually happened. This was generally very different from what was agreed, both sides being guilty of a measure of self-delusion if not substantial hypocrisy. France accepted an independent Algerian state, but sought to bind it to the franc zone and by other economic and cultural provisions; Algeria grudgingly accepted, planning to diversify after independence. The *colons* were to be given full civic rights, political representation in proportion to their numbers, special safeguards in Algiers and Oran, special courts, dual nationality for three years and a promise of no expropriation of property without indemnity; these provisions were all in practice valueless. Joint arrangements for the exploitation of Saharan oil were agreed; these lasted until 1970. The French Navy was granted the use of Mers-el-Kébir for 15 years but in the event left under pressure in 1968. A French garrison of 80,000 was permitted for three years but was also withdrawn earlier. Saharan nuclear weapon test facilities, to which de Gaulle attached great importance, were granted but came under increasing criticism, leading France to move these tests out of Algeria after four years. There was to be an immediate cease-fire and a provisional executive for the transition to independence. In France a massive referendum *oui* was returned in support of the agreements.

17 Boumedienne's arguments received added force when a private *colon*-owned aircraft flown by club airmen machine-gunned an FLN base and hospital in Morocco.

News of the detail negotiations and, after 18 March, the agreements themselves unleashed a wave of OAS carnage in Algiers and Oran, 30 or more being assassinated, or killed in Moslem reprisals, daily in Algiers alone. One OAS Delta Commando specifically targeted a meeting of French and Moslem educationists, killing six, including a well-known liberal writer.

At the end of March the OAS over-reached itself with the killing of a number of French conscripts. In response, General Ailleret, the new French commander, committed 20,000 troops supported by air-to-ground rocket fire against the *colon* Bab-el-Oued area of Algiers, losing 15 killed and 700 injured, *colon* casualties being much higher. This horror was matched by panic in an indigenous *Tirailleurs* unit that under pressure from a mob and perhaps provoked by an OAS sniper, opened fire, killing 46 and wounding many more.

In April Salan and Degueldre were both caught. Jouhaud had been tracked down earlier, but the bloodshed continued with a further series of OAS mass killings – on one occasion 24 Moslems, on another 62 – and the destruction of institutions such as the Library of the University of Algiers. The FLN in reply also returned to killings, in turn bringing further OAS massacres until, surprisingly, in June, the OAS and the FLN agreed a truce. Some 1,450,000 people, mostly *colons* but also including many loyalist Moslems, streamed down to Algeria's ports *en route* for France or elsewhere with the permitted baggage allowance of two cases per person, one of the twentieth century's least well-recorded but worst cases of mass misery. Homes, businesses, shops, cars were all abandoned, families burned furniture in huge street bonfires. The vast majority of the *colons*, some 1,380,000, opted to settle in France, though others chose Spain, Canada, or in a few cases Argentina.

After the March cease-fire the French Army was bound by its non-intervention provisions. The French thought – or deluded themselves – that the presence of French forces in Algeria for three years would provide security for *colons* and loyalists alike while passions cooled. In practice, the French Army had to stand as helpless spectators at atrocities, one of the worst being in Oran where the local commander, General Katz, forbade intervention during a massacre of *colons*; elsewhere they were sometimes ordered to disarm *harkis* prior to their being handed over to the FLN. In other areas French units just withdrew at night abandoning the *harkis*, or remained in camps while *harkis* were massacred. The *harkis* spokesman, Bachaga Boualem, spoke bitterly of betrayal. De Gaulle eventually allowed his Prime Minister, Debré, to resign in chagrin.

For honour's sake some French regiments and officers ignored the strict instructions given that the *harkis* were not to be allowed to escape to France, an order repeated after independence in the full knowledge of the fate befalling the *harkis*.[18] Some were hurriedly 'recruited' as soldiers and some concealed in lorries and stores. Others swam out to troopships, some being picked up and some left in the sea. Officers found condoning rescue and escape were cashiered or severely disciplined. Joxe even issued a secret circular attempting to have returned to Algeria those found in France, an instruction ignored. Metropolitan regiments returning to Marseille found no welcome, poor arrangements, and a city decorated with Communist and FLN flags.

In a further referendum held in Algeria on 1 July, 5,993,754 voted for the agreements, 16,478 voting against, the mass of *colons* being either departed or too traumatized to vote. Three days later, Fouchet, who had replaced Morin and was to be France's last Algerian proconsul, departed for Paris and the French Tricolour was lowered for the last time.

The long war was almost over. Since 1954 the French had lost some 13,000 soldiers of European origin together with 3,500 non-European soldiers killed in action, with a further 7,000 and 1,000 respectively killed in accidents, and a combined total of 11,000 dead from disease or suicide. Some 50 per cent of these deaths occurred after April 1961. In respect of civilians, 2,788 Europeans and 16,738 indigenous were killed by the FLN, with a further 875 Europeans and 13,296 indigenous missing, all up to April 1961. The French estimated that between April 1961 and independence 50,000 indigenous were killed, with, in revenge killings of loyalists and *harkis* after the ceasefire, a further 150,000. French estimates of ALN casualties were 141,000 killed in action, 12,000 killed by Amirouche and others in internal purges, at least 1,500 killed by the Moroccans and Tunisians in trying to maintain order, and 4,000 killed in metropolitan France.[19] These figures do not include the thousands who died in the resettlement camps. Algerian nationalists suggest higher figures, a total of 300,000 dead. For some, too, the war was not over. Captured *harkis* were put to work on the Moroccan and Tunisian frontier lines, clearing wire

18 Excerpts from this post-independence order, issued by General de Brébisson, appear in François Porteu de la Morandière, *Soldats du Djebel* (Paris, Société de Production Littéraire, n.d.), p.359. A feeble justification offered was that the *harkis* were grouped in camps simply for the food provided there. More revealing was a statement that France could not be further saturated with refugees.

19 These figures are based on those in Morandière, *Soldats du Djebel*, p.374, and Horne, *Savage War*, pp.537–8.

and mine-fields with neither safety equipment nor aid for the injured; hundreds of others were tortured to death in a variety of atrocious ways.

The more fortunate *harkis* who managed to escape to France were, after some confusion, re-settled in the southern Massif Central. The *colons* scattered all over France, but large concentrations settled in small towns, or new estates especially built in Provence. The OAS vendetta against de Gaulle continued for a further year though the OAS itself was (like the FLN) weakened by internal dissensions, interior versus exterior, and some splintering. Salan, in particular, tried to prevent the worst excesses. The four senior generals were all put on trial, initially *in absentia*. Jouhaud and a number of other officers received death sentences, but after the capture of Salan, Jouhaud's sentence was commuted following a skilful defence by Salan's lawyer when he was tried in person. Zeller and Challe received lesser sentences, though Degueldre was shot.[20] De Gaulle's actions in June 1940 were cited as justification, perception of a higher national need justifying disobedience to authority. The French Army long suffered hatred and bitter divisions within its officer corps. Despite its military successes, it saw Algeria as another in the succession of misfortunes that had befallen it since 1940.

Victory immediately also opened rifts – some ideological, some purely personal – among the victors. Ben Bella, supported by Boumedienne, provoked a major crisis in the CNRA, meeting in Tripoli at the end of June. He attacked both the collective leadership and the ideology of the GPRA. A second rift was opened by attacks on the General Staff from the heads of the *Wilayas* furthest from the frontiers who accused the General Staff of failing to support them. Amid open, bitter and violent polemical argument the GPRA dissolved the General Staff and dismissed Boumedienne. Ben Khedda, the head of the GPRA, however, failed to assert authority, while Boumedienne, ignoring the GPRA, began to move his units from Tunisia into Algeria, creating a 'Political Bureau' almost as a rival authority. Ben Bella allied himself with Boumedienne's followers in the west, arriving from Morocco. July and August were months of the utmost confusion as the Evian

---

20   Challe's defence included the obligations he felt arising from the *Wilaya* 4 events. The prosecution objected. The presiding judge, Catroux, refused to uphold the objection.

Generals Pigot, Nicot and Gourand, and Colonel de Saint-Marc of the 1er REP all received prison sentences, as did some of their subordinate officers. Challe, Zeller and Jouhand were all released early. Salan and others still detained were released and restored to their honours and pensions in 1968, a move generally believed to have been the Army's price for supporting de Gaulle at the time of the student-worker riots.

interim executive, Ben Khedda and the GPRA, Ben Bella and Boumedienne's Political Bureau and various other *Wilaya* leaders, notably Krim and Boudiaf in the Kabyle *Wilaya* 3, all struggled for power. The struggle involved a final round of killing off political rivals and any suspected of collaboration with the French, and also many of those *colons* who had unwisely hoped to remain, probably as many as 1,600. Armed bands of the different factions took to the hills and city streets machine-gunning and murdering.

Eventually Mohammed Khider arranged a cease-fire between the *Wilayas* on 7 September. This enabled Boumedienne's ALN to enter the strife-torn and looted Algiers three days later. On 25 September a newly elected Constituent Assembly, whose candidates had all been approved by Boumedienne's Political Bureau and Ben Bella, proclaimed a Democratic and Popular Republic of Algeria. The Assembly further approved a Ben Bella government, including Boumedienne but no member of the former GPRA. Two years later, in 1964, Boumedienne completed the process of ensuring the control of the external ALN both over those leaders who had been held by the French and the internal ALN when, in a *coup*, he removed Ben Bella.

The longer-term consequences of this loss of the last of France's major imperial possessions will be considered in the next chapter. This chapter, terminating at Algeria's independence, should as a conclusion note that, however tortuous de Gaulle's policies had been, however bitter the resentments they created, withdrawal from Algeria left vendetta only, not civil war. Stepping from his bomb-splintered car in September 1961 de Gaulle could well have echoed Edgar in *King Lear*: 'Think that the clearest gods, who make them honours of men's impossibilities, have preserv'd thee.'

10 CONCLUSION

In the previous chapters some of the main consequences for the territories concerned of the respective conflicts have been set out. This chapter seeks to examine further results of the two major conflicts, in Indochina and Algeria, both for the countries concerned and for France. The chapter will also seek to extract and identify certain other themes relating to decolonization in general.

One of these latter themes relates to the general strategy of counter-insurgency warfare. A leading British administrator and theoretician, Sir Robert Thompson, set out five fundamental principles which had to be observed for the successful conduct of a counter-insurgency campaign: the need for a co-ordinated overall plan and co-ordinated local plans at local levels; the need to establish secure base areas; the need to concentrate initially on destroying the political infrastructure of the insurgent movement; the need to adhere to the rule of law; and the need for a government to have a clear political aim towards which its military and political work is directed. This aim should be one that would command sufficient popular acceptability to isolate the insurgent. These principles were recognized in and formulated as a result of Great Britain's most successful counter-insurgency campaign, that of Malaya, in 1948–60. There General Sir Gerald Templer, the British High Commissioner and Commander-in-Chief, clearly recognized his priorities, remarking on one occasion in 1953, 'The shooting side of the business is only 25 per cent of the trouble, and the other 75 per cent lies in getting this country behind us.' Of the French campaign commanders only Leclerc, de Lattre and perhaps Soustelle seemed able fully to grasp this essential truth. Elsewhere it was obscured by traditional French centralism, and the exaggerated arguments of theorists of the counter-revolutionary warfare school.

This failure leads on to another major difference between the British and French experience, the way the nature of the independence struggle laid the foundations of the new successor states. British success in counter-insurgency campaigning enabled Britain to control the pace and nature of decolonization, most notably in Malaya and Kenya, and play an influential role in constructing the constitutions, politics and economies of the successor states. France was able to exercise this influence in colonies where there was little unrest, most notably in Black Africa and even in territories where there had been military operations but where she had maintained military advantage, Madagascar, Laos and Cambodia; in these decolonization was in the end accomplished smoothly even if troubles followed later. But when France was enfeebled, as in Syria and Lebanon, defeated as in Vietnam, or simply wearied, as in Algeria (and to a lesser extent in Tunisia and Morocco), the successor states reflected the aims of France's opponents even in their variety, with Tunisia as a bourgeois oligarchy, Morocco a monarch-driven government and Algeria a socialist republic.

In the case of Vietnam only two out of the three issues over which the war had been fought, French control, the unity of the three *kys*, and the ideology of the successor regime were settled. French control was ended, but what should have been a relatively manageable and local issue, unity, remained complicated by ideology with all its unmanageable international ramifications. The 1954 Sainteny mission in Hanoi failed, but its actual presence amid the victors illustrated another unusual facet of the 1946–54 Indochina war. Many Vietnamese, including a surprising number among the Viet Minh, hated the colonial French in Indochina but admired France, in particular for her revolutionary and Second World War resistance traditions which they saw as inspiration. Examples of this almost love–hate relationship appeared at the end of the war with Viet Minh requests for French technical aid. The conversion to Communism was for many either opportunism or a very skin-deep adherence. No such involved a relationship existed during the second Indochina war against the United States.

Algeria, too, was left at independence with a major problem still to be resolved, that of identity, a problem evident as early as 1963 in political controversy over Algerian nationality. Some writers have described the Algerian was as 'the war without a name'; in common use during the campaign was the French term of reference for an insurgent as an HLL, *Hors La Loi* or outlaw. No specific geographic name, such as 'Viet' could be given to them. This absence of a specific identity was a result of the artefactual nature of Algeria, a creation of French nineteenth-century military power encapsulating a wide variety of northern and Saharan peoples with in common nothing more than Islam and growing opposition to the French. Ferhat Abbas had recognized this in the 1930s when he had commented on the absence of any specific Algerian personality. The governments of Algeria that followed independence were formed from successive cliques of the guerrilla war FLN; most of these saw, in perspectives more purely functional than those of the Viet Minh, merit in French-patterned institutions and some continuing use of the French language so long as metropolitan French control was removed. But in face of the country's ever-worsening economic difficulties compounded by rapid population growth and a squandering of oil profits, men who had little or nothing other than their religious faith became disillusioned. They began to turn against the increasingly corrupt FLN politico-military establishment and its remaining French-patterned structures and cultural links; when these latter were replaced under the government's Arabization policy Kabyle resentment became evident. A male-dominated Moslem fundamentalism appeared as a new solution offering a new and more real national and moral identity, and opening a challenge in both the ballot box and the streets.

France herself had no will left for any further colonial assertion. The Fourth Republic's *loi cadre* of 1956 provided each Black African territory with a political framework; this was followed by de Gaulle's Community institutions of 1958. Nevertheless, increasing nationalist demand obliged France to grant flag independence for all the Black African colonies in 1960. Prudently, the leading African politicians had been restrained in their criticism of French policies in Algeria, to the disgust of the FLN. The transition was generally smooth with the exception of Mauritania, in which there were very minor military operations, and Cameroun, whose status presented particular problems.

Cameroun had been a German colony; after the First World War it became a League of Nations mandated territory almost all allocated to France. After the Second World War Cameroun became a United Nations Trust Territory. This especial status encouraged the emergency of a militant nationalist movement, the *Union des Populations du Cameroun* (UPC), under a radical leader, Um Nyobe. Riots broke out in 1955 and the UPC was banned. Underground, the UPC turned to insurgency, launching a sabotage campaign in December 1956. This campaign, in which communications in the southern Sanaga maritime province were the chief target, lasted for two years, effectively ending with the killing of Um Nyobe in September 1958. The scale of operations was never large, the most spectacular event being a two-company *Coloniale* parachute drop on Eseka airport to secure communications between Douala and Yaoundé. Elsewhere *Tirailleurs Sénégalais* detachments operated with the police; at the most 100 people were killed. The issues at stake were complicated by rival factions within Bamileke and Bassa society; the nationalist impulse was in any case defused by the evident moves towards independence.

In any record of the wider consequences of France's wars of decolonization mention should also be made of the impression created by the cost and casualties in both Belgium and Britain. Belgium's political leaders were influenced in their decision for a speedy flag independence for their Congo colony by the fear that if they remained they would face a guerrilla war; they lost their nerve in face of disorders still controllable and gave their colony independence without proper preparation. The results were disastrous for the Congo and unsettling in Belgium herself. In Britain a variety of reasons was leading the Conservative Party to accept decolonization: colonial nationalist demands, the example of India, domestic lack of will to assert continuing imperial rule, a belief that British commercial interests would be best secured by economic development in partnership with moderate nationalists, the wish to end conscription and de Gaulle's post-1958 'Wind of change'. The perceptions of the Algerian war added to these pressures, playing their small but recognizable part in the decision that dismantling of the Federation of Rhodesia and Nyasaland was inevitable if a large-scale insurrection was to be averted.

One nation that unfortunately failed to heed the lessons from the French experience, especially that in Indochina, was the United States. It became only too clear, during America's Vietnam war, that the American command never properly grasped the social and political structure of the Viet Cong. Vietnam was seen as another peninsula, like Korea, where Communism could be stopped by superior technology in a brief local war. Like the French, the Americans were slow in attempting to create local South Vietnamese forces; further, they denied their own regular ground forces any opportunity to attack Viet Cong supply and reinforcement routes in and from safe rest areas in Laos. The American command structure was confused, with different services pulling in different directions and uncertain political direction, the Army relied too much on fire power – where heavy bombardments warned the Viet Cong of attacks to come – and on mechanization. Front-line foot soldiers were rarely available in adequate numbers. Again like the French, the American generals set too much store on a kill-rate attrition and on hopes of a set-piece battle; their preference for operations by day left the nights free for Viet Cong action and political indoctrination. The United States might also have drawn two lessons from France's campaign in Algeria: that reluctant conscripts, especially those from the under-privileged sections of society, make poor counter-insurgency soldiers; and the need for responsible, professional command and control if excess and atrocity are to be averted. From both campaigns the United States might have appreciated earlier the demoralizing effects of domestic anti-war political protest.

Of France herself it is tempting to say that she was on the winning side in the Second World War but was nevertheless a loser, and was on the losing side in her two major wars of decolonization but emerged, paradoxically, as the winner. These colonial wars were not on this occasion on her soil, but France was, nevertheless, having to cope with the triple problems of costly reconstruction from the devastation of the Second World War, the campaigns themselves, and the Cold War which for France was domestic as well as external. That she emerged triumphant, economically very strong and politically rejuvenated is attributable to three factors. The first, the widest context, was the general strength and balance of the French economy whose rich and varied resource base left her relatively free from a need for costly imports, in particular staple foods. The major weakness of the French economy, oil, was not fully recognized as such in the 1950s; hopes of Saharan oil obscured the issue.

The second was wise planning of the economy despite all the political turbulence and ever-changing administrations of the Fourth Republic. This planning had been authorized by de Gaulle in January 1946 when Monnet, an exceptionally able administrator, was appointed to head the *Commissariat Général au Plan* and prepare a blueprint for the complete modernization of France. Monnet and his staff concentrated their work upon investment, output, productivity and production in six priority sectors: coal, steel, cement, transport, agricultural machinery and chemical fertilizers. Assisted by Marshall Plan funding and other parallel developments such as the great Rhône dams, the development of natural gas, and later the European Coal and Steel Community (in origin also an idea of Monnet's), the French economy experienced a recovery second only to that of Germany. Industrial production between 1945 and 1958 more than quadrupled. By the late 1950s motor-cars or motor bicycles filled the streets of French towns, whole communities had moved into new housing and France was building first-line military and civil aircraft with the world's largest passenger liner to follow. Thousands left the land, the farmers who remained replaced the old horse-drawn farm cart with a new tractor. For the mass of the population, now increasingly suburban, economic prosperity provided the comforts of the consumer society. The ending of the Algerian war released men and money for yet further economic expansion.

The third was the stature and prestige of de Gaulle, who was able to enjoy the fruits of Monnet's planning and provide France with a greater international status than at any other time in the twentieth century. His presidential style and firm assertion of France's national interests in all international issues gave France a renewed sense of *gloire*, national self-respect. With the ending of the Algerian war de Gaulle was free to pursue his personal national and strategic objectives without any need to secure goodwill from any quarter. Central to these objectives was the French independent nuclear deterrent. Atomic weaponry gave weight to France's claim to great power status and both freed France from the need for American nuclear protection and, by French perceptions, also reduced the risk of her being a target for Soviet blackmail. Anti-American sentiment, the view that the United States had been unhelpful in the final stages of the Indochina war and hostile over the Algerian war, was strengthened by the American rejection of de Gaulle's troika project of a NATO led jointly by the United States, Britain and France. In its stead de Gaulle turned to a Napoleonic vision of a 'European Europe' led by France as strong as either the United States or the Soviet Union.

To escape from institutional American control de Gaulle first withdrew the Mediterranean and then the Atlantic fleets from NATO commands, in 1959 and 1964 respectively. In 1963 Army units returning from Algeria were grouped into a 1st Army Corps sited in France, under national and not NATO command. In 1966 France withdrew entirely from the NATO integrated commands and directed that all NATO institutions in France be relocated elsewhere; these included two major NATO commands, the Supreme Headquarters Allied Powers in Europe (SHAPE) and the Allied Forces in Central Europe (AFCENT), together with numerous logistic systems. In 1967 de Gaulle's Chief of Staff, General Ailleret, proclaimed the *à tous azimuts* strategy – the targeting of French nuclear weaponry in all directions, by implication including the United States.

Much of this strategic policy was for show. De Gaulle did not withdraw France from the North Atlantic Treaty Alliance, and he continued to stress that France would come to the help of any NATO ally under attack. This promise was given more substantial form in a secret agreement, the Lemnitzer-Ailleret accord of 1968, and would almost certainly have been renewed even if de Gaulle had withdrawn France totally from NATO. *Tous azimuts* in any case did not survive the departure of de Gaulle, Ailleret's successor, Fourquet, revising the strategy to one of an independent French co-operation with NATO.

Within the French Army itself a number of officers, at least one-sixth of the officer corps, resigned; these included the majority of those who felt Algeria should not have been given independence. Others, for the sake of their careers, kept their opinions to themselves. Divisions and recriminations within the officer corps were, however, to last for most of the 1960s, though the events of 1968 provided some release. De Gaulle correctly perceived the changing nature of the French Army; the new high-technology Army that he planned came to provide a fresh range of intellectual, material, cultural and sporting rewards. Its officers, too, came from a wider, less squirearchical, social base. They lived, in France, alongside their civilian counterparts sharing many of the same day-to-day problems and needs, if not quite the same moral values. In this way the links between people and Army, badly fractured from 1940 to 1962, were re-cemented. The conscript soldier, too, was freed from risks to his life and was required to serve for a shorter period of time, both boons accepted with relief and gratitude. For the adventurous, *Coloniale*, returned to its pre-1900 title of *Troupes de Marine*, was given the lead role in the new intervention forces. Overall, at general officer level, one major lesson appears to have been drawn, not only from the experiences of 1945 to 1962 but the wider experience of the inter-World War years onwards. This lesson is that Theatre Commanders and Service Chiefs of Staff must be well educated politically so that they are sensitive to the politics of any military situation, but not themselves become involved politically – a wise lesson for any army at any time.

In sum, the colonial Empire had developed from the linkage of nineteenth-century metropolitan agricultural and merchant company capitalism together with influential military interests, in a partnership with the colonies. Monnet and de Gaulle replaced these with new visions of a larger, European-scale capitalism, sophisticated life styles and a France secured by the Common External Tariff, her UN veto and atomic weapons. So, empire, which had never greatly interested *la France profonde*, the small farmer and local businessman, even in its heyday, was relegated to the past and in daily life the nation's 'return to the hexagon' accepted.

At a deeper level it has proved more difficult for Frenchmen to 'walk away' from the Algerian war, just as it has proved difficult for France to come to terms with the events of 1940 to 1945. For long many of those involved preferred neither to write about nor even discuss Algeria; the few documents that have been released concern events up to 1946 only. A sense of shame and guilt remains.

Nevertheless, as part of the price she had to pay, France, like the other combatants, had had to adopt a regime structured to meet the needs of the wars. In France's case the structure reflected a need for authority to contain the consequences of apparent defeat rather than one to enjoy the fruits of military victory. The Fourth Republic would certainly have lasted longer, and in the climate of economic recovery might even have survived permanently, had it not been for the Algerian war. Its successor, the Fifth Republic, was a constitutional and political system designed not to be blown off course by urban demonstrations, civil unrest or parliamentary turbulence. So designed, the Fifth Republic, dominated in particular in the Senate by the rural areas, proved a system slow to respond to the need for change or to manage change when necessary. Early evidence of this weakness appeared in 1968.

In purely political terms the wars of decolonization left two currents which were to flow continuously at varying strengths. Domestically, after the end of OAS activities and the departure and death of de Gaulle, there still remained a measure of resentment at the loss of Algeria, particularly among the *colon* population despite their generally comfortable resettlement in the metropole. Large *colon* communities, settled along the French Mediterranean coast, passed on the *colon* 'culture' to successive generations. The *colon* dialect *patouette* was preserved by local groups and associations by means of local radio and papers. This resentment, by the late 1980s, added strength to the non-Gaullist political Right, especially the extreme Right whose leader, Le Pen, was a former parachute soldier, *'un Bigeard boy'*. De Gaulle remained the target of hatred. In international affairs the current was one of on-going anti-Americanism. Resentment over American attitudes to the Algerian war was a contributory cause to the French withdrawal from NATO's military structures and de Gaulle's project, never fulfilled, to withdraw altogether from the Alliance.

A more serious domestic consequence of the period of French rule in North Africa, and one sharpened by the Algerian war, was the presence in France of a large Maghreb population that increased rapidly following independence. The totals are:

	1940	1946	1954	1962	1968	1980
Algeria	22,114	–	211,675	350,484	473,812	805,355
Morocco	–	16,458	10,734	33,320	84,236	421,369
Tunisia	–	1,916	4,800	26,569	61,028	181,618

These include descendants of labourers of the first half of the century, in the case of Algeria loyalists and the descendants of loyalists of the Algerian war period, and more recent arrivals. The majority live in conditions of illiteracy, poverty, often squalor; few, even from among the descendants of the *harkis*, show any sign of cultural assimilation to France, and incidents of friction or violence increased in the 1980s.

In conclusion, a few general observations may be made in respect of decolonization in its widest context. The word itself was not in circulation in the 1950s or early 1960s and connotes a rationalization not wholly deserved. This work has examined France's attitudes to the loss of empire and her difficulties in adjusting to the process in the years 1940 to 1962. A lengthened historical view is, however, necessary. The mid-twentieth-century years saw the military process at its most dramatic but it was one that had actually begun very much earlier, with the final French eviction from Haiti in 1809 following military defeat in 1802–3 at the hands of a Black revolutionary army. Also, French military interventions and operations in former colonies were to continue for many years after flag independence of the early 1960s, notably in Chad from 1968 onwards, in Gabon in 1962 and 1964, in the Central African Republic in 1967 and 1979, in Niger in 1963, in Cameroun in the late 1960s, and in Togo in 1986. While most of these were relatively small-scale, the 1983 operations in Chad involved as many as 4,000 French troops.

Much academic debate in Britain has revolved around the relative importance of the initiatives and motivation for British decolonization: far-seeing India and Colonial Office officials, changed views on empire in Britain herself, international pressures, nationalist challenge. This debate is largely irrelevant in the case of the French Empire; the previous chapters have clearly illustrated the lead role of the nationalists in achieving flag independence.

Finally, what is actually meant by 'decolonization'? For whatever the manner of decolonization, and after the departure of the colonial administrators, much that is less easily repatriated is left behind: the frontiers established by colonial rule encapsulating different peoples within the Western concept of a nation state; patterns, sometimes uneven or skewed, of economic development and trade; transport networks; bureaucratic infrastructures; medical, agricultural veterinary research; miscellaneous science and technology contributions of a very wide variety; social structures together with customary law sometimes drastically reconstituted; educational systems, language and cultural or even sporting activities or graftings. Some of these visible colonial legacies were to be changed; others, some beneficial, some harmful, can never be reversed. In the field of the history of ideas, too, theorists on colonial dependency discourse have claimed that colonialism was not simply a matter of political governance or even conscious culture impacts but was also about states of mind and clashes, sometimes sub-conscious, over meanings. The quest for an Algerian identity seems to support this view, as does the rejection of French institutions as well as French rule by the Madagascar rebels. The argument may also throw some further light on the apparently ready acceptance of Communism by so many Vietnamese. In the 'seamless web' of history the military campaigns form only one of the wide variety of strands contributed by the processes of decolonization.

CHRONOLOGY

1941
18 May   Founding of Viet Minh

1942
5 May   British occupy Diego Suarez in Madagascar
10 September   British campaign to occupy all Madagascar opens
5 November   Vichy French governor of Madagascar surrenders
8 November   Allied landings in Morocco and Algeria

1943
3 June   Formation of French Committee of National
                  Liberation (De Gaulle and Giraud) in Algiers
9 November   De Gaulle assumes sole leadership of Committee
                  of National Liberation

1944
30 January   Brazzaville Conference opens
3 June   Formation of French provisional government in
                  Algiers
19–25 August   Liberation of Paris
9 September   De Gaulle establishes provisional government for
                  liberated France in Paris
23 October   US recognition of the provisional government

1945
9 March   Japanese *coup* destroys French authority in
                  Indochina
11 March   Bao Dai proclaims independence in Vietnam
24 March   De Gaulle government's Indochina policy
                  statement
8 May   Uprising at Sétif and in Constantine region of
                  Algeria
9 May   Surrender of German forces: end of war in
                  Europe

2 *August*	Potsdam Conference concludes
13–14 *August*	Japanese surrender. Opening of uprising in Vietnam
25 *August*	Abdication of Bao Dai
2 *September*	Signing of formal surrender by Japan
2 *September*	Declaration of independence by Republic of Vietnam
11 *September*	Arrival of Chinese in Hanoi
25 *September*	Heyraud massacre in Saigon
5 *October*	General Leclerc de Hauteclocque arrives in Saigon
21 *October*	National Referendum on abolition of Third Republic. Constitution and General Election for Constituent Assembly
31 *October*	Admiral d'Argenlieu arrives in Saigon
21 *November*	De Gaulle forms a new government

1946

6 *January*	Monnet officially authorized to commence planning for modernization of France
20 *January*	De Gaulle resigns
24 *January*	Tripartite agreement between MRP, Socialists and Communists
26 *January*	Gouin (Socialist) forms government
28 *February*	Franco-Chinese agreements
6 *March*	French troops arrive at Haiphong, Ho Chi Minh–Sainteny agreement
18 *March*	Leclerc arrives in Hanoi
5 *May*	New Draft Constitution rejected in National Referendum
1 *June*	Proclamation of Republic of Cochinchina
2 *June*	General Election for Second Constituent Assembly
11 *June*	Gouin government resigns
19–23 *June*	Bidault (MRP) forms government
6 *July*	Opening of Fontainebleau Conference
14 *September*	*Modus vivendi* working agreement between Moutet and Ho Chi Minh
13 *October*	Second Draft Constitution approved in National Referendum
10 *November*	General Election
20 *November*	Clash in Haiphong
23 *November*	French warships bombard Haiphong
12–16 *December*	Blum (Socialist) forms government

19 December	Uprising in Hanoi

1947

2 January	Viet Minh invest Nam Dinh
16 January	Auriol elected as President of Republic
21–22 January	Ramadier (Socialist) forms government
5 March	Bollaert replaces d'Argenlieu in Indochina
11 March	French forces relieve Nam Dinh
22 March	Vote on military supplies for Indochina
29 March	Outbreak of uprising in Madagascar
10 April	Sultan of Morocco's Tangiers speech
4 May	Communist ministers depart from Ramadier government
27 May	General Juin arrives in Morocco as Resident-General
15 August	Independence of India and Pakistan
20 September	New Statute for Algeria finally enacted
12 November	Widespread transport and industrial unrest in France begins
19 November	Ramadier government resigns
22–24 November	Schuman (MRP) forms government
23 December	Laos and Cambodia join the French Union. Paris rejects any dialogue with Ho Chi Minh

1948

11 February	Departure of Valluy. General Salan deputizes
21 April	General Blaizot arrives to replace Valluy
19 July	Schuman government resigns
24–26 July	Marie (Radical) forms government
27 August	Marie government resigns
1 September	Schuman (MRP) forms government
4 September	Schuman resigns
9 September	Bourguiba returns to Tunis
10–12 September	Queuille (Radical) forms government
24 September	General strike in Paris
20 October	Pignon replaces Bollaert in Indochina

1949

20 January	Chinese Communists enter Peking
8 March	Elysée Agreement between Bao Dai and Auriol
4 April	NATO Treaty signed
16 May–17 June	General Revers's mission in Indochina
13 June	Bao Dai arrives in Saigon

2 July	'State of Vietnam' proclaimed by France
19 July	Laos becomes an Associated State
3 September	General Carpentier arrives, replacing Blaizot
18 September	Street scuffle in Paris, copy of Revers's report found in possession of Vietnamese student
6 October	Queuille government resigns following internal differences in economic policy
27–28 October	Bidault (MRP) forms government
8 November	Cambodia becomes an Associated State
30 December	Vietnam becomes an Associated State
1950	
19 January	Chinese recognition of Ho Chi Minh's government
30 January	Soviet recognition of Ho Chi Minh's government
7 February	US and British governments recognize the three Associated States
21 February	Ho Chi Minh orders general mobilization
25–30 May	Attack upon, fall and re-occupation of Dong Khe
11–18 June	First US military aid arrives at Saigon
24 June	Bidault government resigns
25 June	Outbreak of Korean war
30 June–2 July	Queuille (Radical) forms government
4 July	Queuille government resigns
11–12 July	Pleven (UDSR) forms government
2 September	Carpentier decides to evacuate Cao Bang
16 September	Dong Khe recaptured by Viet Minh
1–8 October	Fall of Cao Bang
17 October	Evacuation of Lang Son
19 October	Paris Assembly debates Indochina. Mendès-France launches effective non-Communist criticism of French policy
17 December	Arrival of General de Lattre de Tassigny in Saigon
1951	
13–17 January	Battle of Vinh Yen
January–February	El Glaoui's Berber followers mount crisis in Morocco
28 February	Pleven government resigns
7–10 March	Queuille (Radical) forms government
23 March–1 April	Battle of Dong Trieu
28 May–7 June	Battle of Ninh Binh

17 June	General Election in France
10 July	Queuille government resigns
31 July	Assassination of General Chanson
11 August	Pleven (UDSR) forms government
7–25 September	De Lattre's visit to the United States
End September–	
6 October	Defeat of Viet Minh at Nghia Lo
10 November	Opening of battle of Hoa Binh

1952

6 January	General Salan appointed interim Commander-in-Chief
7 January	Pleven government resigns
11 January	Death of de Lattre
17–20 January	Faure (Radical) forms government
February	Evacuation of Hoa Binh
29 February	Faure government resigns
6–8 March	Pinay (Independent) forms government
1 April	Letourneau appointed High Commissioner for Indochina
9 April	Salan becomes Commander-in-Chief
June	Sihanouk's *coup* in Cambodia
20 July	Massacre of French women and children at Cap Saint-Jacques in Cochinchina
14–18 September	Viet Minh offensive at Nghia Lo
1–2 December	Viet Minh repulsed at Na San
23 December	Pinay government resigns

1953

7–8 January	Mayer (Radical) forms government
5 March	Death of Stalin
March–April	King Sihanouk opens independence crusade
15 April	Laotian government appeals for help
8 May	General Navarre appointed to succeed Salan
21 May	Mayer government resigns
26 June	Laniel (Independent) forms government
3 July	Dejean appointed Commissioner-General in Indochina
27 July	Armistice in Korea
12 August	Evacuation of Na San
20 August	Sultan of Morocco deposed
20 November	Occupation of Dien Bien Phu begins
23 December	Coty elected President of Republic

1954

25 January	Opening of Berlin Conference
18 February	Notification of forthcoming Geneva Conference
13 March	Opening of battle of Dien Bien Phu
April–August	Secret meetings of the Algerian *Comité Révolutionnaire d'Unité et d'Action*
26 April	Opening of the Geneva Conference
7 May	Fall of Dien Bien Phu
3 June	Navarre replaced by General Ely in Indochina
12 June	Laniel government resigns
16 June	Ngo Dinh Diem becomes head of Vietnam government
18 June	Mendès-France (Radical) forms government
20–24 June	Battle of An Khê
20 July	Geneva agreements on Indochina
27 July	Cease-fire in North Vietnam
31 July	Mendès-France and Declaration of Carthage
1 August	Cease-fire in central Vietnam
6 August	Cease-fire in Laos
7 August	Cease-fire in Cambodia
11 August	Cease-fire in South Vietnam
9 October	French withdrawal from Hanoi
27 October	Eisenhower promises Diem unconditional US support
1 November	Algerian Rebellion opens
10–30 November	Viet Minh troops withdraw from Laos and Cambodia
30 December	Signing of agreements between France, Cambodia, Laos and Vietnam

1955

25 January	Soustelle appointed Governor-General of Algiers
5 February	Mendès-France government resigns
19–23 February	Faure (Radical) forms government
2 April	State of Emergency in Algeria
17–24 April	Bandung Conference
15 May	Last French troops leave North Vietnam
20 August	Massacre of French miners and families in Middle Atlas; 75 killed in total in different locations
20 August	Philippeville massacre in Algeria, 71 Europeans killed

23 October	Referendum in South Vietnam rejects Bao Dai
26 October	Diem proclaims himself President of South Vietnam
5 November	Sultan of Morocco restored to throne
25 November	19 French soldiers killed in Morocco
29 November	Faure government defeated in Assembly
2 December	National Assembly dissolved

1956
2 January	General Election
31 January	Mollet (Socialist) forms government
2 February	Lacoste replaces Soustelle in Algeria
6 February	Mollet humiliated in Algiers
29 February	*Loi Cadre* for Black Africa introduced
7 March	Moroccan independence
4 March	Election of South Vietnam Constituent Assembly
20 March	Tunisian independence
End April	French troops leave South Vietnam
18 May	Palestro massacre of conscripts in Algeria
20 August	FLN Soummam Valley Conference
30 September	FLN bombings open Battle of Algiers
22 October	Ben Bella and others hijacked by French
5 November	Anglo-French attack upon Suez
14 December	Salan appointed Commander-in-Chief in Algeria
20 December	Creation of new Front for National Liberation in Vietnam

1957
7 January	General Massu given responsibility for Algiers
16 January	Attempt to assassinate Salan fails
28 January	Massu's troops break strike in Algiers
21 May	Mollet government resigns
11–13 June	Bourgès-Maunoury (Radical) forms government
2 July	Kennedy talks of 'independent personality' of Algeria
24 September	Yacef captured by French; end of battle of Algiers
30 September	Bourgès-Maunoury government resigns
29 October–	
5 November	Gaillard (Radical) forms government
26 December	Killing of Ramdane Abane

1958
8 February	French aircraft bomb Sakiet in Tunisia

15 April	Gaillard government resigns
26 April	*Colon* street demonstrations in Algiers
13 May	Pflimlin (MRP) forms government
28 May	Pflimlin government resigns
29 May	Coty invites de Gaulle to form government
1 June	De Gaulle government formed
28 September	Fifth Republic Constitution approved in National Referendum
3 October	De Gaulle launches Constantine plan
23 October	De Gaulle offers *paix des braves*
23 and	
30 November	General Election
19 December	Delouvrier and General Challe arrive in Algeria
21 December	De Gaulle elected President of Republic

1959

6 February	Challe's offensive in western Algeria opens
23 March	Amirouche killed
18 April	Challe's offensive in Algiers hinterland opens
22 July	Challe's offensives in the Kabyles and Hodna opens
16 September	De Gaulle offers 'self-determination' to Algeria
19 September	GPRA proclaimed in Cairo
Early November	Challe's offensives in the north Constantine area open

1960

1 January	Independence of Cameroun
19 January	Massu posted out of Algeria
24 January	'Barricades Week' begins
29 January	De Gaulle's speech
23 April	Challe posted out of Algeria
10 June	*Wilaya* 4 leaders meet de Gaulle
25 June	Melun talks with FLN open
29 June	Melun talks fail
1 July	Independence of Belgian Congo
28–29 September	Ferhat Abbas in Moscow and Peking
23 November	Delouvrier replaced by Joxe and Morin
20 December	UN recognition of Algeria's right to self-determination

1961

25 January	First major OAS assassination in Algiers
20–26 April	General's *coup* attempt in Algiers

25 April	First French atomic weapon exploded in the Sahara
20 May	Evian talks with FLN open
19–23 July	French–Tunisian fighting at Bizerta
28 July	Evian talks fail
8 September	Assassination attempt on de Gaulle near Paris

1962
7 March	Evian talks resumed
18 March	Agreement reached at Evian
19 March	Cease-fire between French and FLN
20 April	Salan captured by French
17 June	OAS and FLN conclude truce
1 July	Referendum on independence in Algeria
3 July	Algeria formally granted independence
15 September	Ben Bella becomes President of Algeria
25 September	Democratic and Popular Republic of Algeria proclaimed

ABBREVIATIONS

ALM	Armée de Libération Marocaine
ALN	Armée de Libération Nationale
AML	Les Amis du Manifeste et de la Liberté
CCE	Comité de Coordination et d'Exécution
CNRA	Conseil National de la Révolution Algérienne
CRUA	Comité Révolutionnaire d'Unité et d'Action
FAF	Front d'Algérie Française
FLN	Front de Libération Nationale
FNF	Front National Français
GPRA	Gouvernement Provisoire de la République Algérienne
JINA	Jeunesse Nationaliste Malgache
MDRM	Mouvement Démocratique de la Rénovation Malgache
MNA	Mouvement Nationaliste Algérien
MRP	Mouvement Républicain Populaire
MSM	Mouvement Social Malgache
MTLD	Mouvement pour la Triomphe des Libertés Démocratiques
OAS	Organisation Armée Secrète
ODA-T	Organisation de Défense Anti-Terroriste
OPA	Organisation Politico-Administrative
OS	Organisation Spéciale
PADESM	Parti des Déshérités de Madagascar
PANAMA	Parti Nationaliste Malgache
PDM	Parti Démocratique Malgache
PPA	Parti du Peuple Algérien
PSD	Parti Social Démocrate
RGR	Rassemblement des Gauches Républicans
RPF	Rassemblement du Peuple Français
SAS	Sections Administratives Spécialisées
SFIO	Section Française de l'Internationale Ouvrière
UDMA	Union Démocratique du Manifeste Algérien
UDSR	Union Démocratique et Socialiste de la Résistance

UFNA	Union Française Nord-Africaine
UGTT	Union Générale Tunisienne du Travail
UPC	Union des Populations du Cameroun
VNQDD	Viet Nam Quoc Dan Dang
VVS	*Vy, Vato, Sakeliko*

BIOGRAPHICAL NOTES

ABBAS, FERHAT   Ferhat was born in 1899, the son of a local official; he attended schools and the University of Algiers, where he studied pharmacy; he also served in the French North African Army. He began his political career in the 1930s, his aims at the time limited to the emancipation of the Moslem population within the French framework.

The defeat of France in 1940 and the failure of the Pétain and later the interim post-Allied landings French administrations to grant any concessions led him to make a formal demand for internal autonomy in a famous manifesto in 1943, and to lead a political organization to support the demand. Briefly detained after the May 1945 Sétif uprising, Ferhat on his release formed a new moderate nationalist political movement, the UDMA, which won 11 of the 13 seats in the 1946 Constituent Assembly allotted to Moslems. Under the 1947 *Statut*, however, and with elections ruthlessly gerrymandered by the French administration, the UDMA lost strength and credibility. Initially critical of the 1954 uprising, by 1955 Ferhat had developed contacts with the FLN and in Cairo in 1956 formally joined them. When the FLN formed its provisional Algerian government in 1958 Ferhat was elected President, but he was set aside in 1961 in favour of the more radical Ben Khedda. After independence, Ferhat served briefly as President of the Assembly but was placed under arrest by Ben Bella in 1964. After the Boumedienne *coup* Ferhat was released but was again placed under house arrest in 1976. In 1984 he was restored to civic rights, and in 1985 he died.

ARGENLIEU, ADMIRAL THIERRY D'   D'Argenlieu was born at Brest in 1889 and was commissioned as a naval officer in 1908. He served until 1920, when he entered a Carmelite monastery as Father Louis of the Trinity. On the collapse of France in 1940 he rejoined the Navy and was appointed by de Gaulle first as High Commissioner in the Pacific from 1941 to 1943, and then from 1944 as Commander of Free French naval forces. In 1945 de Gaulle appointed d'Argenlieu as

High Commissioner in Indochina; his increasingly hard line led to his replacement in 1947. He then returned to religious life, dying in 1964.

BAO DAI Bao Dai was born in 1913, becoming titular Emperor in 1925, confirmed in 1932. He was educated in France. In the Second World War Bao Dai was initially prepared to work with the Japanese; supported by them he proclaimed an independent government for all Vietnam in March 1945. But the mistakes of this government, and Bao Dai's status, led Ho Chi Minh and the Viet Minh to demand his abdication. To preserve a façade of a broad front he was, however, briefly a 'councillor' in Ho's government. This arrangement broke down and Bao Dai left Indochina to live abroad, largely in Paris, from 1945 to 1949, during which time he tried to secure sufficient concessions from the French to enable him to return to Indochina as a credible non-Communist nationalist alternative to the Viet Minh. He agreed to return in 1949, but the status he was accorded by the French, except perhaps that briefly given by de Lattre in 1951, was never sufficient to secure any patriotic following. After the French defeat at Dien Bien Phu in 1954 Bao Dai lost all support and was deposed; following a national referendum in South Vietnam organized by Ngo Dinh Diem a republic was proclaimed. Bao Dai departed into exile in the south of France.

BEN BELLA, MOHAMMED Ben Bella was born at Marnia in 1919. He served in the French *Armée d'Afrique*, becoming a warrant officer and being awarded the *Médaille Militaire* for his conduct in the Italian campaign. After the war he became a member of the MTLD, from which he moved on to the insurrectionary OS, participating in acts of violence from 1949 onwards. In 1950 he was arrested but escaped, and in 1954 became a member of the CRUA and one of the 'historic nine' who planned the outbreak of the rebellion. His next role was that of organizing the supply of arms to the FLN from outside. In 1956 Ben Bella and other 'external' FLN leaders were hijacked by the French while on a flight from Morocco to Tunis, and he remained in detention until the final stages of the 1962 negotiations, in which he took a hard line. After independence Ben Bella and Boumedienne progressively undermined and then overthrew the provisional government of Ben Khedda, and after the September 1962 single-list election Ben Bella was elected Prime Minister. Ben Bella's government was, however, in turn overthrown by Boumedienne in a *coup* in 1965. Ben Bella himself was placed under arrest but was released in 1979, when he went into voluntary exile in Switzerland. There he was associated with groupings opposed to the government of Boumedienne's successor, Bendjedid.

BEN KHEDDA, YOUSSEF   Ben Khedda was born in Algeria and studied pharmacy in Algiers University. A follower of Messali Hadj, he was arrested in 1943 for eight months. On his release he was one of the founder members and Secretary-General of the MTLD. He was again arrested by the French in April 1955 but released a little later, after which he joined the FLN, in which he was one of the organizers of the Soummam Valley Congress and a leading member of the CNRA. Holding a key liaison post, Ben Khedda played a leading role in preparing the FLN challenge in Algiers in 1956–57. After the failure of the FLN offensive in Algiers Ben Khedda fled to Cairo, where he was an important figure in the GPRA government in exile, becoming its President in 1961, and one of the leading negotiators in the Evian negotiations. After Algeria's independence Ben Khedda was unable to maintain his position and authority against the challenge of Ben Bella and Boumedienne, and was neither a member of the government formed in September 1962 nor even a member of the Assembly. Ben Khedda then retired from public life, emerging only to criticize some of Boumedienne's policies in 1976, for which he was placed under house arrest. He died shortly afterwards.

BIDAULT, GEORGES   Bidault was born in 1899; he served as a conscript soldier in the First World War and then became a teacher of history, also interesting himself in politics. He played an outstanding role as head of the Resistance in France during the Second World War, after which he became a leading figure in the MRP. Here the paradox of his views, a liberal, pro-Europe, pro-NATO, in favour of reconciliation with Germany on the one hand, with a total opposition to any form of colonial nationalism on the other, soon became evident. As Prime Minister (twice), and Foreign Minister in a number of governments, Bidault actively worked for the Treaty of Dunkirk and Western European Union, for NATO and for the European Coal and Steel Community. At the same time he took an uncompromising attitude towards events in Morocco and Indochina, though in the case of the latter he became realistic as well as skilful in the 1954 Geneva negotiations after the defeat at Dien Bien Phu. At first welcoming de Gaulle's return to power, Bidault quickly became disillusioned and increasingly critical of de Gaulle's policies in Algeria. He sympathized with the aims, if not the methods, of the OAS to the extent that he was charged with conspiracy. Before the formal charge he had, however, gone underground and later went into exile in Brazil. In 1968 the charges against him were dropped and he returned to France. He lived in retirement until his death in 1983.

BOUDIAF, MOHAMMED   Boudiaf was born in 1919; his education was curtailed by illness. He served in the French Army where in 1943 he organized nationalist cells among Algerian soldiers. He was an MTLD party organizer and a member of the OS before the outbreak of the rebellion, and one of the rebellion's 'historic nine' organizers. With Ben Bella he was imprisoned by the French after the 1956 airliner hijacking. After independence Boudiaf was arrested by Ben Bella, but later released. He went into exile in Morocco where he led an organization opposed to Boumedienne. After the Algerian political crisis of December 1991–January 1992, Boudiaf, as a national hero, became Chairman of a High Committee of State, effectively Head of State. He was, however, assassinated later in the year in circumstances that remain unclear.

BOUMEDIENNE, HOUARI   Born in the mid-1920s as Mohammed ben Brahin Boukharouba, Boumedienne came from a poor peasant family of the Guelma area. He joined the FLN in 1955, quickly displaying marked organizational ability, first as a guerrilla leader and then as Chief of Staff of the ALN in Tunis, awaiting its moment. At independence Boumedienne joined with Ben Bella to oppose the provisional Algerian government of Ben Khedda. He served in several of Ben Bella's governments until 1965 when he overthrew Ben Bella in a military *coup* and became President of Algeria. In office he nationalized the mines in 1966 and the oil companies in 1971, and through his support for Arab nations in the 1967 Six Day war became a leader of Third World nations. He died in office in 1978.

BOURGUIBA, HABIB   Bourguiba was born in Tunisia in 1903, the son of a Tunisian officer in the French Army. He was educated at schools in Tunisia and studied law in Paris. From his youth a nationalist, he was a leading member of the early nationalist *Destour* Party, and from 1934 Secretary-General of the more radical break-away *Néo-Destour*. He was arrested in 1934, released in 1936, re-arrested in 1938 and taken by the Germans in 1942. Axis efforts to woo him to their cause failed but French surveillance of his activities drove him into exile, mostly in Cairo, between 1945 and 1949. Returning to Tunisia in 1949 he resumed active nationalist political activity, for which he was arrested again early in 1952. After Dien Bien Phu and the accession to power of the Mendès-France government in Paris, Bourguiba was allowed to return to Tunisia in 1955 where his main problems were challenges from more militant rivals in the *Néo-Destour*, some of these taking the form of insurgency. Bourguiba triumphed, obtaining independence from the French in 1956 with himself as Premier. In 1957 the Tunisian monarchy was abolished, Bourguiba becoming President. He was re-elected President in 1959, 1964, 1969 and 1974; in 1975 he was proclaimed President for life. In 1987, aged and infirm, he was removed from office and placed under house arrest.

BOYER DE LATOUR DU MOULIN, GENERAL PIERRE   Born in 1896, Boyer spent most of his military career in North Africa, especially in Morocco. He served with distinction in the North-west Europe campaign of 1944–45, and in the Indochina war proved a successful military commander in Cochinchina. He was appointed military commander in Tunisia in 1953, and then in 1954 elevated to the post of Resident-General. He was, however, quickly moved to be Resident-General in Morocco in 1955. He resigned from this post later in the same year, following the decision by the Faure government that Sultan Mohammed V be allowed to return. He died in 1976.

CATROUX, GENERAL GEORGES   Catroux was born in 1877 and joined the Army in 1896, later entering Saint-Cyr. He quickly made a reputation as a highly intellectual colonial soldier. He served in the *Légion Etrangère* and *Tirailleurs Algériens* prior to the First World War, in which he was wounded and taken prisoner in 1914. In the inter-war years Catroux held important appointments in North Africa and Syria. He was appointed Governor-General of Indochina early in 1940 but resigned the appointment to rally to de Gaulle after the fall of France, the most senior French officer to do so. After the Allied occupation of Syria and Lebanon in 1941, de Gaulle first appointed Catroux to be High Commissioner in the Levant, then from 1943 to 1944 Governor-General of Algeria, where he found his efforts towards reform thwarted by the strength of the *colons*, and lastly as a minister in the interim French government. After the war Catroux served as Ambassador to Moscow from 1945 to 1948. Because of his known liberal views he was used successfully by the Laniel government to persuade Sultan Mohammed V to return peacefully to Morocco in 1955. The Mollet government tried to appoint him Governor-General of Algeria in 1956 but *colon* objection forced cancellation of the appointment. After the abortive generals' *coup* in Algiers in 1961 Catroux was appointed by de Gaulle to be a member of the military tribunal to try the offenders. Here, without in any way condoning the subsequent actions of the OAS, Catroux argued for clemency, understanding if not agreeing with the sentiments of the accused and anxious not to open any blood feud within the Army that would follow death sentences. This lenient approach, accepted by the tribunal, was unacceptable to de Gaulle, who reconstituted the court. Catroux continued university-level teaching until 1963; he died in 1969, a remarkable if somewhat neglected figure in French twentieth-century history.

CHALLE, GENERAL MAURICE   Born in 1905, Challe had been a pre-war Air Force officer. After the fall of France Challe was first a member of the Resistance, in which he performed several notable services, and then a bomber commander. Although an airman, he was selected by de Gaulle in 1958 to be Commander-in-Chief in Algeria, where he proved to be one of the most successful of France's counter-insurgency generals, conducting a series of major operations in 1959. After the events of 1960, Barricades Week, a reluctant Challe was brought back to France on promotion to a major NATO command. In January 1961, increasingly concerned over de Gaulle's Algerian policies, Challe resigned from the armed forces and in April he headed the abortive generals' *coup* in Algiers. His motive was one of responsibility towards Algerians fighting on the French side whom he felt must not be abandoned. He refused to order French personnel to fire on other French personnel, and on the failure of the *coup* gave himself up. Arrested, tried and imprisoned, Challe was released on medical grounds in 1966 and amnestied in 1968. He died in 1979.

FAURE, EDGAR   Born in 1908, Faure studied law and became a Radical Deputy in 1946. He served twice as Prime Minister, in 1952 and in 1955–56, and as a minister in several other governments. In 1950 he was expelled from the Radical Party following his decision to call an election (and also as a result of his approval of the return of the Sultan of Morocco). He then became leader of the RGR and as such served as Finance Minister in the short-lived Pflimlin government of May 1958. After the accession to power of de Gaulle, Faure became a Senator, Minister for Agriculture in 1965, Minister for Education 1968–69, and President of the *Assemblée Nationale* from 1973 to 1978. In 1979 he was elected a member of the European Parliament. He was also, at the same time, Professor of Law at Dijon University from 1962. He died in 1988.

GAULLE, PRESIDENT CHARLES DE   De Gaulle was born in 1890 and after training at Saint-Cyr served as an infantry officer, being wounded on the Western Front and taken prisoner. After the war he served in France, Poland and Lebanon. In the 1930s he wrote on the need for the modernization and mechanization of the French Army, and in 1940 he commanded a small French armoured formation. Rejecting the concept of an armistice, de Gaulle, still only an unknown briga-dier-general, launched his Free French movement from London, at the same time from the start asserting his own independence from Britain. After the Allied landings in North Africa, and despite strenuous Amer-ican opposition, de Gaulle progressively extended his claim to the leadership of all French forces serving with the Allies and to the headship of a provisional French government; as head of this provi-sional government he rendered his second great achievement for France, the containment of the very powerful Communist movement. He resigned in January 1946 in protest against the emerging style of political life. This style, the *régime d'Assemblée*, was to remain the target of his bitter criticism until events in Algeria led to his return to power, first as Prime Minister and then as executive President in 1958. He remained President until 1969, giving France great interna-tional prestige. In his third major achievement for his country, finalized only amid violent controversy and assassination attempts, he withdrew France from Algeria in 1962. When de Gaulle died in 1970 his successor, Pompidou, commented 'France is a widow'.

GIAP, GENERAL VO NGUYEN Giap was born in 1911, the son of a peasant farmer. He attended schools in Hué and Hanoi and read law at Hanoi University. From his early years a political activist, Giap soon joined the Vietnam Communist Party; his militant beliefs were strengthened after the death in prison of his first wife and the execution of her sister by the French. In 1941 he joined Ho Chi Minh's partisans, where he quickly acquired military skills to add to his organizing abilities. These he used initially against non-Communist nationalist leaders and groups. From 1945 onwards he commanded Viet Minh and later Viet Cong forces in both Indochina wars. Of his campaigns Giap later remarked, 'For us there is never a single strategy. Ours is always a synthesis, military, political, diplomatic.' Although suffering some reverses and at enormous cost in human life, Giap's skilful use of this synthesis ensured him a place in history as one of the most successful field insurgent leaders of any age.

GUILLAUME, GENERAL AUGUSTIN Born in 1895, Guillaume spent al-most all his pre-1939 military service in North Africa, mostly in Morocco. He led the *goums*, irregular levies, in the Italian campaign with notable success, and became a divisional commander in the 1944–45 North-west Europe campaign. After service as Military Attache in Moscow and Commander-in-Chief of French forces in Germany, Guillaume was appointed Resident-General in Morocco; in this appointment he deposed Sultan Mohammed V. In 1953 he became Chief of Staff of the French Armed Forces, from which he retired in 1956. He died in 1983.

HO CHI MINH Born in or about 1890 as Nguyen Tat Tanh, Ho Chi Minh was the son of a minor official dismissed by the French. He spent the years 1912–18 as a ship's steward, dishwasher in a London hotel and a photographer in Paris. Under the name Nguyen Ai Quoc he became immersed in revolutionary politics, becoming a founder member of the French Communist Party. He studied in Moscow in the 1920s; in 1930 he founded the Vietnam Communist Party. Arrested briefly by the British in Hong Kong in 1930, he was released in 1932. He moved between the Soviet Union and China for the remainder of the 1930s. In 1941 he formed the Viet Minh but was detained for over a year by the Chinese Nationalists. On his release, and under the name of Ho Chi Minh, he quickly assumed the formal leadership of the Viet Minh, proclaiming Vietnam's independence in September 1945. Throughout the years of conflict with the French, Ho remained the effective leader. After the Geneva Conference, and in the subsequent war with the United States, Ho's personal authority as Democratic President of the Republic of Vietnam appears to have been reduced perhaps on account of his age. His name, however, continued to appear on all official communications. Ho's ruthlessness and dedication to Communism were often concealed behind an overtly mild, benevolent manner, charm and humour. One of the outstanding figures of twentieth-century Communism, Ho died in 1969. After the final collapse of the South Vietnam regime Saigon was re-named Ho Chi Minh City in his honour.

JUIN, MARSHAL ALPHONSE Juin was born, the son of a gendarme, at Bône in Algeria in 1888. He attended schools in Algeria and France before entering Saint-Cyr, where, at an early age, he first displayed his exceptional military abilities by passing out first. Juin's military service before 1939 was spent almost entirely in North Africa or with Moroccan troops on the Western Front. After the fall of France in 1940 Juin was appointed Commander of all Land Forces in North Africa by the Vichy government. After the Allied landings in North Africa Juin commanded first the French forces in the Tunisian campaign and then with notable success, the French Expeditionary Corps in the

Italian campaign. In 1944 de Gaulle appointed him Chief of Defence Staff. From 1947 to 1951 Juin was Resident-General in Morocco, from where he returned to France to be Inspector-General of the Armed Forces, Commander-in-Chief NATO Land Forces, and France's only marshal. He retired in 1956. His opposition to de Gaulle's Algerian policies became outspoken and led to his briefly being placed under a loose form of house arrest in 1962. He died in 1967.

KRIM, BELKACEM Krim was born in 1922 and served as a junior non-commissioned officer in the French Army. He became an insurgent leader from 1947 onwards and was one of the 'historic nine' leaders of the CRUA. After the battle of Algiers Krim joined the 'external' FLN leadership, serving as a minister in the Provisional Government, GPRA. He was the chief negotiator for most of the Evian negotiations and an opponent of Ben Bella at independence. He stayed out of politics for three years but in 1965 was accused of attempting to assassinate Boumedienne. He departed into exile and was himself assassinated in Germany in 1970.

LATTRE DE TASSIGNY, MARSHAL JEAN DE De Lattre was born in 1889, and after training at Saint-Cyr served in the cavalry and later the infantry on the Western Front. He was wounded on several occasions. In the years 1919–39 de Lattre served in Morocco and France; in 1940 he commanded a division with notable valour. In November 1942, virtually alone of the officers of the Vichy Army, de Lattre tried to organize resistance to the German forces entering Unoccupied France. For this, seen by the Vichy authorities as disobedience, he was imprisoned. He escaped from prison and was flown secretly out of France. He commanded the French army that landed with the Allied forces in the south of France in August 1944; this army formed the right flank of the Allied armies in the final North-west Europe campaign. After the war, de Lattre became Inspector-General of the Armed Forces and in 1948 Commander of the Land Forces of the Western European Union. In 1950 he was appointed High Commissioner and Commander-in-Chief in Indochina, where by personal ability he retrieved the French forces from a potentially disastrous situation. He continued to serve in Indochina until his death in 1952. His personality, charismatic but mercurial, often aroused controversy, but he remains one of the most outstanding commanders ever produced by the French Army.

LECLERC DE HAUTECLOCQUE, MARSHAL PHILIPPE De Hauteclocque was born in 1902 into a Catholic conservative family of the country aristocracy. After training at Saint-Cyr de Hauteclocque served in the cavalry in France and Morocco. In 1940 his fiery patriotism led him immediately to rally to de Gaulle under the alias of Leclerc. De Gaulle directed him to secure French Equatorial Africa for Free France and then to lead a column across the Sahara from Chad to Tripoli. Leclerc next commanded an armoured division in the Liberation and North-west Europe campaigns, units of this division being the first to enter Paris. In 1945 de Gaulle appointed Leclerc Commander of French forces in Indochina. There his liberal views were at variance with those of the High Commissioner, Admiral d'Argenlieu. Leclerc, a man of total integrity, returned to France in 1946 and was given a North African command. He died in an aircraft accident in Algeria in 1947.

MASSU, GENERAL JACQUES   Massu was born in 1908 and, after training at Saint-Cyr, joined the colonial infantry. In 1940 he immediately joined Leclerc's Free French forces in West Africa, and served with Leclerc's armoured division, a column commanded by him forming the vanguard of the French entry into Paris in August 1944. In 1945–46, again under Leclerc, Massu led columns in the re-occupation of Cochinchina. In 1955 Massu was appointed to command the elite 10th Parachute Division, which he led at Suez and in the battle of Algiers. He was promoted to be Commander of the Algiers Region Corps in 1958, but in January 1960 he was recalled and retired following critical remarks about de Gaulle that he made to a journalist. In 1961, however, he was reinstated, first as Military Governor of Metz from 1961 to 1966, and then as Commander-in-Chief of the French troops in Germany from 1966 to 1969. In this latter role, when so besought by de Gaulle, he promised military support to restore the authority of the President at the time of the May 1968 student-worker riots. In the event the support was not needed. Massu retired in 1969.

MENDES-FRANCE, PIERRE   Mendès-France was born in 1907, his part-Jewish family having emigrated to France from Portugal in the sixteenth century. An outstanding Paris University law student, Mendès-France qualified as France's youngest lawyer in 1928. He became a Radical Deputy in 1932 and rallied to de Gaulle in 1941 after escaping from Vichy custody, becoming a minister in de Gaulle's provisional government in the years 1944–45. He returned to the Assembly as a Deputy in 1946. These events led him to develop increasingly critical views on French colonial policies in Indochina and North Africa. He became Prime Minister after the May 1954 Dien Bien Phu disaster, securing a dignified French withdrawal from the area. He also set Tunisia on the road to independence with the July 1954 Declaration of Carthage. He served as a minister in Mollet's 1956 Socialist government, but resigned when Mollet appointed Lacoste as Governor-General of Algeria in place of General Catroux; he lost his seat in the 1958 election. He was opposed to de Gaulle, and assumed the leadership of the non-Communist Left in the Assembly in 1967–68. He died in 1982. He has been described as 'the most memorable statesman of the Fourth Republic'.

MOHAMMED V, SULTAN, from 1957 King, of Morocco Sidi Mohammed, as he was known in the French Protectorate period, was born in 1910. He was the third son of Sultan Moulay Youssef, who died in 1927, when a Regency was proclaimed. Mohammed was instructed by French tutors, but as a young man indicated his own personal commitment to nationalism, though not one that was anti-French. A reluctant client of Vichy, Mohammed was pleased with the arrival of the Americans in November 1942 and from then on, notably in Tangier in 1947, expressed a demand for Moroccan independence. This demand led Mohammed into increasing confrontation with the French authorities and in 1953 he was deposed and exiled. The deposition led to a breakdown of order in Morocco and open insurgency in the mountains, with the result that the French were obliged to restore Mohammed in 1955 and concede independence in 1956. The King continued to play the lead role in the politics of Morocco until his death in 1961.

MOLLET, GUY Mollet was born in north France in 1905 and became a secondary school teacher. Mobilized in 1940, he was taken prisoner but later released. He joined the Resistance, served with distinction and was thrice arrested by the Germans. After the war he entered politics as a Socialist, becoming Mayor of Arras, a Deputy Secretary-General of the SFIO (Socialist Party) and briefly a Minister of State in de Gaulle's provisional government. He became Prime Minister in January 1956 and headed the longest-lasting government of the Fourth Republic, surviving until May 1957. His premiership included his abortive attempt to install General Catroux as Governor-General of Algeria, the Suez crisis and much of the Battle of Algiers. He was, however, defeated on a financial question. In the crisis of May 1958 Mollet supported the return of de Gaulle to power, and he continued to support de Gaulle's Algerian policies. In the Fifth Republic years Mollet lost influence, and when in 1971 the Socialist Party was re-formed with Mitterrand as leader, Mollet withdrew into the background. He died in 1975.

NAVARRE, GENERAL HENRI   Navarre was born in 1898; his father was at the time Dean of the Faculty of Letters at Toulouse University. During the First World War he served in both the infantry and the cavalry and attended Saint-Cyr. In the Second World War, in which he followed Vichy until the Allied landings in North Africa, Navarre was an intelligence specialist and a regimental commander. After the war he served in Algeria and in Germany, before being appointed to command in Indochina in 1953. After the disaster of Dien Bien Phu and the subsequent enquiries Navarre embarked on a new career in the brick industry. He died in 1983.

NGO DINH DIEM   Diem was born in Hué in 1901, the son of one of the ministers of Emperor Thanh Thai. His personality and upbringing were an uneasy mixture of Catholicism, modernization and traditional Confucian Mandarin authoritarianism. He was profoundly antagonistic to the French and refused to participate in public life under them. He believed that their ejection from Indochina and the future of Vietnam could best be secured by means of American help. Supported by the Americans he became Premier in Emperor Bao Dai's Vietnam government in June 1954. After the collapse of French rule Diem deposed Bao Dai and organized a referendum, which in a 98 per-cent vote nominated him as President of the Republic of Vietnam. At first successful in suppressing the semi-independent religious sects in the country, his rule became increasingly despotic, his regime corrupt, and at the same time unable to secure itself against Communist infiltration and subversion from the north. Diem survived two *coup* attempts, but fell victim to a third in 1963, in which covert American involvement has been alleged. In the course of this *coup* Diem was killed.

RABEMANANJARA, JACQUES   Rabemananjara was born in 1913 in Maroantsetra; he was educated in Madagascar, and in France during the war years. In 1946 he was elected a Deputy for Madagascar to the French National Assembly. He was the first Secretary-General of the MDRM. After the 1947 Madagascar uprising Rabemananjara was sentenced to forced labour for life, but was later removed to France in detention. At independence in 1960 he returned to Madagascar and became a minister and later Vice-President. Rabemananjara, a journalist and author, has written extensively; his works include poetry and drama as well as political commentary.

RAMADIER, PAUL   Ramadier was born into a bourgeois family in 1888, and studied law in Toulouse and Paris. As a sergeant he won a decoration for bravery in the First World War. He became a Socialist Deputy in 1928, and a junior minister in 1937. He opposed the granting of full powers to Pétain in 1940; as a reward for this he became Minister for Food in de Gaulle's 1944 government. He was a minister in Blum's 1946 government and became Prime Minister in 1947. Later he served as a minister in the 1948 Queuille and 1956 Mollet governments. He opposed the return of de Gaulle in 1958 and lost his seat in the election of that year, after which he retired from politics. He died in 1961.

RAVOAHANGY, JOSEPH Joseph Ravoahangy Andrianavolon, a Merina, was born in 1893 and educated at a Norwegian Protestant mission school before embarking on a medical course at Tamatave. Ravoahangy's medical studies were interrupted by a period of exile in the Comores because of his involvement with the *Vy, Vato, Sakelika* proto-nationalist movement. After qualification, he involved himself in trade-union and nationalist activities, becoming after 1945 a founder member of the MDRM and being elected a Deputy for Madagascar to the French National Assembly. After the 1947 uprising, Ravoahangy was sentenced to death, a sentence later commuted to imprisonment. At independence in 1960 Ravoahangy became Minister for Public Health and Population; later in 1965 he was appointed Minister without Portfolio in the President's Office.

SALAN, GENERAL RAOUL Salan was born in 1899 the son of a junior official. He was commissioned from Saint-Cyr in 1919. After a distinguished career as a front-line soldier in the Second World War Salan served in Indochina, succeeding de Lattre as Commander-in-Chief in late 1951. He commanded with considerable ability but was unable to prevent a progressive decline in the French military position and was recalled in 1953. In 1956 he was appointed to command in Algeria, where he again showed ability but with an increasing ruthlessness. After the accession to power of de Gaulle, Salan was recalled, de Gaulle believing that he had attempted to rig the November 1958 elections. He was given a sinecure appointment in France. There Salan's penchant for intrigue, and support for hard-line officers known to be critical of de Gaulle's policies, brought him under surveillance and he fled to Spain in 1960. From Spain he travelled to Algeria secretly in 1961 to place himself as one of the heads of the abortive generals' *coup*. After the failure of the *coup* Salan went underground as head of the extreme Right-wing, anti-de Gaulle OAS, which was conducting a campaign of terror in Algiers. Caught by French forces in 1962,

Salan was placed on trial and sentenced to life imprisonment. He was released after the 1968 amnesty and died in 1984.

SOUSTELLE, JACQUES Soustelle was born in 1912 into a Protestant working-class family. After university he became an anthropologist and a member of a number of Left-wing, anti-fascist intellectual groups. After the fall of France in 1940 Soustelle rallied to de Gaulle and became head of de Gaulle's intelligence services. After the war he became Secretary-General of the MRP from 1947 to 1951. In 1955 he was appointed Governor-General of Algeria. He initially planned a radical reform and integrationist policy but was opposed by the *colon* lobby and he himself was converted to a more cautious approach by FLN brutality, especially the Philippeville massacres of 1955. Recalled to France in 1956, he campaigned actively for the return to power of de Gaulle and served in de Gaulle's first cabinet. He, however, became increasingly opposed to de Gaulle's Algerian policies and went into exile in 1961. In 1962 a warrant for his arrest was issued. Soustelle accordingly lived abroad until the 1968 amnesty, after which he returned to Paris in an academic appointment. He later returned to the National Assembly and served as French representative to the Council of Europe in 1973, after which he returned to academic anthropological work. He died in 1990.

NOTES ON FURTHER READING

These notes must necessarily limit themselves to the more important standard works; any complete bibliographical survey of all the military operations set in their wider contexts would extend to several volumes. The titles that follow will, however, serve as a further step within which, in turn, titles of studies more extended or specialized studies can be found.

In respect of France herself, Alfred Cobban, *A History of Modern France*, vol. 3, 1871–1962 (London, 1979) forms a foundation. For further metropolitan political studies, Jean Pierre Roux, *The Fourth Republic 1944–1958* (Cambridge, 1968); Frank Giles, *The Locust Years, the story of the Fourth French Republic 1946–1958* (London, 1991); and P.M. Williams, *Crisis and Compromise: Politics in the Fourth Republic* (London, 1964) will carry readers further. The most important French texts are A. Grosser, *La Quatrième République et sa politique extérieure* (Paris, 1961); G. Elgey, *La République des illusions, 1945–51* and *La République des contradictions 1951–54* (Paris, 1965 and 1968), and President V. Auriol, *Journal du Septennat, 1947–54* (Paris, 1970–71, seven volumes).

For the French Empire, D.B. Marshall, *The French Colonial Myth and Constitution Making in the Fourth Republic* (New Haven, 1973); Raoul Girardet, *L'Idée coloniale en France* (Paris, 1972); and Jacques Thobie and others, *Histoire de la France coloniale*, Vol. II (Paris, 1990), are all valuable.

The French Army merits special examination. For English readers, Anthony Clayton, *France, Soldiers and Africa* and *Three Marshals of France* (London, 1988 and 1981) will both be found useful, as well, in wider context, as Alistair Horne, *The French Army and Politics 1870–1970* (London, 1987) and J.S. Ambler, *The French Army in Politics 1945–1962* (Ohio, University Press, 1962). The earlier significance of the Army, and especially that of the *Troupes de Marine* (*La Coloniale*) and colonial forces generally is well set out in Christopher

213

M. Andrew and A.S. Kanya-Forstner, *France Overseas: the Great War and the Climax of French Imperial Expansion* (London, 1981).

De Gaulle, of course, towers over historiography as in most other matters; the best biographies are Bernard Ledwidge, *De Gaulle* (London, 1982), and the English version of Jean Lacouture, *De Gaulle, the Rebel, 1890–1944* and *De Gaulle, the Ruler 1945–1970* (both London, 1992).

Colonial and decolonization campaign strategies attract theoretical writers. Of especial value as an overview is Ian Beckett and John Pimlott, *Armed Forces and Modern Counter-Insurgency* (London, 1985). In respect of revolutionary theory, Mao Tse-tung, *Selected Military Writings*, (Peking, 1967) or S.B. Griffith (ed.), *Mao Tse Tung on Guerilla Warfare* (New York, 1978), Vo Nguyen Giap, *People's War, People's Army* (New York, 1962), Truong Chinh, *The Resistance Will Win* (Hanoi, 1960), and Frantz Fanon, *The Wretched of the Earth* (London, 1965) are important in the context of campaigns studied here. French theories are well summarized in G.A. Kelly, *Lost Soldiers* (Cambridge MA., 1964), and P. Paret, *French Revolutionary Warfare from Indo-China to Algeria* (London, 1964), and in French in Roger Trinquier's *La Guerre moderne* (Paris, 1961) and *Guerre, Subversion, Révolution* (Paris, 1968).

Each of the two major campaigns, Indochina and Algeria, is now covered by numerous works. For Indochina, J. Davidson, *Indochina Signposts in the Storm* (Kuala Lumpur, 1979) is an excellent basic introduction, after which Jacques Dalloz, *The War in Indochina 1945–54* (Dublin, 1990), Joseph Butlinger, *Vietnam: a Political History* (London, 1969), and Anthony Short, *The Origins of the Vietnam War* (London, 1989) all provide much further information. Also useful are chapters in Dennis J. Duncanson, *Government and Revolution in Vietnam* (London, 1968), D. Lancaster, *The Emancipation of French Indochina* (London, 1961), and P.J. Honey, *Genesis of a Tragedy: the Historical Background to the Vietnam War* (London, 1968). Of especial value in its detailed analysis of the French domestic political activity resulting from the Indochina war is R.E.M. Irving, *The First Indochina War* (London, 1975).

For overall accounts of the fighting, Bernard Fall, *Street Without Joy: Indochina at War 1946–54* (Harrisburg, PA, 1961), Edgar O'Ballance, *The Indochina War, 1945–54* (London, 1964), and an excellent French study, General Yves Gras, *Histoire de la Guerre d'Indochine* (Paris, 1979) are outstanding. Of particular specialist interest because it draws on memoirs and personal accounts is

Philippe Heduy, *La Guerre d'Indochine 1945–54* (Paris, 1981). There is also a stimulating over-view in the first chapters of Elizabeth Jane Errington and B.J.C. McKercher, *The Vietnam War as History* (New York, 1990).

For particular phases of the war, two *Service Historique de l'Armée de Terre* collections of documents in book form are useful: *Le Retour de la France en Indochine, 1945–46* (Vincennes, 1987), and *Indochine 1947, règlement politique et solution militaire* (Vincennes, 1989). A third volume, *Indochine, l'année 1948* is expected. Other volumes may follow. General Vezinet, *Le Général Leclerc* (Paris, 1982), and Bernard Simiot, *De Lattre* (Paris, 1954) contain accounts of their respective commands, as do Raoul Salan, *Mémoires, II* (Paris, 1971), General Henri Navarre, *Agonie de l'Indochine 1953–54* (Paris, 1956), General Paul Ely, *L'Indochine dans la tourmente* (Paris, 1964), and General Giap, *Dien Bien Phu* (Hanoi 1964).

For Indochina political events and the international facets of the conflict among the most informative are J. Sainteny, *Histoire d'une paix manquée, Indochine 1945–47* (Paris, 1953), King Chen, *Vietnam and China 1938–54* (Princeton, 1964), Arthur M. Schlesinger, Jr, *The Bitter Heritage: Vietnam and American Democracy* (London, 1967), Robert F. Randle, *Geneva 1954* (Princeton, 1969), J. Lacouture, *Ho Chi Minh* (Paris, 1967), and Bernard Fall, *The Viet-Minh Regime* (New York, 1954).

The three indispensable basic books for Algeria are Charles-Robert Ageron's history of Algeria since 1830, *Modern Algeria* (London, 1991), John Ruedy, *Modern Algeria, the Origins and Development of a Nation*, (Bloomington, IN, 1992) and one of the finest overall accounts of the campaign, Alistair Horne, *A Savage War of Peace: Algeria 1954–1962* (London, 1987). These can usefully be supplemented by Alf Andrew Heggoy, *Insurgency and Counter-insurgency in Algeria* (Bloomington, IN, 1972) and in French by B. Droz and E. Lever, *Histoire de la guerre d'Algérie 1954–62* (Paris, 1982), and Pierre Le Goyet, *La Guerre d'Algérie* (Paris, 1989).

A *Service historique* collection of documents, *La Guerre d'Algérie par les documents, I, L'Avertissement 1943–1946* (Vincennes, 1990) portrays a fascinating picture of Algeria before, during and after the Sétif uprising of May 1945. Unfortunately, further volumes of documents are not now to be produced, Algeria remaining highly sensitive. The four volumes of Yves Courrière; *La Guerre d'Algérie, Les fils de la Toussaint* (Paris, 1968), *Les Temps des léopards* (Paris, 1969), *L'Heure des colonels* (Paris, 1970) and *Les Feux du désespoir, la fin d'un empire* (Paris, 1971) provide a richly detailed journalist-style narrative of the events. H. Alleg and others provide another, three-volume, history in *La Guerre d'Algérie* (Paris, 1981); also useful are J. Talbott, *The War Without a Name, France in Algeria 1954–62* (London, 1981), David C. Gordon, *The Passing of French Algeria* (London, 1966), and Michael Kettle, *De Gaulle and Algeria 1940–1960* (London, 1993).

Specifically military works of note are André Beaufre, *La Guerre Révolutionnaire* (Paris, 1972), Raoul Salan, *Mémoires, III* (Paris, 1972) and IV, (Paris, 1974), and Jacques Massu, *La Vraie Bataille d'Alger* (Paris, 1971). Another very full collection of personal accounts of French soldiers of all ranks serving in the widest variety of duties appears in François Porteu de la Morandière, *Soldats du Djebel* (Paris, 1979).

Algerian contributions include Ferhat Abbas, *Guerre et Révolution d'Algérie* (Paris, 1962), Hocine Ait Ahmed, *La Guerre et l'après-guerre* (Paris, 1964), and Saadi Yacef, *Souvenirs de la bataille d'Alger*, (Paris, 1964); the loyalist case is presented in Bachaga Boualem, *Les Harkis au service de la France* (Paris, 1963).

French protest against the war appears in two translated works: H. Alleg, *The Question* (London, 1958), and Jean-Jacques Servan-Schreiber, *Lieutenant in Algeria* (London, 1956). Also important is Simone de Beauvoir, *La Force des choses* (Paris, 1963).

Among biographies of note are Georges Bidault, *Resistance, the Political Autobiography* (New York, 1967) and R. Merle, *Ahmed Ben Bella* (London, 1967).

Some of the international ramifications of the Algerian war appear in Hugh Thomas, *The Suez Affair* (London, 1967), and in sections of Harold Macmillan, *Riding the Storm, 1956–1959*, (London, 1971) and *Pointing the Way, 1959–1961* (London, 1972).

Polemical writing illustrating the passions aroused by the war is unfortunately mostly in French. Two of the 1961 abortive *coup* generals have put their views on record in Maurice Challe, *Notre Révolte* (Paris, 1968), and Edmond Jouhaud, *O Mon Pays Perdu* (Paris, 1988). A more intellectually argued rejection of the general wisdom concerning the end of the Algerian war appears, succinctly and in English, in *The Times Literary Supplement* of 10 July 1992, in which Professor Elie Kedourie reviewed Ageron's *Modern Algeria* noted above. Two paragraphs from Kedourie's long review merit quotation:

De Gaulle climbed to power on the shoulders of the French Army in Algeria whom he duped into imagining that he was in favour of maintaining the French position there. In reality, however, he believed that Algeria was no more than an *affaire de quatre sous*, to be liquidated as soon as possible. This was done a bare four years after the hurrahs with which Algiers, Mostaganem and Oran had welcomed him.

This liquidation made the European settlers from one day to the next into panic-stricken and penniless refugees – vicarious sacrifices to decades of impolicy by their own leaders, of clashing ambitions on the part of Paris politicians, and of the grandiosity of the de Gaullian *Weltpolitik*. Above all, the liquidation was to the great detriment of the Algerian people who were cruelly abandoned to the mercies of the FLN. Professor Ageron's whig history gives the reader no feel for the ambiguous and tragic complications of the French adventure in Algeria.

Earlier in this review Kedourie had commented that it was of course true that the French had invaded Algeria, seized land and committed misdeeds, but so had their Arab and Turkish predecessors; that the FLN victory was the work of a handful of *purs et durs*, and that the successor regimes, which he goes on to criticize, had not been exemplars of freedom, prosperity and justice.

Morocco and Tunisia have attracted little anglophone historical writing. In English, a useful if somewhat journalistic introduction to the events in Morocco is Rom Landau, *Moroccan Drama 1900–1955* (London, 1956). The most informative book on Morocco, with important detailed chapters on the last years of French rule, remains Charles-André Julien, *Le Maroc face aux impérialismes 1415–1956* (Paris, 1978). Also very interesting is General Georges Spillman, *Du Protectorat à l'indépendance* (Paris, 1967). For both Morocco and Tunisia, Pierre Boyer de Latour du Moulin, *Vérités sur l'Afrique du Nord* (Paris, 1956) sets out French perspectives in the final colonial years.

For Madagascar there is, unfortunately, even less writing in English, only two titles being at all relevant: Mervyn Brown, *Madagascar Revisited* (London, 1978), and Maureen Covelle, *Madagascar, Politics, Economics and Society* (London, 1987). For any fuller understanding of the revolt, recourse to J. Tronchon, *L'Insurrection malgache de 1947* (Paris, 1974) is necessary.

The Second World War events and developments in Syria and

217

Lebanon are well covered in Ariel Roshwald, *Estranged Bedfellows, Britain and France in the Middle East during the Second World War* (New York, 1990), and S.H. Longrigg, *Syria and Lebanon under French Mandate* (London, 1958). The French position is readably argued in Henri Lerner, *Catroux* (Paris, 1990).

There is an ever-growing library of books devoted to the general theme of decolonization. Among the most useful are Henri Grimal, (trans. S. de Vos), *Decolonization* (London, 1978); R.F. Holland, *European Decolonization 1918–1981* (London, 1985); W.H. Morris-Jones and Georges Fischer (eds), *Decolonization and After: the British and French Experience* (London, 1980); J.D. Hargreaves, *Decolonization in Africa* (London, 1988); Jacques Thobie and others, *Histoire de la France coloniale 1914–1990* (Paris, 1990); and Raymond F. Betts, *France and Decolonization, 1900–1960* (London, 1991).

An especially valuable French text is J. Marseille, *Empire colonial et capitalisme français, histoire d'une divorce* (Paris, 1984); a convenient English language summary of Marseille's argument appears in his 'The phases of French colonial imperialism', *Journal of Imperial and Commonwealth History*, XIII (1985), 3.

Finally, three works of fiction and one film will add greatly to understanding, offering atmosphere and local colour not easily found in textbooks. The works of fiction (which do require a level of knowledge of the events) are all translations of novels by Jean Lartéguy: *Yellow Fever* (London, 1965), *The Centurions* (London, 1961) and *The Praetorians* (London, 1963). The first concerns Indochina in 1954, the second both Indochina and Algeria, and the third Algeria only. The film is Pontecorvo's classic *The Battle of Algiers*, originally produced in 1965 under its Italian title, *La Battaglia di Algeri*.

MAPS

1.   Syria and Lebanon, 1945–1946

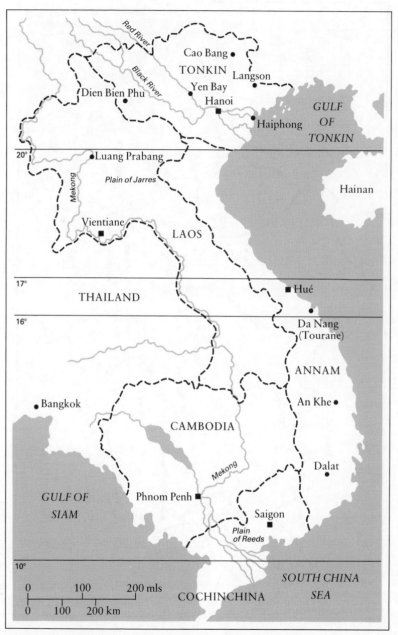

2. French Indochina

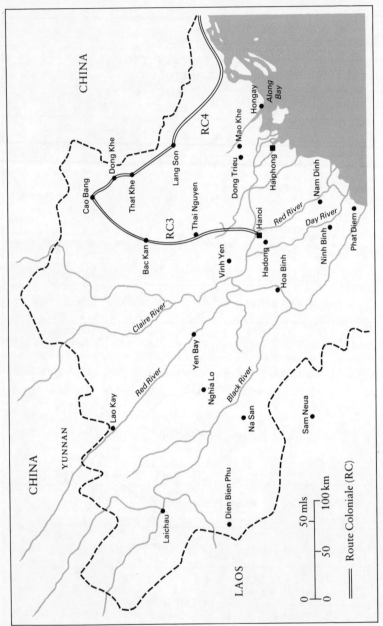

CHINA

Hongay

Along Bay

RC4

Mao Khe

Dong Khe

Lang Son

Dong Trieu

Cao Bang

That Khe

Thai Nguyen

Haiphong

Nam Dinh

RC3

Bac Kan

Vinh Yen

Hanoi

Red River

Day River

Hadong

Phat Diem

Hoa Binh

Ninh Binh

Claire River

Yen Bay

Red River

Nghia Lo

Black River

Lao Kay

Na San

Sam Neua

CHINA

YUNNAN

Dien Bien Phu

Laichau

LAOS

50 mls

50

100 km

0

0

══ Route Coloniale (RC)

3. Tonkin, 1945–1954

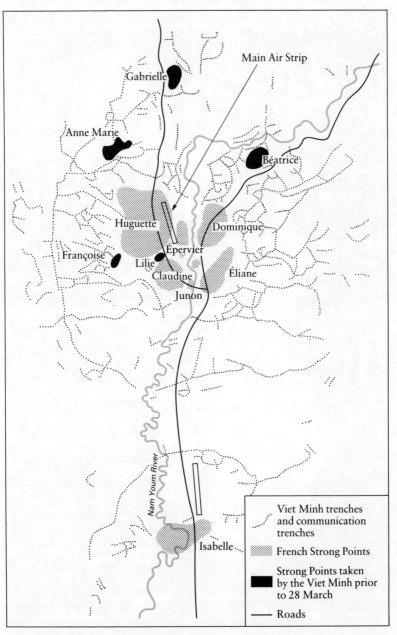

Main Air Strip

Gabrielle

Anne Marie

Béatrice

Huguette

Dominique

Françoise

Épervier

Lilie

Claudine

Éliane

Junon

Nam Youm River

Isabelle

Viet Minh trenches
and communication
trenches

French Strong Points

Strong Points taken
by the Viet Minh prior
to 28 March

Roads

4. Dien Bien Phu as at 28 March 1954

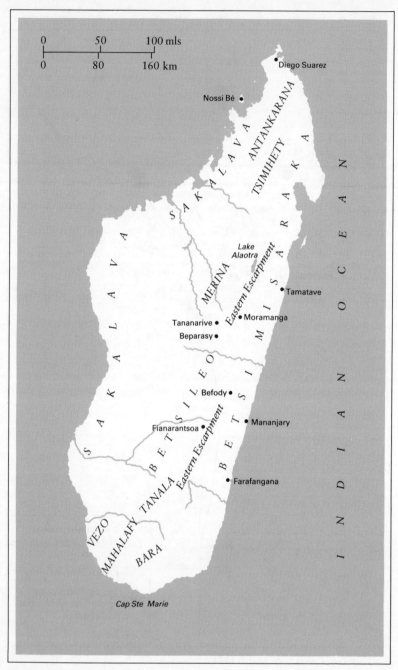

5. Madagascar (Ethnic groups are in italic caps)

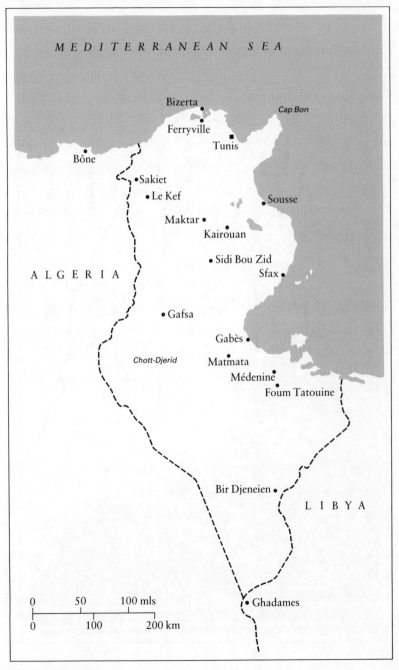

MEDITERRANEAN SEA

Bizerta

Cap Bon

Ferryville

Tunis

Bône

Sakiet

Le Kef

Sousse

Maktar

Kairouan

Sidi Bou Zid

Sfax

ALGERIA

Gafsa

Gabès

Chott-Djerid

Matmata

Médenine

Foum Tatouine

Bir Djeneien

LIBYA

| 0 | 50 | 100 mls |
| 0 | 100 | 200 km |

Ghadames

6. French Tunisia

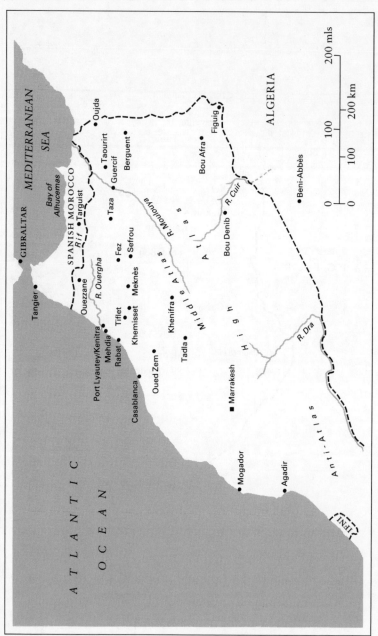

MEDITERRANEAN SEA

Bay of Alhucemas

GIBRALTAR

ALGERIA

200 mls

200 km

100

100

0

0

Oujda

Taourirt

Guercif

Berguent

Figuig

Bou Afra

Beni-Abbès

Taza

SPANISH MOROCCO

Rif • Targuist

Fez • Sefrou

Meknès

Ouezzane

R. Ouergha

Tiflet

Rabat

Khemisset

Port Lyautey/Kenitra

Mehdia

Tangier

Khenifra

Tadla

Oued Zem

Casablanca

Marrakesh

Mogador

Agadir

Middle Atlas

High

Anti-Atlas

Atlas

R. Moulouya

R. Cuir

Bou Denib

R. Dra

IFNI

ATLANTIC OCEAN

7. French Morocco

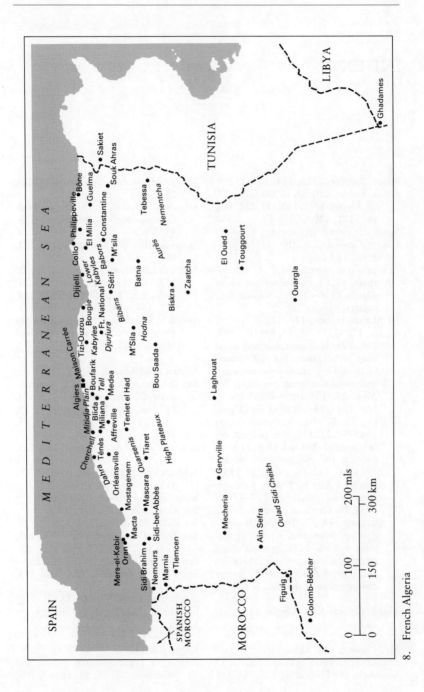

8. French Algeria

227

INDEX

Abane, Ramdane, 123, 128, 137, 153
Abbas, Ferhat: activities to 1945, 26, 27, 32, 33; post-1945, 110, 117, 122, 153, 167, 171, 180
Agostini, General: in Morocco, 103
Ailleret, General C: in Algeria, 174; post-1962, 183
air support: in Algeria 1945, 31; in Indochina, 57, 61; in Madagascar, 85; in Algeria 1954–62, 159. *See also* helicopters, napalm
Ait Ahmed, Hocine, 112, 124
Algeria, 12, 64, 75, 81, 88, 89, 102, 103, 104, 105, 107: economic and social links with France, 7–8, 109; status to 1939, 13; administrative, economic and social conditions pre-1945, 14, 25–6, 28, 108–10; political life to May 1945, 26–30; 1945 Sétif Uprising 30–3; constitutional status 1945–54, 15, 110, 116; political developments, OS and CRUA, 110–12; political and military developments 1954–56, 112–16; events in 1957, Battle of Algiers, Morice Line, international pressures, 127–43; in 1958, De Gaulle in power, early initiatives 144–57; 1959–62, policies develop, Barricades Week, negotiations with the FLN, generals' coup attempt, ethnic cleansing, casualties and independence, 158–77; further consequences of the war, 178, 179–80
Allard, General J: in Algeria, 117, 131, 157
Alleg, H, 134
Aly la Pointe, 128, 133
Allessandri, General: in Indochina, 53, 55
Amirouche (Ait Hamouda), 127, 161, 165

Amis du Manifeste et de la Liberté (AML), 28
Argenlieu, Admiral G Thierry d', High Commissioner in Indochina, 41–7, 49, 50n
Armée de Libération Marocaine, 101, 103, 106
Armée de Libération Nationale (ALN), 32, 112, 115, 118: organization, 122–31; operations, 136, 138, 145, 153, 154, 155, 156, 158, 160, 161, 166, 171
Auriol, V, President, 47: Elysée agreement 1949, 51; and Cambodia, 65–6; and Morocco, 95, 96

Balafry, Hajd Ahmed, 25
Bao Dai, Emperor, 18, 20, 21: as instrument of French policy, 50–1, 52, 53, 54, 58n, 59, 62, 63, 64, 65–6, 69, 73, 77, 114; chief ministers, 58n, 59, 67
Beaufre, General A: in Algeria, 117, 121, 128
Belgium: lessons learnt from French Wars, 181
Bellounis, Mohammed, 122, 136, 155
Ben Arafa, Sultan, 98, 101, 103
Ben Badis, Abdel Hamid, 26, 29
Ben Bella, President Ahmed, 103, 115, 124, 137, 166, 173, 176, 177
Ben Goulaid, Mostafa, 112, 116, 123
Ben Khedder, President, 123, 136, 171, 173, 176
Ben M'hidi, Larbi, 32, 128, 133
Ben Tobbal, Lakhdar, 118, 136, 153
Beynet, General, Delegate-General in Syria, 37
Biaggi, J-B, 147
Bidault, G, Prime Minister, 10, 15: and Indochina, 45, 46, 51, 66, 67, 70n,